DATE DUE

Sol

D E

Problems

Solving
DEER
Problems

HOW TO DEERPROOF YOUR YARD AND GARDEN

Peter Loewer

Skyhorse Publishing

First Skyhorse Publishing edition copyright © 2015 by Peter Loewer

Skyhorse Publishing books may be purchased in bulk at special discounts for sales promotion, corporate gifts, fund-raising, or educational purposes. Special editions can also be created to specifications. For details, contact the Special Sales Department, Skyhorse Publishing, 307 West 36th Street, 11th Floor, New York, NY 10018 or info@skyhorsepublishing.com.

Skyhorse® and Skyhorse Publishing® are registered trademarks of Skyhorse Publishing, Inc.®, a Delaware corporation.

Visit our website at www.skyhorsepublishing.com.

10 9 8 7 6 5 4 3 2 1

Library of Congress Cataloging-in-Publication Data is available on file.

Cover design by Richard Rossiter
Cover photo credit Thinkstock
All interior uncredited art is by the author. Images in chapter 10 courtesy of Annie's Annuals.

Print ISBN: 978-1-63220-535-3
Ebook ISBN: 978-1-63220-936-8

Printed in China

CONTENTS

This book is dedicated to my wife, Jean, who fed them,
The late Ben Wechsler who talked to them,
To Peter Gentling for knowing them and also being a friend of
the mighty bear,
The Birdwells, *père et fils*, for thought and counsel,
And to the Deer of America, for surviving it all.

Quarry mine, blessed am I
In the luck of the chase.
Comes the deer to my singing.

—Old Navaho Hunting Song

Introduction

I teach a class in botanical art at Asheville-Buncombe Technical College, and one of my students lives and gardens in Biltmore Forest, here in Asheville, North Carolina.

Biltmore Forest is a separate enclave within the city with a unique history. It was incorporated in 1923 and became a historic preservation district in 1990.

In the late 1920s, Mrs. Edith Vanderbilt sold 1,500 acres to establish as a suburb of Asheville designed with spacious lots and featuring all the modern amenities. The area was known as the Town of Biltmore Forest, and boasted of planning that underlined being a low-density and master-planned community with all the grace and style evidenced by Biltmore Estate's first architect and planner, Frederick Law Olmsted.

And for all the years I've lived in Asheville (twenty-three), Biltmore Forest has been under attack by hoards of deer. The town has sponsored many public meetings where discussions leapt around the room as subjects changed from hiring bow-hunters to sterilizing the bucks, and opinions were shouted out from home-owners, both pro and con, but, in the end, the final solution was left up to the individual homeowner.

"What can I do?" my student asked. "They're attacking everything I've planted and, I swear, they know that I'm a dedicated gardener and will continue to set out plants, even when I know I might lose everything! What can I do?"

"There are solutions," I answered, "but they are not always cheap, and like life in general, they work most of the time but there are no guarantees."

"What can I do?"

So I told her a few snippets of what's in this book.

I also told her that deer are really intelligent creatures who are not only mirroring the world around them (a world suffering from overpopulation and lack of habitat), but among all the pest animals of America, seem to know just how to convince gardeners in particular and landowners in general that they have personally picked on their gardens for destruction. They can do this because they are beautiful creatures and are symbols of the development of America.

Before I spent twenty years in Sullivan County, New York, where the deer began their attack on our first garden when it was still in the planting stage, I thought that deer were best represented by the final scene of that 1955 soaper, *All That Heaven Allows*, where a deer walks into the backyard of a trendy home built by Rock Hudson for the older Jane Wyman, and nibbles at an apple.

There was not a dry eye in the theatre.

But during those twenty years, my wife and I gardened on a small cleared area measuring a little over two acres. Our civilized room was the front part of thirty-three acres, acreage surrounded by second-growth forest (but forest just the same), located between Cochecton Center and Lake Huntington in Western Sullivan County. Geographically, we were in the southwestern corner of New York State, but almost everybody considered our home upstate New York because it was not within an hour's commute of Manhattan.

After a year spent in making our house (a combination of abandoned farmhouse and resort hotel) livable, we sought escape from carpentry and finishing in working the land.

When the battle with red shale and red clay was close to an end (thanks to compost, lime, and more compost) we began to grow vegetables for the table and the larder.

Soon we two were knee-deep in all sorts of incredible garden pests. In the insect world they ranged from armyworms to tent caterpillars to gypsy moths to Japanese beetles, and finally, ants. In the animal world, the threats came from chipmunks, woodchucks (some call them groundhogs), voles (not moles as moles were never a problem), rabbits, and deer. Of all, the deer were the worst.

Why? It seemed as though they ate all within their path.

It seemed that whatever the season, the local deer population looked upon our land as a trendy restaurant, a place meant to provide endless reserves of food for these very intelligent goats.

So instead of bowing to rising tides of anger, I decided to try a few new (to me) procedures to stop the deer in their tracks. So I asked local farmers and hunters for their advice.

Years passed. Gardens grow—and gardens come and go.

We now live in Asheville, North Carolina, protected by surrounding highways from problems with deer in the garden. But as The Wild Gardener radio host, I'm deluged with questions about how to control deer, what products are available, are there any plants that deer dislike, and many more.

Again I asked farmers and hunters, but this time I also asked highway departments, experts on deer, doctors, vets, and searched out new products on the World Wide Web.

When trying to ferret out plants that deer dislike, I'm reminded of the following answer to that question, provided by Joe Seals, my good garden friend from California: "After an extensive survey of gardeners in badly deer-infested areas (after a bad winter drought that forced record numbers of wild deer into urban areas), we shortened our list to the following: oleander and old brick."

One more thing: In addition to being a gardener, I'm a naturalist. The gardener in me resents the damage that deer do to gardens, while the naturalist always wants to point out that whatever happens, it is not the fault of the deer. As Shakespeare wrote in *Julius Caesar*, "The fault, dear Brutus, is not in our stars, But in our selves—."

For we are the disturbers of the environment, we did away with the predators, we took the land for development that deer once lived upon, we did away with the small farm and opened the path to the mega-farm, and we built the highways that they must cross.

Let's not forget!

CHAPTER ONE

All About Deer

The Typical Deer

If dandelions were rare plants everybody would want at least one plant in their garden. And the same holds true for deer. Endangered, they would be desired by all, but in today's numbers they've become suburban pests. All thoughts of their graceful beauty are gone. Deer are now looked upon like intelligent goats, ready and willing to eat their way through your garden and landscaping.

Deer are herbivorous mammals; like cows, they are cud-chewers that eat vegetation and not meat. They walk upon cloven hooves, and have trotted into the hearts of many folks in our culture because of books like Felix Salten's *Bambi*, and the marvelous 1942 Disney movie of the same name that first introduced America, and then the world, to the cycles of life in the forest—not to mention Thumper, the rabbit.

In order to get a firsthand account of a typical deer, in this case a whitetail, I talked to Dr. Leonard Lee Rue III, the author of many books about deer, including the authoritative volumes *The Deer of North America* and *Whitetail Savvy*.

"They are," said Dr. Rue, "incredible animals worthy of our admiration. Today, the three groups, whitetails, muleys, and black-tails, probably total about twenty-five million deer—and that's a lot

A pair of white-tailed deer in a lithograph by John James Audubon in 1844.

of any single kind of wildlife. Whether or not there were more deer wandering North America before the Europeans came, nobody really knows, but from the time of man's first arrivals on this continent, deer have been important to the survival of mankind.

"When you think of what deer represented, first to the existence of the American Indians and then to the first settlers, you begin to wonder if mankind could have managed without them. Venison was a dietary staple, they used deer hides for clothing, the sinews were used to sew the skins, the bones fashioned into awls to poke holes in the leather so the sewing could commence, the hair was used as insulation when stuffed into deer-leather moccasins, the hooves were turned into glue and ornaments, and finally the bones and antlers became tools, weapons, decorations, and religious objects.

"And never forget, the settlers were far more aggressive than the Indians when it came to the deer harvest. They didn't limit their kills to personal needs but began killing deer for both meat and deerskins, with Europe as an expanding market."

"I never thought," I said, "of the professional hunters of that time. Do you have any figures as to the kills?"

"There was," said Dr. Rue, "a gentleman, one Thomas Meacham of Hopkinton, in St. Lawrence County, New York, who kept exact records of his victims. When he died in 1850, he had killed 214 wolves, 77 cougars, 219 bears, and 2,550 deer. There were others but I think he probably holds the record.

"And it is easy today," he added, "to condemn the professional hunters of the past but remember, these men were a product of their time and thought that the wealth provided by nature would go on forever. They were respected for their hunting skill."

"I live," I said, "about fifty miles from Jonesborough, Tennessee, the capital of the short-lived state of Franklin, and I seem to remember that at that time official salaries were made in multiples of deerskins and not greenbacks."

"That's right," he said, "but remember that in 1646, Rhode Island became the first colony to pass a law protecting deer from the hunt for at least part of the year. The laws didn't always work but at least they tried."

Dr. Rue went on to tell me that the late 1800s were the blackest period for all sorts of wildlife on the American continent with the north eastern states hit the hardest. By the end of the nineteenth century, New Jersey had fewer than two hundred deer while in Massachusetts, Vermont, and New Hampshire, deer were so scarce that just the sight of hoof prints made newspaper headlines.

Now, thanks mainly to the increased awareness of the general public, more rigid game laws, better enforcement of those laws, and moving deer abound to fill in gaps where they were once scarce, that old pendulum is beginning to swing the other way—although both mule deer and blacktails have declined slightly in recent years.

"I think," said Dr. Rue, "that much of the problem is one of habitat loss. Where once there were fields and woods, there are now housing developments, not to mention the decline of the predator. Wolves, bobcats, lynx, even bear are effective hunters of deer. But dogs probably take a greater toll than all other predators combined. And let's not forget the automobile, too."

Dr. Rue on Deer through the Year

A year is a long time. If it's spring in your backyard and some violets, or perhaps trilliums, are blooming, when you think back to the last time you saw those blooms, and you remember all the passing days and the events they saw, a year is a long time. And it's a long time from a deer's point of view.

So I again called Dr. Rue and asked him about a year in the life of a deer.

Dr. Rue is an imposing man: A craggy face, piercing eyes, a face surrounded with a salt and pepper beard and mustache plus a head full of long gray hair. He's the author of thirty books on wildlife, his photographs have appeared in countless magazines, from *Field & Stream* to *Newsweek*. He lives in Blairstown, New Jersey. And he doesn't accept email—which is a laudable trait.

The Spring

"In the spring," he said, "snows melt and days get longer. It's a clue to the whitetails of the North to move. Many deer have been yarding up, a term that means they've wintered in a sheltered area, like a gully, a swamp, or just a protected place in the woods, to get out of the wind. These are warmer spots where the sun by day and the tree canopy by night both make and hold a bit of heat. In the West, mule deer and blacktails move to lowlands rather than yarding up.

"The driving force is food. Now more than any other time of the year, sprouting vegetation provides nutrition. Believe it or not, throughout all of North America, wherever it's grown (over thirty

A white-tailed deer drinking in a watercolor by Winslow Homer in 1892.

million acres in the United States), in early spring deer feed on alfalfa."

"Are there distinct behavior patterns between males and females at this time of the year?" I asked.

"All over the country, bucks bed down earlier in the morning and look for heavier cover. They're generally less active by day and only come out to feed later in the evening. And don't forget, in the springtime white-tailed bucks are often solitary or sometimes a big buck is followed about by several younger bucks. Blacktails are usually the same. Remember, their antlers are growing now and they take special care not to injure themselves.

"Does, on the other hand, usually start feeding around dawn, until about 9:00 A.M. Pregnant females have additional demands on their systems and they need a long time to cram in all the food necessary. Then they rest until around 11:00 A.M."

"I remember, "I said, "that up in our Sullivan County farm, their activities often had clockwork precision."

"That's right," answered Dr. Rue, "and they start to feed again around 4:00 P.M., the time when they eat the most. Once they have their fawns, the does usually nurse them before each of their own feeding periods begin.

"As birthing time approaches, a doe seeks solitude. When a fawn is born, it's out of proportion to an adult: The legs are much longer at birth than later in life, in fact they seem to be all legs. And remember, a doe can give birth to identical twins, fraternal twins, triplets, or even quadruplets—although fraternal twins are more common than identical twins. Recent research shows that 25 percent of twins were sired by different bucks."

"There is in people," I said, "something psychologists call the cuteness response. It's why even the most masculine of men will ooh and aah over a baby, or any young animal or sometimes an adult that has no adult features, no sharp edges, but has a bulging forehead with big round eyes. And if ever there was such an animal, it's a fawn. I can just imagine their responses to twins."

"Every year," he continued," game departments across the country are deluged with reports of folks picking up 'orphan' fawns. They are obviously under the spell of being both protective and caught by the fawn's beauty. Unless the doe has been killed, these fawns are not orphans, but once touched and petted, there's a 10 percent chance that they may become orphans. If the mother is afraid of a human scent, she might abandon the fawns.

"Upon birth, when a doe washes her fawn, she soon leads them away from the birthing spot. That washing not only cleans the fawn but leaves a doe's individual odor so she can tell her offspring from others.

"Now, she must nurse the fawn. At the same time, fawns spend about 96 percent of their time curled up in their beds. When bedded, they hold their heads up and are very, very alert. When detecting danger they lower their head, curl up and hold their breath for as much as several minutes."

"I know the spotted coat makes excellent camouflage," I added, "because I remember that one spring Jean and I were walking in the woods and passed an area of beautiful ferns, all dappled with sunlight, and we suddenly saw a fawn. It didn't move a muscle but we looked into those baleful eyes and quickly, but quietly, walked on."

"I've often seen dogs run unawares right past fawns that were curled up in the forest," Dr. Rue noted. "Many biologists claim there is no discernable odor to very young fawns."

The Summer

Soon it's summer in the forest. When walking in the Catskill woods, even in the shade of old oaks, you can smell the scent of pitch from the pines.

"It's the only time of the year," said Dr. Rue, "that deer, including the doe with her young, can take it slow and easy.

"At birth, fawns are on a milk diet. But when about three weeks old, they follow their mother and sample all sorts of vegetation. By the age of five weeks, they've become quite selective in what they eat and actually begin to develop taste preferences. Research has shown that fawns are dependent on milk until they are about three months old but I think the speed of weaning depends on the individual doe.

"And let's not forget play! Play is conditioning for later life and most mammals engage in it. Even a solitary fawn will suddenly run, buck, kick out, jump, and dash around in circles. If there's more than one, they'll play tag, all the while developing muscles, expanding lung capacity, and learning the dexterity needed to escape from predators in later life.

"By the end of August, the fawns begin to lose their spots and all deer begin to shed their thin, red summer coats, taking on their hollow-haired (for insulation), grayish-brown winter coats."

Dr. Rue stopped for moment.

"Ever been bitten by a deer fly?"

"Certainly," I answered, "and up in the Catskills they get pretty big, too."

"Well," he said, "deer are subject to all the discomforts of a camper in the wood, in addition to many internal parasites. Deerflies, midges, blackflies, and mosquitoes do their worst, not to mention ticks and their connection to Lyme disease.

"And they are subject to an army of different worms, flukes, and general diseases including anthrax. They evenget tumors."

"When you really think about it," I said, "it's a wonder as many survive as do. They fight nature, man, diseases, the loss of range, predators, famine, cold, and automobiles. But they still go on."

"Yes, it is, and in the summer nature lets out a bit of slack. While the does and fawns may come out just before sunset, the bucks feed at dusk. The deer begin to feed around 11:00 P.M. and again after 1:00 A.M. with another major feeding effort just before dawn. And by midsummer, the buck's antlers have reached their maximum growth, with daylight stimulating the pituitary gland which, in turn, causes testicles to enlarge and produce live sperm. Now the antlers harden and the velvet covering dries up. The velvet is always stripped from the antlers, starting at the tips. A buck picks a bendable sapling—not a tree—and rubs his antlers along the trunk.

"Now with hardened antlers and testosterone in his blood, a buck becomes the quintessence of being male."

The Autumn

Days are shorter and in the mountains, cool air flows down the valleys; at higher elevations leaves begin to be touched by frost while on clear, moonless nights, the stars glow as though touched by special lighting.

"Deer are greatly influenced by weather," said Dr. Rue. "They know that winter is on the way so they begin to eat compulsively, taking advantage of the available food. I can state, unequivocally, that in the northeastern, central, southern, and west coast regions of the

United States, acorns, when available, are the favorite food of white-tailed deer. Acorns are also very important to both the mule deer and blacktails, as well.

"And just like people get indigestion, deer can suffer from over-eating, especially from too much high-carbohydrate foods, like corn, sugar beets, grapes, pears, or wheat. When autumn winds cause a surplus of apples to fall, the deer eat too many and get indigestion."

"We had a number of apple trees on our property," I said. "And often, when the apples were upon the ground too long, they began to ferment with the result that an occasional grouse would become blotto and on two afternoons, we had deer stumble and flounce about just like people who have too many drinks."

"I've never seen it myself," he said, "but I've read many reports of such actions.

"About this time the fawns are two-thirds the size of their mothers, and are perfect little carbon copies. They actually will stop growing now and wait until the following spring because all the nutrition they now get is necessary for winter survival.

"And now rutting begins. Sexual activity peaks in November and December, although timing depends on the latitude. It's a dangerous time and about three weeks before the first females come into estrus, the bucks start to run the does. When the country was primarily rural, and more people lived on farms than in cities, it was said that the most dangerous animal was a Jersey bull. With the passing of the farms, the most dangerous animal is now a pet white-tailed buck. Every year there are stories of people being killed or injured by a buck they raised in captivity.

"Then hunting season begins with some states only permitting the shooting of bucks. But whatever the rules, the game is afoot."

"When we lived in the Catskills, we dreaded hunting season," I said. "Not because of the genuine hunters, but the men (and unfortunately some women), who you term 'slob' hunters. They came up to the mountains to prove their manhood, using a lot of beer and noise for cover, and every year, shot as many of each other as they did the deer."

"I know," he said, "I know the slob is the one who blazed away at anything, at any time, and at any distance. Decent hunters will never try for a 'pot' or 'luck' shot but are always sure their weapons kill the game cleanly and quickly if they shoot.

"Finally," he said, "when you realize how many wounded deer are lost every year, the figures become appalling, ranging all the way to 8 percent of the total hunter's take."

The Winter

The chill winds blow, the cold rains pelt the earth, and the snows fall.

"Some deer will yard up, others roam a small area of woods, and food becomes scarce. It's now that farms, nurseries, and gardens are hit harder. The deer are forced to do more browsing in the winter, although browsing can become a sort of pruning and most plants survive.

"But when the easily reached food is gone, deer can stand on their hind legs and reach overhead branches. A seven-month-old fawn standing on its hind legs can reach up about five feet, and an adult doe can get up to six feet, a buck up to seven."

"And people must remember," I said, "that these habit patterns were set long before farms and gardens dotted the countryside. Under nature's eyes, a shorn tree that lives is still a tree and not a blot on the aesthetic landscape of a gardener."

"And with so many deer," he said, "and habitats decreasing, the saddest thing of all is the starvation that haunts so many of these animals. Sure, some fawns have been known to go a month without food and still survive; some adults have gone up to two months, but more than that and starvation can cause up to a one-third weight loss and then death is inevitable.

"Then enter winter recreation with snowmobiles forcing frightened deer to use scant reserves of energy just to escape what they perceive as a major threat.

"The Native Americans called the month of February, "Starvation Moon"; it was thought to be the month of the greatest winter hardships, and the effects of a severe winter are insidious. The obvious loss is the carcasses of starved deer found in the spring, their bleaching bones scattered about. But less obvious is the lowered fawn production rate the following spring."

Dr. Rue paused for a moment and his tight mouth produced a slight smile.

"But deer," he said, "have a tremendous tenacity; they are tough. Although many will die, more will live, and it has always been so. They've lived with adversity for many millions of years, and have evolved because of it."

Anatomy of a Deer

Deer are mammalian, cloven-hoofed quadrupeds. They are the only hoofed mammals that bear antlers that shed every year. The females are smaller and lack antlers. They have a potential life of eleven to twelve years (sometimes longer), but except for those in captivity, few ever last that long in the wild.

A leaping long-tailed deer in a 1851 lithograph by John James Audubon.

Deer have excellent, but not perfect, eyesight, although it's aimed at detecting motion. You can prove this yourself by being downwind of a deer and moving ever so slowly.

They have a great sense of smell. It's thought it might be better than a dog's and everybody knows what a bloodhound can achieve. But, as yet, nobody's found a good way of testing this ability.

Deer are endowed with a sophisticated sense of taste. But it's their hearing that should earn salutes. In the midst of a blowing breeze, with rustling leaves, buzzing bees, and a few bird calls thrown in for good measure, just dare to step on a stick and you'll see deer activity stop as heads are alert and ears go up to find the cause of the disturbance.

Deer learn the warning sounds that other animal make when danger threatens, especially birdcalls. Yet, the milk truck rumbling up the hill to Lake Huntington never got their attention when eating in the front part of our Cochecton home. So again, like people, they can adapt to noises, whether loud or just insistent.

Just like people, an adult deer has thirty-two teeth. But unlike humans, in deer the teeth are distributed in a pattern to aid in chewing vegetation instead of meat.

Deer can weigh up to three hundred pounds, which explains why a car or a truck hitting a deer often results in a great deal of damage to both participants—but most weigh far less. And counter to most widely held beliefs (especially among hunters who have lost a potential trophy), deer rarely stand above three-and-a-half feet high at the shoulder and are only about six feet long.

Whitetails breed from the middle of September to late February, with the fawns being born in early summer. There is a two-hundred-day gestation period. At the first birthing, does usually have a single birth; in later years, as long as food is abundant, twins are common.

Deer are ruminants, and have, like cows, four-chambered stomachs, and, like other ruminants, chew a cud. Four-chambered stomachs are very valuable for animals on the go (and I'm sure there are a few stockbrokers out there who, if the operation were possible, would divide their stomachs in the same way). This stomach arrangement lets a deer ingest a lot of food, quickly, then digest it later, in a more leisurely manner.

While most gardeners would disagree, unlike many animals, deer amble when they eat. They take a bite of food, walk a few feet then nibble again.

They eat twigs, branches, and bark in the winter, lush grasses and new leaves in the spring and summer (in addition to farm

A white-tailed deer nibbles on winter produce; below is a hoof print in the snow.

crops), and in the fall, turn to their favorite food: acorns. I well remember the Grund Family in Cochecton who, every summer, fought to keep the deer from the cornfields, as the deer would often bite the stalks with the tassels, thus preventing formation of a good corn crop.

A deer's coat changes color according to the season. In summer they have a short dense coat while in winter they grow longer, hollow hairs, well-insulated against the cold.

The Varieties of Deer

There are a number of varieties of deer in North America. They all belong to the genus *Odocoileus*, a name bestowed by Constantine Samuel Rafinesque (1700–1800), a French-American naturalist who is usually described as being gifted but eccentric.

Just as in the scientific names given to plants, the same rules hold true for animals. This seems like a good rule but it often leads to almost laughable mistakes in nomenclature.

For example, in 1832, Rafinesque was exploring some caves in Virginia where he found the fossilized tooth of a remote ancestor of the present white-tailed deer. He probably meant to name the genus *Odontocoelus*, meaning hollow tooth, strangely a word often used to describe the denture of lizards, so it's not clear why he chose this word. Perhaps Greek was not his strong suit. But the result was the genus *Odocoileus*. And thanks to that word being the first on record, it's the one that science today must deal with.

Deer descend from a 10-million-year-old common ancestor of the Pliocene Period but about a million years ago migrated across our continent and wound up as three distinct species: the white-tailed deer (*O. virginianus*), the mule deer (*Odocoileus hemionus*), and the black-tailed deer (*O. hemionus columbianus*).

The White-tailed Deer

The white-tailed deer makes its home in all forty-eight contiguous states, a large part of Canada, and is divided into seventeen subspecies or races. In the mid-1600s there were some twenty million deer in North America. They were generally shot by the combined forces of the Native Americans, the settlers, in addition to having their habitats denuded so that by the end of the 1800s, about fifty thousand survived.

Then conservation entered the scene, a philosophy that worked with such success that today, there are now some twenty million white-tailed deer at large in this area. Whitetails are divided into the following subspecies:

1. Virginia whitetail (*Odocoileus virginianus virginianus*) eat their way across Virginia, West Virginia, Kentucky, Tennessee, North

A white-tailed fawn in an 1846 lithograph by John James Audubon.

and South Carolina, Georgia, Alabama, and Mississippi. This moderately large deer with fairly heavy antlers has adapted to an astounding number of habitats ranging from the Piedmont's coastal marshes, woodlands, and swamps to the tops of the Great Smoky Mountains. The Virginia whitetail makes its home just a few miles from my city garden in Asheville, and has become a thorn in the side of suburbanites in Western North Carolina.

2. The northern whitetail (*O. virginianus borealis*) is the largest of the subspecies and the animal that made garden life so difficult for my twenty years in Sullivan County. This animal is found in Maryland, Delaware, New Jersey, Pennsylvania, Ohio, Indiana, Illinois, Minnesota, Wisconsin, Michigan, New York, Connecticut, Rhode Island, Massachusetts, New Hampshire, Maine, Vermont, and the Canadian provinces of New Brunswick, Nova Scotia, Quebec, Ontario, and part of Manitoba. Not bad for a subspecies.

3. The Dakota whitetail (*O. virginianus dacotensis*) is slightly smaller in stature, and in winter has a paler coat than the northern whitetail. Its range covers North and South Dakota, parts of Nebraska, Kansas, Wyoming, Montana, and the Canadian provinces of Manitoba, Saskatchewan, and Alberta.

4. The Northwest whitetail (*O. virginianus ochrourus*), is another large deer with a winter coat of a pale cinnamon-brown. It ranges parts of Montana, Idaho, Washington, Oregon, California, Nevada, Utah, and the Canadian provinces of British Columbia and Alberta.

5. The Columbia whitetail (*O. virginianus leucurus*) is presently on the endangered species list and found only on the Federal Columbian White-tailed Deer Refuge, and along the Columbia River near Cathlamet, Washington. There are presently fewer than five hundred animals alive.

6. The Coues or Arizona whitetail (*O. virginianus couesi*) is a small deer with larger ears and tail in proportion to its body size. It lives in the dry, desert regions of southeastern California, southern Arizona, southwestern New Mexico, and into Mexico proper.

7. The Texas whitetail (*O. virginianus texanus*) is the largest of the southern deer and lives in western Texas, Oklahoma, Kansas, southeastern Colorado, eastern New Mexico, and the northern portion of Mexico proper.

8. The Carmen Mountains whitetail (*O. virginianus carminis*) is a larger deer but still smaller than the northern whitetail, making its home in the Big Bend region of Texas, limited to the Carmen Mountains on both sides of the Rio Grande.

9. The Avery Island whitetail (*O. virginianus mcilhennyi*) is known as the deer of the Texas Big Thicket Country. It's a large deer with a brownish winter coat with a range that stretches along the Gulf Coast in Texas and Louisiana.

10. The Kansas whitetail (*O. virginianus macrourus*) represents the fourth subspecies in Texas, being a large deer at home in eastern Texas, Oklahoma, Kansas, Nebraska, Iowa, Missouri, Arkansas, and Louisiana.

The following four subspecies live on islands far enough from the mainland to prevent interbreeding with one another or with mainland subspecies.

11. The Bull's Island whitetail (*O. virginianus taurinsulae*) is found only on Bull's Island of South Carolina.
12. The Hunting Island whitetail (*O. virginianus venatorius*) is another island habitant of South Carolina, found only on Hunting Island.
13. The Hilton Head Island whitetail (*O. virginianus hiltonensis*) ran across my headlights on a lecture tour in Sea Island, and is another island variation.
14. The Blackbeard Island whitetail (*O. virginianus nigribarbis*) claims Georgia as its home state and lives only on the islands of Blackbeard and Sapelo.
15. As you can tell from the species name, the Florida whitetail (*O. virginianus seminolus*) is the home deer of the Everglades.
16. The Florida coastal whitetail (*O. virginianus osceola*), lives on the Florida panhandle, southern Alabama, and Mississippi. It is not as large as the Florida or Virginia whitetail.
17. And finally, the smallest of them all, the diminutive Florida Key deer (*O. virginianus clavium*) is another animal on the endangered species list. If ever the word cute applied to an animal, it's here. After decades of losing its habitat to immigrants plus the continuing problem of being hit by cars, this deer, the smallest of all native deer, now numbers about 350.

The Mule Deer and the Blacktail Deer

Mule deer and blacktails live west of the Mississippi River. Muleys are often larger than whitetails but it's not a truly reliable characteristic. The dead giveaway is their tail, being narrow and short and tipped with black. There are eight subspecies:

The Rocky Mountain mule deer (*Odocoileus hemionus hemionus*), the northernmost mule deer, is large, the heaviest, and has the darkest colorations. Although you would expect a northern deer to have a paler coat, Mr. Rue suggests that this deer's habitat is forested and they blend quite well into their surroundings. This subspecies is found in the Canadian provinces of British Columbia, Alberta, Saskatchewan, Manitoba, and the Northwest Territories, in addition to Washington, Idaho, Montana, North and South Dakota, Minnesota, Nebraska, Wyoming, Oregon, California, Nevada, Utah, Colorado, Oklahoma, New Mexico, and Arizona.

The California mule deer (*O. hemionus californicus*) lives only in California, from the Sierras to the Pacific. It's smaller than the Rocky Mountain mule deer and has a smaller white rump patch.

The southern mule deer (*O. hemionus fuliginatus*) lives along the California coast, from south of Los Angeles into Mexico's Baja Peninsula. It's a dark subspecies about the size of the California mule deer.

The Inyo mule deer (*O. hemionus inyoensis*) has a restricted range around Inyo County, California. It's intermediate in size and color between the Rocky Mountain mule deer and the California mule deer.

The burro deer (*O. hemionus eremicus*) lives in the extreme southeastern part of California, there from the southwestern Arizona down into Mexico. It's smaller than the Rocky Mountain mule deer and lighter in coloration.

The desert mule deer (*O. hemionus crooki*), is the kind of animal that songs should be written about. It survives in the harshest of conditions, with a habitat that provides intense heat and harsher cold, limited forage, little water, and when it comes to hiding from enemies, a lack of cover. Even so, this palest of the mule deer survives against all odds—except that increasing whitetail populations will eventually lead to declines in the genetic stock.

The Blacktail Deer

The blacktail deer represent two more subspecies:

The Columbian blacktail deer (*O. hemionus columbianus*) lives in California, Washington, Oregon, and British Columbia. It runs the gamut of climate from high mountains to dry chaparral, and makes its home in the densest and wettest forests of North America. Columbian blacktails have a redder coat than mule deers and are smaller than the average whitetail.

The Sitka blacktail deer (*O. hemionus sitkensis*) sports a cinnamon brown coat and is smaller, on average, than the Columbian. It was originally found in the coastal rain forests, from the Queen Charlotte Islands, off British Columbia, and up to the southeastern Alaska Panhandle. But back in 1916, herds were introduced to islands in Prince William Sound and later to the Kodiak Islands and the Yakutat area.

CHAPTER TWO

Thoughts About Deer (and a Few Other Garden Animals)

The following essays deal mostly with deer, but the garden antics of both buck and doe are so closely linked to, for example, those of woodchucks and chipmunks. I've included some thoughts of some writers and naturalists (including myself) on a choice of mammalian pests.

I begin with Henry David Thoreau, a man whom most credit with originating America's naturalist tradition. The essay is an imaginary interview I held with Thoreau, written for a study on garden animals, and based on actual Thoreau quotations taken from his journals (*The Journal of Henry D. Thoreau*, edited by Torrey and Allen, Dover Publications, New York, 1962).

The second is another conversation, this time with the late Benjamin Wechsler, a noted conservationist who had studied deer and maintained a hunting camp for many years.

The last is one of my favorite garden columns about deer written in 1985.

A Conversation with Thoreau on Garden Animals

Since the invention of *Star Trek*'s warp drive, a number of things have become possible that were impossible in times past.

For example, one day a few summers ago Henry David Thoreau visited my garden. The mountains were seething under the blanket of a late-spring Bermuda high. By nine o'clock in the morning, the mercury hit 85°F, and for our garden, that's hot.

There's a spot under an archway of bittersweet vines (the offending berries are always removed before they become a threat) where the sun is filtered twice: once through a high canopy of oak leaves and once through the bittersweet. Earlier in the morning, I put two French garden chairs there plus a small table set for tea.

We settled into place and he put his straw hat down by the side of the chair.

"Just as the sun was rising this morning," he said, "I saw a rainbow in the west horizon, and I thought of,

Rainbow in the morning,
Sailors take warning;
Rainbow at night
Sailor's delight."

"We need the rain," I said, "so if it comes, it'll be welcome."

We stirred the cups of tea.

Late the day before, while driving along the River Road, a busy two-lane highway that parallels the Swannanoa River in South Asheville, I saw a woodchuck eating grass and clover, not one foot from the roar of traffic. The trucks and cars didn't bother him at all; he just kept chewing.

So I asked Thoreau about woodchucks because I knew they were a favorite animal in his scheme of things.

The Woodchuck

"One June morning in 1854," he said, "while rambling in the grassy hollows north of Goose Pond, where the woods never seem to grow but the grasses are in blossom around the edges, and small black cherries and sand cherries straggle down into them, I often find woodchucks. They love such places and when disturbed, usually wabble off with that peculiar loud squeak like the sharp bark of a red squirrel, then stand erect at the entrance of their holes, ready to dive into it as soon as you approach. Are there any in your garden?"

"No. We're cut off from the open land along the river by a highway that's busy twenty-four hours a day, so a woodchuck would be unlikely to make it across the road. But I have fond memories of them from our garden in the Catskills and from walking in the woods."

"Do you remember their scientific name?"

"Yes, it's *Marmota monax*, the genus because of the animal's resemblance to the marmot found in the Black Hills of South Dakota. The species is from the Delaware Indian word *monachgen*, for woodchuck. They hibernate in the winter, but not always too deeply and are most active in the morning and late afternoon. And they can both climb and swim."

"I knew they could swim, but climb?"

"When we lived in the Catskill Mountains, we surrounded a new vegetable bed with a snow-fence made of wooden slats about four feet high, and held together by twisted wire at the top, the bottom, and along the middle. One morning I watched a big chuck climb up using his claws in the wood and clicking on the wire, until reaching the top, he jumped down and walked to the beans."

"They love beans. Back in July of 1845, I remember writing in the journal that my enemies in the garden were worms, cool days, and most of all woodchucks. They nibbled an eighth of an acre clean. I planted in faith but they reaped. When they run they look like a ripe fruit mellowed by winter."

"I know I read in your journal about meeting a woodchuck."

"I've been very friendly with woodchucks," he said, as he sipped his tea. "One April morning in 1852, I turned round the corner of Hubbard' Grove, and saw a woodchuck, the first of the season.

He was sitting in the middle of the field, about thirty-five feet from the fence that bounds the woods and a few hundred feet from me. I ran along the fence and cut him off even though we both started running at the same time. When I was only about twenty feet away, he stopped, and I did the same; then he ran again, and I ran up to within three feet of him, when he stopped again.

"I squatted down and surveyed him at my leisure. His eyes were dull black with a faint chestnut iris, with but little expression and that more of resignation than of anger. The general aspect of the coarse grayish-brown fur was a sort of gristle with a lighter brown next to the skin. The head of a woodchuck is between that of a squirrel and a bear, flat on the top and dark brown and darker still or black on the tip of the nose. The whiskers are black about two inches long and the ears are very small and rounded, set far back and nearly buried in the fur. His feet are black with long, slender claws for digging.

"He appeared to tremble or was shivering with the cold. When I moved, he gritted its teeth quite loud, sometimes striking the under jaw against the other chatteringly, sometimes grinding one jaw on the other, yet as if more from instinct than anger. Whichever way I turned, that's the way he headed. I took a foot-long twig and touched his snout, at which it started forward and bit the stick, lessening the distance between us to two feet, and still held its ground. I played with it tenderly awhile with the stick, trying to open its gritting jaws. Ever its long incisors, two above and two below, were presented. But I thought it would go to sleep if I stayed long enough. He stood there, half sitting, half standing, and we looked at each other for about a half hour, till I swear we began to feel mesmeric influences. When I was tired, I moved away, wishing to see him run, but I could not get him started. He wouldn't stir as long as I was looking at him or could see him.

"I walked around him but he turned as fast and continued to front me. So I sat down by his side within a foot. I talked to him in quasi-forest-lingo, a kind of baby talk, at any rate in a conciliatory tone, and thought that I had some influence on him. He gritted his teeth less. I chewed checkerberry leaves and presented them to his nose and was met with a grit. With a little stick I lifted one of his paws to examine it, and held it up at pleasure. I turned him over to see what color he was beneath—more purely brown—though he turned himself back again sooner than I could have wished. His tail was also all brown, though not very dark, rat-tail like, with loose hairs standing out on all sides like a caterpillar brush. He really had a rather mild look. I spoke kindly to him. I reached checkerberry leaves to his mouth. If I had a few fresh bean leaves from my bean garden, I'm sure I could have tamed him completely. I finally had to leave him without seeing him move from the place.

"I respect woodchucks as one of the natives and I think I might learn some wisdom from him. His ancestors have lived here longer than mine, or yours. He is more thoroughly acclimated and naturalized than we are."

The Eastern Chipmunk

There's a three-foot-high wall of field stone about ten feet away from where we sat and runs the length of the perennial border. We both saw a quick movement, a living streak of brown race along the wall, then suddenly disappeared in the leaves of a spirea bush.

"It's a chipmunk," I said. "They have tunnels behind that wall and no matter how I try to keep them away, they keep coming back. If I fill a tunnel in the morning, it's back by mid-afternoon but I never find a hint of the soil they move."

"Neither have I. How do they do it?"

"According to Lawrence Wishner in his book *Eastern Chipmunks, Secrets of Their Solitary Lives* (Washington, DC: Smithsonian Institution Press, 1982), their tunnel construction is carried out with a 'working tunnel,' where they push the dirt along with their noses and their feet, opening everything from below. The last thing they do is excavate the entrance tunnel, using that dirt to fill in the working tunnel. Their tunnels are, of course, complicated, and contain food storage chambers, and nesting chambers are lined with dry leaves. Droppings are never found in the chambers."

"And," I added, "chipmunks are so clean they seldom have a hair out of place and according to many observers their almost obsessive cleanliness means they have few, if any, external parasites."

"I never had a formal garden like yours, so I wonder how much damage they do?"

"Oh, some gardeners claim chipmunks are major pests, but to me, they're one of the most intelligent creatures in the garden, with a unique social system all their own, so I don't begrudge them their holes, although I do swear a bit when I'm forced to fill them up."

"Their scientific name," said Thoreau, "is *Tamias striatus*, the genus from the Greek word for a steward, and could either refer to their food-gathering capabilities, or the way they run their existences. The species, of course, refers to their striped coat. I, on occasion, called them chipmunks but usually striped squirrels."

The lone chipper on the garden wall surfaced for just a moment.

"Although they are usually unsocial among themselves," I said, "I've always been delighted by their antics, especially when they put tails in air, and leap from log to log or along a wall."

"In very early spring of 1855, I was walking along the sunny hillside on the south of Fair Haven Pond, which unfortunately the choppers had just laid bare, when I heard a rustling amid the dry leaves on the hillside and saw a striped squirrel eyeing us from its resting place on the bare ground. It sat there till we were within some fifteen feet, then suddenly dived into its hole.

"I once saw a striped squirrel on a rail fence with some kind of weed in his mouth—it could have been a milkweed seed—at any length, he scudded swiftly along the middle rail past me, and, instead of running over or around the posts, he glided through the little hole in the post left above the rails, as swiftly as if there had been no post in the way. So he sped through five posts in succession in a straight line! But, you say they are not social creatures?

"Why I can remember one October afternoon in 1857, when I saw as many as twenty striped squirrels busily running out to the ends of the twigs, biting off the nuts, running back and taking off the acorn cups, and storing the nuts away in their cheeks."

"I doubt if they were working together. Although they have learned to live in man's vicinity, they are fiercely independent. I've often thought they would be a better symbol for America than the eagle. After all, except for the sheer joy of running about, they continually work. The great naturalist John Burroughs once described one Catskill chipmunk that carried home five quarts of hickory nuts and one quart of chestnuts during a three-day period."

"But why independent?"

"Except for mating season early in the spring or in July, chipmunks live alone. The female takes care of two litters a year, usually consisting of between three and five youngsters, born in an underground chamber. But most of the time, chipmunks are loners."

"I know I've heard the chattering of chipmunks on many occasions. One time in 1853, I heard a striped squirrel in the wall near me, as if he blew a short blast on a dry leaf."

"It's amazing to watch a mother chipmunk raise her young. They continually chatter but if she lowers her voice but just a bit, the youngsters will stop their play and run like the scamps they are into their family hole. Later juvenile chippers move into unoccupied burrows, and if they can't find an old home, they will build anew."

The White-tailed Deer

"What do you think about the deer?" I asked.

"Well, they are regular creatures. I notice that cows never walk abreast, but in single file commonly, making a narrow cow path, or the herd walks in an irregular and loose wedge. They retain still the habit of all the deer tribe, acquired when the earth was all covered with forest, of traveling from necessity in narrow paths in the woods."

He stopped to pour another cup of tea.

"I was once wary of drinking tea or coffee," he said, "but now I find myself less particular in these respects. I carry less religion to the table, ask no blessing, not because I am wiser than I was, but I am obliged to confess, because, however much it is to be regretted, with years I have grown more coarse and indifferent.

"The deer that run in the woods, as the moose for instance, carry perfect trees on their heads. The French call them *bois*. No wonder there are fables of centaurs and the like. No wonder there is a story of a hunter who, when his bullets failed, fired cherry-stones into the heads of his game and so trees sprouted out of them, and the hunter refreshed himself with the cherries. It's a perfect piece of mythology which belongs to these days."

"I looked up," I said, "the scientific name last night. It's *Odocoileus virginianus*, the genus referring to the tooth structure, and the species to Virginia, where they were apparently first spotted.

"Back in January of 1855," said Thoreau, "I was reading William Wood's *New England's Prospect*, the last English edition which appeared in 1639, the edition I read in 1764. Anyway there were then complaints of the wolf as the great devourer of bear, moose, and deer. Of the deer, there were a great many, even more in the Massachusetts Bay, more than in any other place. It was reported that some hunters killed sixteen deer in one day on Deer Island in Boston Harbor, where they had swam to avoid the wolves."

"Well, never fear," I said. "Over the years, thanks to an early twentieth century revulsion to predators, and the decline of the American farm giving way to abandoned fields and pastures, plus the fact that hunting is now a major industry in many states, deer are on the increase. And gardens are continually threatened."

"What do the authorities recommend?"

"Conservation people advise you to put up a fence. Well, gardeners who have tried fences know that it has to be wee-over ten feet high—even with snow on the ground. So for every foot of packed snow, add a foot to your fence. And be sure every inch is staked to the ground, because the little loves can easily crawl under. Fencing for any reasonably sized garden would take enough money to finance a two-month sojourn Paris."

"What would you recommend?"

"I'd like to see the predators return, and if that failed, controlled thinning of the herds, like they do in England."

"I read a book back in 1861," mused Thoreau, "called *Carolina Sports by Land and Water* by one Hon. William Elliott. He described on page 178, being in pursuit of a deer, which he had wounded, and his gun being discharged, he tried to run him down with his horse, but, as he tells us, 'the noble animal refused to trample on his fellow quadruped,' so he made up for it by kicking the deer in the side of the head with his spurred boot. The deer enters a thicket and he is compelled to pursue the panting animal on foot. 'A large fallen oak lies across his path; he gathers himself up for the leap, and falls exhausted directly across it. Before he could recover his legs, and while he lay thus poised on the tree, I fling myself at full length upon the body of the struggling deer—my left hand clasps his neck, while my right detaches the knife; whose fatal blade, in another moment, is buried in his throat. There he lay in his blood, and I remained sole occupant of the field.' There's a picture on the opposite page which shows the hunter in the act of stabbing the deer."

"So much for heroics," I said.

Cats in the Garden

"How do you feel about cats in the garden?" I asked Thoreau.

"I can remember one time back in 1850, when I was working on my journal and somebody in the house shut the cat's tail in the door. She made such a caterwaul as had driven two whole words out of my thoughts. I saw unspeakable things in the sky and looming in the horizon of my mind, and now they were all reduced to a cat's tail. Vast films of thought floated through my brain, like clouds pregnant with rain enough to fertilize and restore a world, and suddenly they were all dissipated."

"That reminds me of a poem from childhood," I told him:

"There is music in the hammer,

There is music in the nail,

There is music in the kitty,

When you step upon its tail."

"I've often wondered how so often a man is more humanely related to a cat or dog than to any human being. What bond is it relates us to any animal we keep in the house but the bond of affection? In a degree we grow to love one another."

"They've done studies in recent years that show having a pet like a cat or a dog extends the life of the owner but so far cannot explain how. But I know that having a good hunting cat in the garden takes care of a number of problems, like keeping the rabbit population down, and the greatest boon, hunting and dispatching voles."

"What are voles?"

"Voles are tail-less mice. You know, Danny Meadow Mouse in the *Burgess Bedtime Stories* by Gelett Burgess. Oh, that's right. He was born four years after you died so you never heard about the purple cow poem or the anthropomorphising of voles?

"They are little brown furry animals under five inches long with a prodigious appetite both for food and reproduction. Each vole can eat its own weight in twenty-four hours and a population of fifteen to an acre can increase to 250 voles in four years. When people talk about mole damage, they usually are describing garden horrors perpetrated by voles, not moles."

"What havoc do they sow?"

"They burrow through hay mulches and tunnel through leaf piles, and eat, eat, then eat some more. Wherever possible they gnaw on tree bark, chew around bushes, and even rip up the leaves of lamb's-tongue in the herb garden, using the shreds for nest linings."

"Moles I know. Back in June of 1856, I remember watching a star-nosed mole endeavoring in vain to bury himself in the sand and gravel while men were repairing a large circular hole at the railroad turntable. Some inhuman fellow had cut off its tail. It was blue-black with much fur, a very thick, plump animal, apparently some four inches long, but he shortened himself a third or more. His forefeet were large and set sidewise on their edges, and he used these to shovel dirt aside, while his large, long, and starred snout was feeling the way and breaking ground. I carried him along to plowed ground where he buried himself in a minute or two."

"Moles are meat-eaters, not plant-eaters. They live almost entirely underground, feeding on smaller animal life, especially earthworms and grubs. They are not vegetarians, only chewing enough roots to clear a path through an underground jungle."

Note: For more on moles and voles, see chapter 7.

The sun was getting higher and even though screened through countless leaves, it was getting warmer. Thoreau adjusted himself on his chair and picked his hat up off the ground, giving it a pat or two before putting it on his head.

"So the cats eat the voles," he said.

"Yes. Our garden cat, Miss Jekyll, always did her bit with the vole menace: Every afternoon, a freshly killed subject showed up on the doormat in front of the back door. And I'm sure she dispatched many more out in the garden and the fields beyond."

"As to cats," continued Thoreau, "I know a characteristic anecdote about our senator's wife, Mrs. Hoar, that I heard just before Christmas of 1857. Her son Edward, who takes his father's place

Miss Jekyll, our garden cat of many years, caught many voles and moles and was named for a great English gardener.

and attends to the same duties, asked his mother the other night, when about retiring, 'Shall I put the cat down cellar?' 'No,' said she, 'you may put her outdoors.' The next night he asked, 'Shall I put the cat outdoors?' 'No,' answered she, 'you may put her down cellar.' The third night he asked, 'Shall I put the cat down cellar or outdoors?' 'Well,' said his mother, 'you may open the cellar door and then open the front door, and let her go just which way she pleases.' Edward suggested that it was a cold night for the cat to be outdoors, but his mother said, 'Who knows but she has a little kitten somewhere to look after?' Mrs. H. is a peculiar woman, who has her own opinion and way, a strong-willed, managing woman."

"For all the talk about cats getting the birds, I would never want a garden without a resident cat. And, I suppose, I could always put a bell on any animal that begins to make too much of a dent in the bird life."

"One morning in October of 1858, the garden was alive with migrating sparrows and the cat came in from an early walk amid the weeds. She was full of sparrows and wanted no breakfast that morning, unless it was a saucer of milk, the dear creature. I saw her studying ornithology between the corn-rows."

An Interview with Benjamin Wechsler

The late Benjamin Wechsler was an old Sullivan County, New York, resident and both a friend and compatriot for forty years. Over those years I served on many Sullivan County committees with Mr. Wechsler, including one group formed by New York State to preserve the future Neversink Gorge State Park, an effort doomed to failure because the state felt it had the moral authority to condemn hunting and fishing rights owned by Mr. Wechsler and, I might add, protected by him, for lo these many years.

I was one of those lucky people who roamed this gorge, in good weather and in bad, and enjoyed walking through age-worn rock that in places looks like Angkor Wat (without the temples), while in others, the forest primeval.

The gorge is located a few miles outside of Monticello, the biggest city in Sullivan County. The county is a large area of land, measuring about one thousand square miles. It's within a two-hour drive of New York City, and since the middle of the 1900s has been a focal point for tourism and hunters of all descriptions.

Mr. Wechsler knew a lot about deer. He operated various hunting clubs since after the Second World War. And he's one of those observers of nature who tries to figure out just what a hungry deer will do, so he can think ahead and outsmart the devils before they invade his garden.

"Deer," he said, "are a cursed species: they eat up to fourteen hours a day, nibbling here, grazing there, then after that's finished they have to chew a cud. They're grazing animals with little time to think but a lot of time spent in survival. Unlike predators, they have no time to really think, no time to develop beyond a certain point, no time to sit around with the pride and digest the food and happenings of the day, just time to eat and in many cases that's being denied to them."

I asked him about the history of deer in that part of New York State as it echoes concerns and conditions found in many places around the country.

"There was staggering over-population in 1960s," he said, "so it's difficult to believe that until the early 1900s, there were no laws as deer were shot for food and hurting crops. The population fell to drastic levels, so to restock the Catskills they brought deer in from the Adirondack Mountains.

"Then subsistence farms were abandoned and dairy farms went into a decline. Open fields soon gave way to second growth, beginning with poplars, birch, sumac, and other fast-growing trees. Then the older-living species arrived, like oaks, maples, beech, and white pines, so the deer now had new food sources.

"History now entered into the equation and by the end of World War II, nine out of ten hunters were away fighting in the armed services.

"By the late 1960s, the deer were once again eating themselves out of house and home. You would actually find dead deer while walking through the woods. They began to eat bark, damaged trees, and went into the orchards. Finally, the climate began to change, resulting in less mast and, except for feral dogs, there were no predators to keep the animals in check.

"Now the predators are back and bears are becoming a nuisance. Coyotes, too. Thirty years ago you saw feral cats and feral dogs but in the last five years they've been attacked by coyotes. In the woods, coyote scat is replacing deer scat. Luckily, coyotes practice a territorial birth control based on packs competing in territories. At some point they produce less puppies per year per pack. So hopefully down the line there will be a new balance in with fewer whitetails."

"Deer," said Ben, "are suspicious creatures. I remember one summer that after a wild thunder and lightning storm a huge branch fell from one of my apples trees, landing in the tall grass next to the trunk. There was no fencing so the local deer herd was free to move about. The first day they just circled and looked at the fallen branch. The second day they ate about a third of the leaves, the next day they finished another third, and finally, on the third day, except for the large branches, they finished it off.

"I know that some people curse the deer as they lose precious plants. I know that if you live in the suburbs or as I do, in the country, you've got to do more than curse if you want to protect your plants."

I can remember visiting Ben in the spring. Whenever he decided to put in a special tree or an interesting plant, the specimen was quickly surrounded by a netting of chicken wire.

"Dogs," said Ben, "are great! Deer do not like dogs and sometimes I wonder if deer have racial memories of past experiences connected to out-running and out-leaping large barking dogs."

"But in the end," he said, "you must fence. It's really the only safe way of protecting your plants and your property."

A Visit with the Wild Gardener

I couldn't let the opportunity go by without printing one of my favorite garden columns from 1985 featuring deer. It was slated for my book *The Wild Gardener* (1991, Stackpole Books, Mechanicsburg, PA) but was dropped due to space limitations.

Our Friends, the Deer: "Klaatu Barada Nikto!"

Sometimes when I once walked my garden up in the Catskill Mountains where the deer roamed as though they had a deed to the entire spread, I felt like one of the unlucky characters in a Steven King novel, not the one about the rabid dog or the giant rats under the New England cotton mill, but more like the man imprisoned by the rabid fan who just won't let him go. Only instead of being human, my fans were the goats of the woods, who (often with reason) usually prune every garden they can find.

With horror I looked out into the garden: Three of them were happily munching on the hyacinths and had chewed back all the Allegheny spurge (*Pachysandra procumbens*), leaving stumps.

I wrapped on the window with such force that my knuckles turned white. I yelled. They turned and batted their limpid eyes—lashes curled to perfection—in my direction and went back to munching.

Running out the back door I screamed: "Out! Out! Out!"

With a flick of their tails, they strutted away.

Not only had they eaten the spurge and the bulbs, they had nibbled the emerging hostas, clipped the daylilies, and chewed off many of the buds on the flowering crabapple.

I remember when we first moved to the country I always thought of the deer in terms of that fine melodrama, *All That Heaven Allows*, where Rock Hudson is a younger man who romances the older widow, Jane Wyman, and faces the irk and ire of her family and friends. In the final scene, Rock and Jane share embraces in the old remodeled mill (a remodeling job, replete with ancient beams and oriental rugs, that probably cost some $250,000 back in 1955) and look out on the garden, as a young doe, oozing cuteness, prances up to the window and gently takes a ripened apple from the snow-swept ground.

Oh, heart! Oh, rapture!

Today I view them as intelligent goats ready to act as tanks with hoofs and mow down anything green except burdocks, crabgrass, and goutweed. Their rule is: If it's valuable or attractive, tear it to shreds!

Since deer conservationists mostly advocate fencing your property, I thought it might be time to report on a few new items of deer research recently published in *Pacific Horticulture*.

"Gardeners," they report, "have experimented with many defenses against deer. Some swear—the gardeners that is—by blood meal sprinkled around plants. Dr. Kenneth Stocking, who heads the arboretum at Sonoma State College, says that an emulsion of blood meal sprinkled on favored plants after each rain or burst of growth helps to repel deer."

(Note that phrase "after each rain." It means that only in areas of minimum rainfall would such treatment be practical; in most places one would need the cooperation of Dracula to get enough blood to do a good job.)

"Big-game repellents sprayed on foliage are reported by some to be effective, but these must be replenished as new growth emerges. A neighbor tried dipping strips of cloth in Deer-Away repeatedly for two weeks. Tied to green garden stakes about four feet high and planted throughout her rose bed, these strips kept deer away for two months before the whole affair had to be repeated. On a larger scale . . . the repellent, however, wore off in the first few rains and repeated use was not cost effective.

"Roy Davidson, a gardener in Seattle, reports that a Bellevue, Washington, firm called INKO has developed a slow-release selenium compound in pellet form that can be applied in big aspirin-like tablets to the soil, where it dissolves slowly and is absorbed by the roots of trees. It is said to be effective in protecting fruit trees, which give off a garlic odor."

The best advice I found in the article is to lay six-foot-wide strips of chicken wire on cleared ground around the garden, as the deer do not like to get their hooves caught in the openings. Or to build a high fence—they can leap over ten feet—or try the New Zealand deer fence that, by being laid at an angle, appears to be three feet wide to an approaching deer.

In years past we always fed the deer with corn. This kept them out of the garden during the winter, leaving all our shrubs and dwarf conifers free from nibbling. Then as the fields greened up they went off and left the plants alone.

The year before last we fed seventeen deer every day, once in the morning and once at night and contrary to the ridiculous claims of many conservation offices, this does not destroy their independence; the minute the grass greens up, they leave the corn, retune their stomachs, and go off to rape and pillage all the farmers in the neighborhood.

We didn't feed them this year because the herd never showed. For a moment I began to believe the cries of many local hunters that the herd was destroyed, weakened, like many politicians, beyond redemption. I patted myself on the shoulder, and decided to rest. After years of angst, I was finally free. Bambi was gone. Hallelujah!

No such luck.

On winter walks I began to see deer tracks where I had not seen them before. Then by the end of February, the dog and I began to see them in the woods. At first there were shadowy outlines, like Kirk and Spock just before "beaming up;" I thought it was my imagination at work. Just past Valentine's Day, the outlines were more vivid and I realized that the deer were still there, merely walking different paths.

In a field down the road from us, I saw great numbers of them, sharing turf with the turkeys, and the count continued to go up.

Four entered out backfield towards the end of March, and I chalked it up to mere caprice. More fool I.

I now wish for Gort. Remember Gort? He was the magnificent robot in *The Day the Earth Stood Still*. A usually peaceful killing machine that could, with the proper code word, wreak havoc beyond description and had the power to totally annihilate the earth.

If Gort were here, I would point to the deer. And unlike Patricia Neal, I would not say: "*Klaatu barada nikto!*"

CHAPTER THREE

The Triple Threat

D eer in all their innocence can cause many problems for people: they are vectors for a number of diseases that affect humanity, notably Lyme disease; they are vectors in thousands of traffic accidents per year; and for whatever the original reason, they cause vast amounts of damage not only to home gardeners but to commercial nurseries, tree farms, and yes, in isolated communities, every garden is at risk.

The Threat of Lyme Disease

Back at the end of the 1970s, many residents of the Northeast first heard local hunters talking about a dread new disease that attacked people, revolved around deer, and was transmitted by ticks. The infection was called Lyme disease, so named because the initial instance of the disease was recorded in Lyme, Connecticut. In that city a group of local children came down with arthritic symptoms that, at first, baffled doctors. Further investigations led to the discovery that Lyme disease was caused by a bacterium, specifically a member of the group known as spirochetes, the same group responsible for syphilis.

Late in the nineteenth century, European doctors had described the disease and experts believe it's been over in America for about a hundred years. Earlier in the twentieth century, European doctors examined patients that evidenced a reddish rash that was associated with tick bites, called *erythema migrans* or EM. Theory suggested it was caused by a tick-borne bacterium. By the 1940s, more tick-borne diseases were observed that often began with EM, and later developed into other illnesses. By the end of that decade, spirochetes were found in skin samples and the new wonder drug penicillin was prescribed as a treatment. In 1969 a doctor in Wisconsin diagnosed a patient with EM and prescribed penicillin for a successful treatment.

But in 1975 those thirty children and adults living in Old Lyme developed what looked like cases of rheumatoid arthritis (the worst type). Because some of the children lived on the same street, the Connecticut State Department of Health was called in to investigate.

The infections around Lyme led researchers to believe that the presence of EM and the arthritis symptoms were linked to tick bites and believed that penicillin treatments not only diminished the EM but reduced the risk of subsequent arthritic symptoms.

In 1982 Dr. Willy Burgdorfer, a scientist from the National Institutes of Health, discovered spirochetes in the mid gut of the adult deer tick (*Ixodes scapularis*). The bacteria were christened *Borrelia burgdorferi* or Bb for short. Since then antibiotics have been the general treatment for the disease.

Lyme disease has been reported in all fifty states (including DC), while New York has the highest rates of Lyme disease in the country (hence the worries in Sullivan County). New York is followed by Connecticut, Pennsylvania, New Jersey, Wisconsin, and Maryland. Massachusetts ranks eighth overall.

The incidence of Lyme disease in the United States has approximately doubled since 1991, from 3.74 reported cases per 100,000 people to 7.01 reported cases per 100,000 people in 2012. Then in 2013, 95 percent of confirmed Lyme disease cases were reported from fourteen states: Connecticut, Delaware, Maine, Maryland, Massachusetts, Minnesota, New Hampshire, New Jersey,

New York, Pennsylvania, Rhode Island, Vermont, Virginia, and Wisconsin. Lyme disease is the most commonly reported vector-borne illness in the United States. In 2013, it was the fifth most common Nationally Notifiable disease. However, this disease does **not** occur nationwide and is concentrated heavily in the Northeast and upper Midwest. Driven by multiple factors, the number and distribution of reported cases of Lyme disease appear to be increasing over time. For continued up-to-date information please contact http://www.cdc.gov/lyme/stats/.

Species of Ticks Involved with Lyme Disease

In the Northeast and the north-central United States, the tick-carrier of choice is the black-legged tick (*Ixodes scapularis*) and on the Pacific Coast, the western black-legged tick (*I. pacificus*) does the job.

The black-legged deer tick is less than a quarter inch in height. Photo courtesy of the Center for Disease Control.

There are over 850 species of tick in the U.S., all belonging to one of five genera: *Amblyomma*, the lone star tick; *Dermacentor*, the American dog tick; *Ixodes*, the black-legged; and *Ornithodoros* or *Rhipicephalus*, the brown dog ticks.

Deer ticks are tiny, much smaller, and harder to find than adult dog ticks. In their juvenile stages they're about the size of a pinhead. Unless engorged with blood, even when attacking they are still so small that people easily miss them. The largest deer tick is less than 3/16 of an inch, legs extended. And to make matters worse, multiple diseases can be contracted from a single tick bite.

Most people classify ticks as insects. They are not. Insects have six legs and three body segments, while ticks, when adult, have eight legs and two body segments, hence ticks are arachnids, and are close relatives of spiders, mites, and chiggers. Ticks are bloodsucking parasites that feed on people, wild and domestic mammals, birds, reptiles, and even other arachnids.

A mature tick usually climbs a tall blade of grass, the fronds of a fern, or leaves of a weed, at a spot slightly above ground level. Then it looks for a host using a number of incredibly complex methods, including monitoring a victim's carbon dioxide levels, body heat, or other chemical alerts. When all systems are go, it uses its forelegs to grab the skin, clothing, or fur of a host.

The female tick requires a blood meal in order to lay eggs, so finding a host is a survival deal. Clutching their victim's skin, ticks draw blood using specialized mouthparts that are adorned with harpoon-like barbs in reverse, designed to first penetrate then attach to skin. They also secrete a cement-like substance that helps them hold fast to their host. They are totally dependent on the blood and tissue fluids of the host. The longer an infective tick feeds, the greater the chance of infection, with infection almost guaranteed if ticks feed in one spot for two or more days.

Ticks go through four life states: egg, larva, nymph, and adult. Eggs hatch into larva, a tiny being with six legs. It feeds and molts or changes into a nymph, a being with eight legs. The nymph feeds and molts into an adult, some male and some female. Remember, in order to infect a victim with a disease, the tick must have the ability to keep its infection through all stages of development. Some ticks can and some ticks cannot. Luckily, although dog ticks can pick up Lyme disease, they do not carry the bacteria from one molt to another.

Who gets a tick? People who work or live in and around tick-infested woods and fields are at risk of getting Lyme disease. Even suburbanites who live in clean and manicured backyards or who use the outdoors for recreation are at risk of picking up Lyme disease.

Getting Rid of a Tick

I referenced the websites of the Lyme Disease Association and the Centers for Disease Control and Prevention for the following up-to-date information on removing a tick once you find one. Check the CDC website for more information on Lyme disease and tick removal: www.cdc.gov/lyme.

Here are the correct procedures for removing a deer tick:

1. Using fine-point tweezers, grasp the tick at the place of attachment, as close to the skin as possible. If you don't have tweezers, protect your fingers with a tissue.
2. Gently pull the tick straight out with even pressure.
3. Avoid squeezing the tick, breaking it, or allowing any blood to remain on your skin.
4. Place the tick in a small vial labeled with the victim's name, address, and the date. Add a bit of moist (not wet) tissue.
5. Wash your hands, disinfect the tweezers and bite site.
6. Have the tick identified and tested by a lab, health department, or veterinarian.
7. Call your doctor to determine if treatment is warranted.
8. Watch the tick-bite site and your general health for signs or symptoms of a tick-borne illness. Make sure you mark any changes in your health status on your calendar.
9. Educate yourself about tick-borne diseases and consult a doctor to see if treatment is warranted.

Having on many occasions botched the job of removing dog ticks (not to mention common slivers), the following question at their website seemed more than pertinent: If the mouthparts break off in the skin, should I dig them out?

There are two competing opinions about this. One viewpoint states that the mouthparts can cause a secondary infection, and should be removed as if it was a splinter (the CDC recommends removal with tweezers if possible). The other opinion they heard came from a pediatrician in a hypodermic area. He stated that parents can do more harm by trying to hold down a child and digging out the mouthparts with a needle. He instructs his families to leave the mouthparts, and as skin sloughs off the tick parts will come out on their own.

You should also observe the following cautions:

1. Children should be taught to seek adult help for tick removal.
2. If you must remove the tick with your fingers, use a tissue or leaf to avoid contact with infected tick fluids.
3. Do not prick, crush, or burn the tick as it may release infected fluids or tissue.
4. Do not try to smother the tick with household preparations like petroleum jelly or nail polish because the attached tick has enough oxygen on its own to complete the feeding.

Why Is Lyme Disease Spreading?

It's not only deer. Studies have shown that migratory birds have helped disperse the infected tick. Then dogs and other animals can run in infected fields and bring infected ticks back to suburban locations and backyards.

Dogs traveling with their owner can spread infected ticks to distant locations. After all, people think nothing of traveling thousands of miles with their pets.

Lyme Disease in Dogs

Just when you thought it was finally safe to come out of the house, now there's another problem on the horizon: Lyme disease in dogs. This disease was first reported in dogs in 1984, and has spread rapidly across the country, affecting more victims every year.

Lyme disease problems have increased sixteen-fold since 1982. It has been reported in forty-seven states, and is being reported with increasing frequency each year. What's more, the incidence in dogs may be six to ten times higher.

Ask yourself these questions:

1. Do you take your dog on walks?
2. Does your dog travel with you?
3. Do you take your dog camping?
4. Does your dog "tag" along?
5. Does your dog hunt with you?
6. Does your dog come along on family picnics?
7. Do you take your dog jogging?
8. Does your dog go to parks?

If you answer yes to any of the above questions, your dog has a potential chance of meeting a tick head on, so to speak. And don't forget to check your cats, too.

How Is Lyme Disease Treated in Dogs?

Several broad spectrum antibiotics have proven effective in treating Lyme disease, especially in its early stages. Your veterinarian will have the most effective remedy available.

Just to be on the safe side, brush your dog after each outing. In fact, routinely check your pets after they have been outdoors, especially if they have been in areas with tall grass and brush. Cut brush and mow the grass where your pet plays. Ask your veterinarian about vaccinating your pet.

More about Lyme Disease

Then I remembered that my sister-in-law, Mrs. Jill Shaw of Bethel, Connecticut, had Lyme disease. I called her about her experiences.

"I thought I had the flu," she said. "It was July 5, 1995, and I woke up in the morning feeling like it was February and I was really sick. So for three days we let the symptoms run their course, but on the fourth day I woke up, my skin dead-white, with a temperature of 105.7°F.

"My husband Greg took me to the hospital. I was barely functioning and continually shuddering. I was also, they tell me, incoherent.

"So they put me in a cooling blanket—the nurses on duty had to learn, on-the-spot, how to use it.

"I was born in Buffalo, New York, and that cooling blanket felt like laying in a pile of wet leaves in that great city, late in October, after a chilling rain. No matter what was wrong with me, the temperature had to fall."

And it did. Jill recovered but until this day, she can remember all that happened.

"And if it ever happens to anybody I know, at least today they are quicker on the diagnosis trigger than ten years ago."

Controlling Ticks on Your Person

Whether you still venture out-of-doors or decide to sit out all the threats by staying inside until winter, the ticks never take a holiday until they freeze. But there are a number of simple things you can do to help in avoiding ticks.

The answer to protection is prevention. Do not go out in the woods of late spring, summer, or before-frost fall dressed in a pair of short-shorts and flip-flop sandals. You will get exactly what you deserve.

If wearing shorts, be sure they are walking shorts and your feet and lower legs are encased in good socks. If at all interested in going off a path, trade in the shorts for long pants and wear a long-sleeved shirt.

Next is textile choice. Here it's necessary to choose light-colored clothing, like khaki, so you or somebody walking close by can see an insect or a tick climbing up your back aiming for the neck. In fact, it's a good idea to stop for a tick check at least every half hour.

For a miticide, tickicide, or insecticide, try DEET. Not pleasant but it generally works. Liberally apply this lotion around your ankles, wrists, and waistline, underneath and on top of clothing, and use more if you are prone to sweating.

Any tick that gets beyond your defenses must be removed. If you have no tweezers or forceps in your first aid pack, use your fingers, but after tick removal, carefully wash your hands. If a tick has been imbedded for more than a few hours, see a doctor.

Finally, upon returning home, check again for ticks. And don't forget to comb the dog because dogs are walking tick magnets.

The Wasting Disease

Believe it or not, there's another tick threat on the horizon and it's called "the wasting disease."

Chronic Wasting Disease, or CWD, attacks the central nervous system of deer and elk, causing fatal damage to the brain. It is spread by a newly discovered disease vector called a prion. Prions are mutated proteins that cause normal proteins to fold in abnormal ways resulting in sponge-like holes in the brain. The disease is similar to, but significantly different from scrapie, a disease found in sheep and documented over 400 years.

In the later stages of infection, deer and elk with CWD exhibit progressive weight loss, listlessness, excessive salivation and urination, increased water intake, depression, and, eventually, death. Animals can be infected with CWD for months or years before outward signs appear.

While the exact method of transmission of CWD is not known, most scientists believe it travels from animal to animal through an exchange of body fluids like feces, urine, or saliva. Animals that are crowded or confined have a greater chance of encountering the body fluids of other animals and, therefore, a higher likelihood of becoming infected if the rogue prion is present. It's also a problem with animals that have social customs that include close contact with herd mates. There is a high probability that CWD prions survive in the environment after infected and exposed animals are removed.

At present, CWD is unique to North America where it's been found in wild deer and elk in Colorado, Wyoming, Nebraska, South Dakota, Wisconsin, and Saskatchewan. In captive deer and elk, it has been found in Colorado, Montana, South Dakota, Oklahoma, Kansas, Nebraska, Saskatchewan, and Alberta.

Currently the only test for the disease is a microscopic examination of an animal's brain stem and to do this, the animal must die.

There is, at present, no scientific evidence that CWD can infect humans, either through direct contact or by eating the meat of infected animals. But while the chance of transmission is extremely small or nonexistent, do not harvest any animal that appears sick or is acting strange.

Note the animal's location and contact the local game commission. Avoid cutting or puncturing the spinal cords or brains of animals taken in the areas where CWD occurs. Do not use household utensils to field dress or process your deer. Wear rubber or latex gloves when handling any harvested animal.

On the Road

Jean and I have experienced traffic accidents involving deer, twice!

The first was back in the late 1970s when we were driving back on a country road returning from Monticello, New York, late on a spring night. The radio was tuned to WQXR out of Manhattan, the air smelled of new foliage and a recent rain, a slim moon was breaking through the clouds, I was driving about 35 mph, and we were talking about a new book I was going to begin the following week.

Up ahead on the left was a local tavern, its parking lot pretty full. And on the right was a yellow road warning sign, with the silhouette of an upright deer, clearly visible, in my headlights.

Suddenly from in front of the sign, a stag lept out of the woods, stopped for a moment as my headlights dazzled his eyes, then proceeded to jump across the road at the same time my right front fender hit him broadside.

I hit the breaks as hard as I could.

The entire front end of the car (a fairly new Plymouth) was smashed, the windshield broke into large shards, the tire went flat, and the poor creature struggled on the black pavement, now stained with blood.

I pulled Jean out of the front seat on the driver's side and we ran to the tavern ahead.

As we came through the door an alert barkeeper already knew something was wrong, as he heard the crash.

"We just hit a deer," I said, my voice shaking with emotion.

"I heard it," he said and reaching above his head, grabbed a rifle that hung on the wall between two bent deer hoofs.

He went out the door and seconds later we heard a shot.

The other folks in the bar came up to find out if we were OK, and the bartender's wife poured us each a shot of whisky. We usual wine-drinkers drank it down.

It was only a half-hour to closing so Frank, the bartender and owner, helped us push the car into his lot, and later drove us the ten miles to home, and the next morning we called our local garage for a tow and a major repair job.

The experience was never forgotten and even today, some thirty years later, I can still smell the night and the blood on the road.

Our next experience was driving up Route 97 from Port Jervis, a picturesque road that winds and curves along the Delaware River on up to the small town of Hancock. This time it was raining as we left Jervis but as we began climbing up hills that lead to Narrowsburg, the rain began to turn to ice. At one particular hill near Grassy Swamp Road, I could feel the wheels begin to slip.

With an effort, I kept the car running along about thirty miles an hour, knowing that if I slowed, we would then slip, and we'd be stuck there for the night.

Suddenly Jean shouted: "Look out your window. My God, there's a deer running beside us!"

With my right hand on the wheel, I opened the driver's window to confront the flared nostrils—steam and all—a terrified eye, and heard the sound of hoofs slipping on the iced macadam in both fast and slow motion.

Before the doe could slip or directly turn into the side of the car, I pressed my foot on the accelerator, and pushed ahead, going over the top of the hill, then majestically sailed over to the right of the road into a snow bank.

Folks who lived in Sullivan County were always prepared for winter problems, so after my breathing returned to normal, I shoveled some of the snow and with my pushing and Jean's rocking the car, we eventually got back to the road, went another half-mile, and parked the car, then walked to a friend's nearby farmhouse to spend the night.

That, too, will never be forgotten.

And, according to the tales I've heard about traffic accidents involving deer, we were very, very lucky.

Warnings for the Road

The following suggestions are not to be glanced over but committed to memory:

1. When driving, be extra vigilant at dawn and dusk, the time of day when deer tend to travel.

2. Pay attention to the side of the road.
3. If one deer is present, there are probably more nearby.
4. If deer are sighted, flash headlights and honk the horn to scare them away from the road.
5. If deer are in the road, do not take evasive action such as hard braking or swerving. If stopping is not possible, it is better to hit the deer than to cross the center-line or leave the road.

Accidents Involving Deer

According to the Insurance Information Institute (III), the increase of car and deer collisions in life, limb, and money, as of October 24, 2012, is $4 billion a year. The statistics point out that cars and deer can be a lethal combination. The increase in urban sprawl, new roads being constructed, often through or close to wildlife habitats, not to mention poor maintenance on existing roads—and don't forget lack of driver education—has led to the rise in man and animal collisions.

An estimated 1.23 million deer-vehicle collisions occurred in the U.S. between July 1, 2011, and June 30, 2012, costing more than $4 billion in vehicle damage, and according to State Farm, the average claim for deer-vehicle collisions between July 1, 2011, and June 30, 2012, was $3,305, a rise of 4.4 percent from the previous year with costs varying depending on the type of vehicle and severity of the damage. Over the last four years, the number of deer-related claims paid out by State Farm increased 7.9 percent, while other claims involving moving vehicles (i.e., first-party, physical damage claims not caused by weather, criminal activity, or fire) declined 8.6 percent. The Insurance Institute for Highway Safety (IIHS) noted that deer-vehicle collisions in the U.S. cause about 200 fatalities annually.

The Proper Placement of Deer Crossing Signs

While searching for deer impact on traffic, I ran across the following information published by the Washtenaw County Road Commission of Ann Arbor, Michigan. I talked with Sheryl Soderholm Siddall, P.E., Supervisor of Traffic and Safety Engineering, who graciously gave me permission to reproduce the following.

The Michigan Manual of Uniform Traffic Control devices lists Deer Crossing signs but it does not provide criteria for the installation and removal of these signs. Therefore, Washtenaw County Road Commission is defining criteria to be used in the installation and removal of Deer Crossing signs.

A deer-car accident history should be looked up for the stretch of road in question. Installation of Deer Crossing signs is warranted if five deer-car accidents have occurred in a twelve-month period.

Placement of the signs should be reviewed every third year. Any necessary adjustments in placement or removal should be made according to the following guidelines:

When the accident study shows that no deer-car accidents have occurred in the study area in a minimum of a twelve-month period, the sign may be removed at the discretion of Washtenaw County Road Commission. When a request for a Deer Crossing Sign is received, the Road Commission reviews crash reports received from the Sheriff's Department to determine if a sign should be installed. A Deer Crossing Sign is warranted if five deer-car accidents have occurred over a twelve-month period.

Nurseries and Gardens

This is supposed to be a book about solutions, and with the world direction being what it is, far be it from me to point out the obvious: read chapter 4 about the many available sources for deer fencing and you will understand that things are getting worse, not better.

For obvious reasons, the life of a nursery, when forced to continually think about and plan for deer invasions, is just part of running a landscape and nursery business. I called my old friend Kate Jayne at Sandy Mush Herb Nursery in Leceister, North Carolina, and asked her about protecting the large number of hostas they grow for sale at their nursery.

Kate thought for a moment, then with a voice that always is pleasant, even if the wolves were at the door and said, "If we didn't have four dogs, mutts that roam free, by the end of the spring we wouldn't have a hosta left, not only for the trade but for our own gardens as well!"

Losing a Garden

The following is a letter from a family friend, Scott Birdwell, who has been waging such a war—and is losing.

"My yard," he wrote, "measures out to be a little less than one acre inside the Washington, DC Beltway in Fairfax County, Virginia. I am up against a herd of deer that continue to frequent my yard and after doing battle with them for about fifteen years, I have learned that deer destroy not only yards, but entire ecosystems.

"The deer in my neighborhood make daily and nightly rounds destroying every edible plant. Ten deer seem far beyond the natural carrying capacity of the neighborhood backyards, so I can only figure that they survive because the homeowners are replenishing the food supply with fresh azaleas, and some feed corn and bird food to the deer."

When Scott began gardening, he planted hundreds of azaleas, hostas, hydrangeas, and daylilies only to have them decimated. The deer picked not only on the ornamentals but also the native plants, too. Now he has high hopes that he's learned a lot more than he knew, and armed with new knowledge, about half of his yard is planted with natives and certified as a wildlife habitat with the National Wildlife Federation. This also means he strives to maintain a diverse ecosystem—but, he added, the deer destroy that too.

"The deer," he continued, "destroy all the native plants that all the other native animal species depend on and the destruction is complete. They clip and girdle new seedling oaks, maples, cherry, magnolia, redbuds, pine, and poplars to make the next generation of forest. The understory of redbuds, fringe trees, viburnums, even a tree with the thorns provided by the devils walking stick, is picked.

Eleven of Scott Birdwell's deer herd look up in amazed wonder as he photographs their quizzical gazes, all in his Washington garden that is inside The Beltway.

"Once the native plants are wiped out, all the native animals that rely so heavily on them will move on—the butterflies, moths, chipmunks, mice, foxes, king snakes, hawks, and owls. The whole ecosystem breaks down and worse yet, the destruction of the native plants allows the exotics to infiltrate and take over my yard. For ten years I have battled the bamboo, multiflora Rose, English ivy, Japanese honeysuckle, and Japanese stilt-grass, all of which seem to be the only deer-resistant plants. Another unfriendly addition to the neighborhood that accompanied the deer is Lyme disease, which a neighbor a few houses down contracted.

"I have sprayed diligently with $30 bottles of deer spray that guarantee results, but responsibility for spraying nearly an acre means that if you are a few days late once, the deer start to slip through and destroy the next generation of yard and forest. Not only is the ecosystem in my yard decimated, I am also mindful that my efforts at 'natural' deer control serve only to drive the deer to someone else's yard where they will do their damage. Not only am I harming my neighbors when I spray, but when the deer eat the natives on their properties they further reduce the diversity of the neighborhood ecosystem.

"Other potential solutions like a dog or an eight-foot fence are just not viable options to me and so my dream garden is impossible. However, there is a greater moral imperative here."

Scott's message to all who struggle with the deer issue, whether counties, neighborhoods, or individuals, is that decisions should not focus on the deer, but on the ecosystems.

"If the deer," he said, "are out of balance, they must be culled. Indeed, the meat from the culling can and should be used to help feed the community. The alternative of course is that the deer will exceed the carrying capacity of the land, which means that they either starve to death or they are hit by cars. Deer-vehicle collisions cost over $4 billion and cause nearly two hundred human fatalities annually. While I have lost the battle in my yard, organized and responsible culling programs are the right thing to do on every level, safety, moral, and aesthetic."

Is It an Honest Approach to Thin Deer Herds?

In July 2002, a story appeared in the *Asheville Citizen-Times,* the headline reading: Biltmore Forest still aiming for shooters to kill deer in town.

The gist of the saga concerned Biltmore Forest town officials meeting with North Carolina Wildlife Resources Commission's Big Game Committee to mull over the town's hiring of a firm, the Connecticut-based White Buffalo Inc., to bait the deer and provide sharpshooters to kill them. Earlier this year, the town proposed hiring White Buffalo but the commission rejected the proposal.

Earlier in the year, Richard Hamilton, deputy director of the commission, said the population control method "is inconsistent with our policy of controlling deer numbers through more conventional and less controversial methods." The commission suggested alternatives, including using plants that deer won't eat and putting up barriers between the town and the Biltmore Estate, where the deer roam.

Brazil said a fence would be too expensive and "unsightly." A fence would cost between $300,000 and $400,000, and would have to be eight feet high, he said.

But now the pressure is building to allow just such a solution.

Years passed and arguments increased from all areas involved in Western North Carolina (WNC) with the problem of deer.

The January 23, 2010, issue of the *Asheville Citizen-Times* reported that "Despite the opinion of a biologist that the killing of deer in this town [Biltmore Forest] is not necessary from a population-management standpoint, town leaders are again trying to cull the herd."

Town workers have killed fifteen white-tailed deer under a state permit issued for 2009 and extended into 2010. The number of bagged deer is way down from previous hunts. Hunters shot 150 deer in 2003 and 90 in 2005, trying to keep the deer from overrunning the heavily wooded town next to sprawling Biltmore Estate.

But a local wildlife biologist for the NC Wildlife Commission said in his opinion the town doesn't need to shoot any deer. "I don't think they have any problem with deer right now," Mike Carraway said. In addition, some residents of the town also have misgivings about the culling scheme.

Still, in the opinion of town leaders: "Every year we want to try to take a small harvest so we can control the population. We don't want to get back up to the four hundred or five hundred deer we had a few years ago," said Mayor George Goosmann.

The meat doesn't go to waste. It is donated through Hunters for the Hungry, and about four thousand pounds of venison has gone to Asheville's MANNA Food Bank since the hunts began in 2003, Goosmann said.

Town officials applied directly to Raleigh for the depredation permit, bypassing Carraway, who can issue permits locally. Carraway typically issues those permits to farmers who can show damage to their property with deer eating soybeans or bear eating corn.

Residential property owners can also apply for depredation permits to kill deer if they can show the animals are eating their shrubbery and landscaping.

Another Part of the State

But the problem isn't just limited to WNC. The website Raleigh Durham About (www.raleighdurham.about.com) issued a report titled, "Deer Control is a Divisive issue in Raleigh-Durham," stating that the Triangle is hit hard by deer overpopulation.

"The idea of controlled deer culling is surfacing more and more around Raleigh-Durham in neighborhood association meetings, at city council and within the University communities. In case you're not familiar with this politically correct term for deer control, culling is the act of bringing in hunters to kill a specific number of deer either with hunting bows or with guns.

"Duke Forest officials estimate their deer population is about eighty animals per square mile. The forest's Resource Manager, James Edeburn, says that number is about four times what is acceptable in order to preserve the forest's viability as a research enviroment. To manage the problem, Duke has taken steps to reduce the deer herd on multiple occasions since 2005 using local, trained hunting groups working under North Carolina Wildlife Resources Commission (NCWRC) guidelines.

"According to Edeburn, 'Similar herd reductions have been conducted in Biltmore Forest, Bald Head Island and Nags Head in North Carolina as well as at a number of locations in other states. Hunting also takes place in a number of other research forests.'

"Opponents of hunting as a means of deer control cite the solution as immoral, inhumane or just plain dangerous. They argue for tactics such as deer-resistant landscaping, deer contraception and eight-foot fences. However, none of these methods has shown to make a significant reduction in the kind of statistics mentioned at the top of this article. Reducing the population, on the other hand, has documented success in reducing the number of deer accidents as well as the cost of clean-up.

"A proposal for deer hunting inside Governor's Club, a large gated community in northern Chatham County, ignited a firestorm. Almost two years of task-force work, study and debate commenced before the issue could even be brought to vote. The deer reduction program was ultimately approved, but a steady stream of vocal opposition on the subject continued to appear in local letters to the editor.

"The subject of deer culling caused a similar community divide in Fearrington, a retirement community between Chapel Hill and Pittsboro. Again more than two years of study and discussion ensued. Their process resulted in the decision not to cull, but instead focus on deer-resistant landscaping, attractive fencing, and a request that no-one in the community actively attract the deer by setting up feeding stations.

"Recently, the Chapel Hill Town Council heard statements from several neighborhoods pleading for deer relief. They voted 8-1 to apply for a 2011 archery permit from the NCWRC, but stopped short of approval for culling pending a public hearing with ecologists, residents and archers.

"It is clear from the differences in decision making and out comes in these situations that the subject of deer culling is one that spurs passionate discourse. But the deer problem is here to stay, so this controversial subject will be under debate for some time to come."

More to the Debate

Meanwhile, others municipalities continue to enter the fray with the insistence that a fence around any community like Biltmore Forest would do the job of keeping the deer out, but of course, the recommended fence is never high enough at eight or even ten feet to do the job because in many situations fourteen feet is the needed height.

One of the solutions offered to Biltmore Forest for controlling their over-the-top deer population concerns a company called White Buffalo, Inc. Their Internet site bills them as the leading expert in control of white-tailed deer especially in highly sensitive areas like suburban communities, city parks, and enclaves where deer seem to outnumber the residents. They are also listed as a non-profit agency.

The debate in Biltmore Forest is, I suspect, the same debate that occurs across the country when a segment of the society wants to control wildlife.

I called Dr. Anthony DeNicola, the director of White Buffalo Inc., when I found out that Biltmore Forest had contacted him about a possible contract to help in their deer control problems.

"After all, it's a philosophical question," said Dr. DeNicola, "over the most humane methods to kill deer. Is it starvation, or their being injured by hitting cars or trucks, or using our sharpshooters who bait selected areas with corn, then shoot the deer from elevated locations, aiming for their head.

"In fact, sometimes we use drop nets to trap animals and captive bolt guns for killing. Then the meat is donated to charities."

Of course many residents of many communities disagree with Dr. DeNicola, including Chuck Rice, the executive director of the North Carolina Wildlife Federation, who said, "My biggest objections have to do with what I consider the ethics of the methods proposed."

Other residents of the town have also disliked the hunt idea, including the proposals made two years ago where bow hunters (who would make less noise) were suggested over rifle bearers.

"There must be," I added, "more reasons for a community to hire you than merely thinning out the herd. What are they?"

"Well, in addition to the cost of vehicle collisions, rising insurance costs, damage to landscapes both public and private, not to mentions damage to the local ecology, there are the humane reasons of killing sick and starving deer because in areas like Biltmore Forest, there is never enough food to go around."

"But there must be steps you must follow?"

"First," he answered, "it's necessary to have a public meeting so private landowners can understand what's involved in a euthanasia program. First, deer distribution is assessed, then access to private properties, and finally safe shoot in the selected areas. A baiting program is established to herd the deer and bring them to these areas. Shooting lanes are then cleared to ensure that there are no obstructions in the trajectory of the bullet. Patterns of human activity like dog walking, school bus routes, joggers, are noted so when the shooting begins, we have maximum safety and, I might add, a sense of discretion.

"For each site, we select one of eleven specialized weapon systems each designed for select site characteristics. This decision is dependent on maximum shooting range, acceptable noise, proximity to homes, and deer abundance. Deer are euthanized with a single shot to the head, ensuring a humane kill."

"How do outside agencies maintain objectivity when communities are in the decision-making phase?"

"We simply review all available deer management options and then determine what is involved logistically, the costs, time frame, and compatibility with the local human activity. This information is then passed on to the powers-that-be so they can make a more informed decision."

"Can agencies implement a control program after an area has been hunted?"

"It's difficult to professionally manage a deer population after they have been pursued by recreational hunters. Prior to any management action, suburban deer are usually easy to approach. Deer that do not readily exhibit alarm behavior can be effectively and efficiently manipulated for the purposes of capture, anti-fertility agents, or what we call remote euthanasia. If deer are hunted they become weary of the threat that humans pose, and any subsequent efforts to manage deer using similar techniques, like tree stands, are often compromised. The only cost-effective way to manage deer effectively uses methods that substantially differ from regular hunting. For example, approaching deer with a vehicle usually remains a viable option."

I asked about trapping and relocating deer.

Dr. DeNicola said that relocation of animals requires trapping, netting, and possibly remote chemical immobilization, always by experienced personnel. Costs can range from $400 to $2,931 per animal. Suitable release sites are necessary but are often difficult to find. Relocating deer can result in stress-related death or disease transmission, like Lyme disease or tuberculosis. Post trapping, you must have experienced personnel so the handling procedures minimize stress and post-release death.

"Now I remember last year there was talk of Biltmore Forest using fertility control to keep the deer population at manageable levels. What is fertility control?"

"Fertility control," he answered, "is the ideal solution. Unfortunately, fertility control agents are limited in their potential for managing overabundant deer populations. Further research is required to review the feasibility and practicality of using fertility control methods. Fertility control agents exist that can prevent reproduction in individual deer, but the need for repeated administration and limited delivery technologies reflect current problems. As a result of the limited management potential of contraceptive vaccines, more research has begun to focus on surgical sterilization given the 100 percent effectiveness and one-time interaction with each animal. Data collected to date racks up a cost of manpower and materials to equal $1,000 per doe. That suggests that contraceptives will be limited to smaller herds."

"So with both trapping and fertility control, that means a community like Biltmore Forest has just three options: sharp shooting, controlled hunting, and trapping linked to euthanasia."

"That's right. The American Veterinary Medical Association approved sharp shooting as a humane form of euthanasia. sharp shooting requires trained personnel to use a variety of techniques to maximize safety, discretion, and efficiency. This method is often implemented in suburban and urban settings with access to both public and private lands. Costs range from $200 to $400 per deer. Typically all meat harvested is donated to area food shelters for distribution.

"Next is controlled hunting. Unfortunately for speed, using hunters to manage overabundant deer populations often requires an approval from a state agency and law enforcement involvement because there's the potential for animal welfare groups to become involved. Costs range from $200 to $400 per deer harvested, depending on the manpower required. Archery is another discreet removal technique but results in a lower success rate because limited shooting ranges require a longer time frame of operation. Where feasible, firearms can be used to maximum efficiency.

"Finally, trapping and euthanasia are available for areas where there's a concern about, or a law prohibiting, the discharge of firearms. Physical restraints like box traps, clover traps, drop nets, or rocket nets are followed by euthanasia using a gunshot or captive bolt to the head. As mentioned above, deer are subjected to great amounts of stress during the restraint operation. The minimum cost is $400 per animal."

As of 2015, the argument goes on.

The Wonderful World of Fencing

When installing a fence around your garden or property, think long range. If you are not a dedicated gardener or plan to retire to Florida in a year or two, perhaps the expense of installing a fence is not the best idea. After all, a good fence is not a cheap solution.

And to make your investment pay, it must be a good fence, carefully planned, specially designed for your site, and installed with care and precision. Consider fencing as a long-term investment. A well-maintained fence should last between five and twenty-some years, depending on the type. Most fences pay for themselves within a few years by reducing losses caused by deer damage.

When researching this book I was amazed at how many sites and organizations suggested a six-foot fence as adequate for protecting a garden. Any healthy adult deer can easily leap six feet without ever breathing hard.

Most healthy deer can easily clear an eight-footer.

Given enough room and the knowledge of where they will land, there are many deer able to vault over a ten-footer. Here in Asheville we have the North Carolina Arboretum, carefully surrounded with a ten-foot-high wire fence. Because of dips and rises in the terrain, in places, it is not high enough.

Deer are careful creatures. They will not purposefully put their lives into harm's way. So in a backyard situation, where on the protected side of the fence, there is limited open space for a deer to land in, you might get by with an eight-foot-high fence. Their caution always works in your favor: unless they are being chased by a known or unknown threat, deer will not jump without knowing they will safely land on the other side of any barrier.

So another solution is to have two rows of fencing with a gap in-between. Let's say you build two four-foot-high fences, parallel to each other, spaced five feet apart. Remember, deer hate enclosed spaces so that five-foot gap would be menacing and it's still wide enough for the gardener to wheel his or her barrow down that protected lane.

And how about packed snow? If you live in an area with high snowfall, and the kind of temperatures that eventually turn snow into solid blocks of ice, then depending on the snow depth, you've lost the same number of feet on your fence.

How about the driveway? I've seen people quarantine their property with an eight-foot fence then block the driveway with a gate, only to leave the gate open because somebody forgot to close it.

Make sure the bottom of the fence is secured to the ground. It is absolutely amazing how a deer, especially when hungry, will limbo his or her way into your garden, particularly fawns.

Non-electric Fences

Today there are two basic types of fencing, non-electric and electric. Let's begin with the non-electric varieties.

I can remember when we first knew the garden must be protected up in Sullivan County. Along with the house and the grounds, we had acquired about one hundred wooden bunk beds, because apparently for many years part of our property had been a summer camp for kids back at the end of the Second World War.

They were sturdily made with mattress supports consisting of long metal straps attached to the bed frame with heavy iron springs.

So until we surrounded the garden with chicken-wire held to wooden posts, we made a fence of two rows of bunk beds, one piled on top of the other. It was unaesthetic but it worked.

In situations in which deer pressure is moderate to high and your garden means a lot to you, fencing becomes a necessity. Remember, you must begin with an eight-foot fence to exclude deer. Many designs of electric and non-electric fence are available to meet specific needs, whether for gardens, nurseries, or tree plantations. They range in cost from pennies per foot to as much as $6 or more per linear foot.

One last thing: Remember to check local zoning laws, especially if you live in a town or a village. It would be a shame to go to the effort and expense of installing a fence only to find out it's illegal.

Wire Mesh Fencing

Because nobody, even a writer on a deadline, wants to reinvent the wheel, it's with great pleasure I thank an article entitled *Controlling Deer Damage in Missouri,* Agricultural publication MP685, November 1, 1997, by Robert A. Pierce II and Ernie P. Wiggers at the School of Natural Resources, for much of the following information on the types of fences available today.

Woven-wire fences are used for year-round protection of high-value crops subject to high deer pressures. While expensive and difficult to construct, they are both easy to maintain and highly effective. It's assembled from two tiers of four-foot woven wire strung together to form an eight-foot barrier. The fence must be tight to the ground so deer are unable to crawl underneath. The tiers of wire are tied together at the seam to prevent penetration. Other designs include six-foot woven wire with strands of high-tensile wire above that to a height of eight to ten feet. Little maintenance is required.

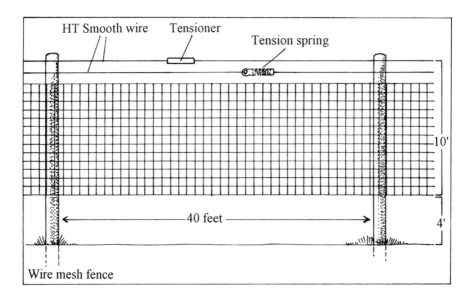

Plastic Mesh Fencing

Non-electric plastic mesh fencing has great residential landscape applications. This type of fencing is lightweight, high-strength, and virtually invisible, so it does not detract from the appearance of the property it protects. The fencing consists of a seven-and-a-half-foot black plastic mesh with an expected life of ten years. This type of fence can be attached to existing trees or hung on pressure-treated posts. The lightweight of the material minimizes the need for many posts. Spaced about a foot apart, twelve-inch white streamers are attached, four feet off the ground, to warn deer of the barrier. Galvanized twelve-inch stakes can be purchased to secure the fencing to the ground every twelve feet.

Deer Blocker Fence (www.nixalite.com/deerfencing .aspx) is extremely strong, long-lasting, virtually invisible, and easy to install. It's strong because the strands are strong, 380 dernier, 36 ply, knotted, virgin (un-recycled) polyethylene mesh. Each UV-resistant strand has a 175-lb. breaking strength. The four-inch square mesh is durable yet inconspicuous and almost invisible at normal viewing distances. The material includes full eight-foot-tall and one-hundred-foot-long pieces for deer exclusion. Construction is seamless and a heavy-duty 5/16" border is woven into all sides of the mesh, eliminating the need for additional hardware. Use Tangle Guard Repeller Ribbon to tie on fencing as avoidance tags.

DeerBusters (www.deerbusters.com) deer fencing is made from the highest quality polypropylene plastic and designed to provide virtually invisible protection around your garden or property for years. This is not the lightweight or folded product available in most big box stores or on other websites. Tenax, the largest and best-known name in the industry, has chosen DeerBusters.com as its preferred distributor. Their product is designed to be virtually invisible so it can be installed around your garden or close to your home without spoiling your view.

Heavy-Duty Deer and Elk Fencing (www.industrialnetting.com) manufactures netting fences for heavy-duty protection from deer and elk. Fences protect feed storage areas from foraging wildlife. They are a passive deterrent near high-traffic right-of-ways. Heights are up to thirteen feet.

A Visit with Patryk Battle

Patryk Battle is an old garden friend and a radio compatriot over many years. The first mention refers to his extensive organic vegetable garden up in Celo, North Carolina, and the second revolves around a radio show we all had in WNC for many more years.

This year Patryk installed an electric fence to protect about an eighth of an acre of his vegetable crop, protection that began with the installation of a fence from Premier 1 Fencing supplies (see image on page 72) that was designed by the company but installed by Patryk and two helpers.

"We did it ourselves," he said, "and the entire job took about three hours to accomplish and it's been one of the brighter moves I've made in my continuing battle against deer taking over the garden.

Patryk Battle checks the layout of his new deer fence in his mountain garden.
Credit photo: Patryk Battle

"The line," he continued, "at the left of the installation is about two feet off the ground, the top line on the right is four feet above the ground, and the bottom line is eighteen inches up. All three are electrified. There is a three-foot aisle between the fences that is mown and wide enough to walk through and use a wheelbarrow, too."

Patryk assured me that installing such a fence is not difficult at all, and the company did individual designs for every client.

"Even if," Patryk said, "you have never installed a fence before in your life, you will become an old pro at your first attempt—and wait until you add the folded metal strips that are baited with apple juice and, naturally, peanut butter!"

Electric Fencing

Electric deer fences are the most common and effective type of fencing used. They do their job because deer, unless chased, prefer to go through or under a fence rather than attempt to jump it. Electric fences are powered by high-voltage, low-impedance chargers, which provide timed pulses (forty-five to sixty-five per minute) of short duration (0.0003 per second). How well a charger performs depends on its power output measured in joules (a unit of energy) under load.

Because deer hair is hollow, it's an effective insulator, and deer hooves, being small and pointed, also lessen the impact of an electric shock. Therefore the type of fence charger used to deter cattle often lack sufficient output to stop deer from moving on. The charger must also be matched to the fence design.

When selecting a charger, a good rule of thumb is one joule of output from a charger will adequately power three thousand feet of fence wire. By determining the perimeter of your fenced area and the number of wires that will be charged, you can get a rough idea of your charger needs.

Remember that unless you live in the middle of the North Woods, with no chance of a stranger every walking onto your property (whether by chance or design), all electric fences must be marked with warning signs.

Chargers can be AC-powered, battery-charged, or solar-powered and should maintain a charge greater than five thousand volts on several miles of fence. It's best to use AC-powered chargers because they have the lowest cost per joule of output and are the most reliable. A power wire can be run to the fence, or aluminum fence wire can be run considerable distances on posts from an AC-powered charger to the remote fence location. The cost of running a well-maintained electric fence with a four-joule energizer for one year is equivalent to the cost of running a 40-watt light bulb for one year. Battery chargers are adequate but must be properly maintained. Solar chargers have a solar panel that keeps a battery charged, but they are expensive and high-joule units must be custom made. In addition, solar chargers need the sun and without adequate sunlight, they will fail.

Fence Maintenance and Effectiveness

Just like the lawnmower or remembering to inflate car tires, after the first year many landowners experience problems with deer penetrating fences because they forget maintenance. Fences must be maintained to remain effective.

Using herbicides or cutting it back by hand, vegetation must be kept off of the lower fence wires to reduce grounding and voltage loss. Voltage must be regularly checked and broken strands quickly repaired. Remember, deer will constantly test the fence and if they are able to penetrate because the power is off or for some other reason, the fence will lose its effectiveness. A common mistake is not electrifying the fence before leaving the area during construction or afterward.

During the off-season some people have mistakenly turned off the power while leaving the fence in place. This renders the fence ineffective even after it is re-electrified, because the deer have learned that they can penetrate it. Fences used for temporary protection should be dismantled during the off-season. It's important to understand that most fences are not true physical barriers but behavioral barriers. The electric shock conditions the deer to stay away. Once deer know they can penetrate this fence, its effectiveness is seriously reduced.

Another problem is not providing a ten-to fifteen-foot cleared buffer outside the fence so deer can see the fence. Without these buffers, deer will run into the fence, breaking it or going right on through. Remember, on steep slopes this buffer must be wider.

Temporary Electric Fencing

Temporary electric fences provide inexpensive protection for many gardens, large or small. They are easy to construct, do not require rigid corners, and use readily available materials. The fences are designed to attract attention and administer a strong but harmless electric shock (high voltage, low amperage) when a deer touches the fence with its nose. Deer soon become conditioned to avoid these fences.

Such fences are easily installed and removed. The major cost associated with temporary electric fencing is the fence charger.

Remember to install fences at the first sign of damage to prevent deer from establishing feeding patterns in your crops. Such fences require weekly inspection and maintenance.

The Peanut Butter Fence

First the peanut butter fence reflects the fact that most animals like peanut butter. This fence is an effective but inexpensive construction best used for gardens or nurseries subject to moderate deer pressures.

A single strand of 17-gauge wire is suspended about thirty inches above the ground by four-foot fiberglass rods at thirty- to sixty-foot intervals. Wood corner posts provide support. Flags of aluminum foil (foil squares four inches by our inches folded over the wire) are attached to the wire at twenty- to fifty-foot intervals, held in place with tape or paper clips. Aluminum flashing can also be used and has the advantage of not being damaged or blown off.

Closer spacing may be necessary near existing deer trails and during the first few months the fence is used, as the gardener attempts to modify deer behavior. The underside of the flags is baited

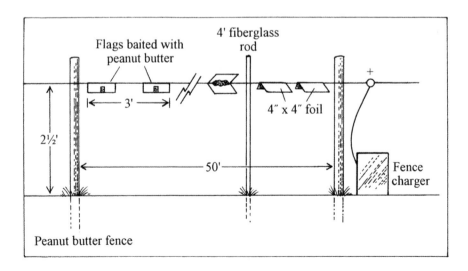

Peanut butter fence

with a one-to-one mixture of peanut butter and vegetable oil. The smell attracts the deer, which touch or sniff the flags and receive an electric shock. The flags should be re-baited every four to eight weeks, depending on weather conditions.

A Polywire and Polytape Fence

The original peanut butter fence is greatly enhanced using polywire or polytape, rather than 17-gauge wire. Poly's have the advantage of being more visible to deer, especially at night. They are also easier to roll up and remove. Polywire has a life expectancy of five to seven years.

Polywire is composed of three, six, or nine strands of metal filament braided with strands of brightly colored polyethylene. A wider polytape is available and has the added advantage of being stronger and more visible—but it's also more expensive. Although both polywire and polytape come in a wide variety of colors, many users claim that white provides the greatest contrast to most backgrounds and is the easiest for deer to see, especially at night. Remember, the loss of voltage over long distances of polywire/polytape can be a problem. Purchase materials with the least electrical resistance (ohms per 1,000 ft) for these applications.

In its simplest application, an electrified single strand of polywire is suspended about thirty inches above the ground by four-foot fiberglass rods at twenty- to fifty-foot intervals and baited in the same way as the original peanut butter fence. A second wire can be added to increase effectiveness: one wire placed eighteen inches from the ground and the top wire at thirty-six inches above the ground. This prevents fawns from walking under the fence and also increases the chance that one wire will remain electrified if deer knock the fence over.

Usually only the top wire is baited. In smaller areas, such as home gardens, more wires can be added on taller poles if desired, and closely spaced bottom wires can keep out rabbits and woodchucks.

It's always important that vegetation is mowed or removed under the fence so it does not short out.

Fiberglass rods do not provide enough support for use as corner posts. At corners it's better to use four-foot metal fence stakes with a bottom plate that provides stability when it is pounded into the ground. A piece of thin-walled one-inch PVC pipe can be slipped over the metal stake to act as an insulator with the polywire or polytape wrapped around a few times. This allows the stringing of the wire with sufficient tension to hold the flags. A variety of wooden posts with plastic insulators will also work.

The use of electric fences around the home often leads to concern for children and visitor safety. One option is to time the fence charger so it turns on from dusk to dawn.

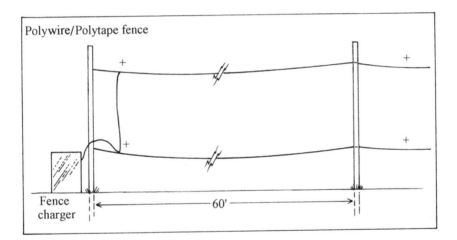

Permanent and Semi-permanent Electric Fencing
High-tensile fencing can provide year-round protection from deer damage. Many designs are available to fit specific needs. All require strict adherence to construction guidelines concerning rigid corner assemblies and fence configurations. Frequent inspection and maintenance are necessary. High-tensile fences have a twenty- to thirty-year life expectancy.

The Offset or Double Fence

Here's an effective fence design best suited for gardens, nurseries, or truck farms under forty acres in size. The fence's electric shock coupled with its three-dimensional design repel the deer. More wires can be added if deer pressures increase.

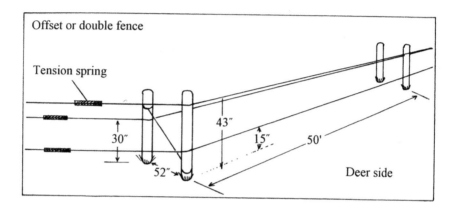

A Vertical Electric Deer Fence

Here's a permanent fence for protecting large truck gardens, orchards, and other fields from moderate to high deer pressures. It offers highly effective protection for areas up to twenty to twenty-five acres. A wide variety of fence materials and specific designs are available, including variation in the number of wires (five, seven, nine, or more) and fence height (five to ten feet). Posts are usually driven into the ground and high-tensile 12-gauge wire is applied and maintained under high tension, hence the need for good support.

This fence is powered by a high-voltage, low-impedance, New Zealand–style charger. Because of the prescribed wire spacing, deer try to go through the fence and are effectively shocked. Vertical fences use less ground space than three-dimensional fences, but are probably less effective at keeping deer from jumping over. It is recommended that you employ a local fence contractor.

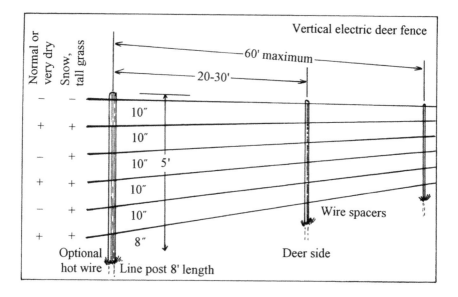

A Slanted Seven-Wire Fence

Here's a fence that differs from the vertical fence in both post alignment and wire barrier. It's constructed at a thirty-degree angle to the ground with the result that a deer must carefully consider the jump. Its three-dimensional design (five feet high by eight feet wide) plus an electric shock present a formidable barrier. It's used primarily where high deer pressures threaten moderate-sized to large orchards, nurseries, and other high-value crops.

Construct the fence using 12-gauge wire. The wires are attached to slanted fence battens at fifty-foot intervals to achieve the three-dimensional effect. One drawback to this fence is that it requires eight feet of space along its entire length, which increases maintenance cost.

The Electric Spider Fence

The spider fence is a relatively new fencing concept that combines multi-wire electric fencing technology with medium cost and offers good protection. This five-wire fence is four feet tall and uses a

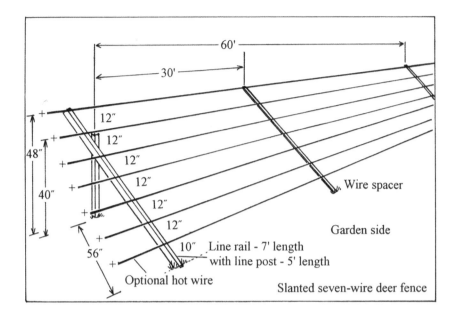

<- 60' ->

<- 30' ->

12"

12"

48"

12"

12"

40"

12"

12"

Wire spacer

Garden side

56"

10" Line rail - 7' length
with line post - 5' length

Optional hot wire

Slanted seven-wire deer fence

17-gauge wire, not held under high tension. The only driven posts
are the corners, and intermediate fiberglass posts are used periodi-
cally to maintain wire spacing and height. Minimal wire tension is
increased or decreased by wrappings on the Spider G-Spring at the

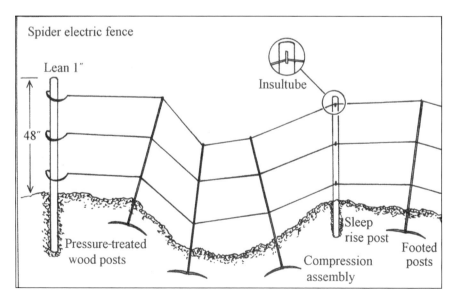

Spider electric fence

Lean 1"

Insultube

48"

Pressure-treated
wood posts

Sleep
rise post

Footed
posts

Compression
assembly

gate opening system. Because there are few driven posts and low tension, the fence is semi-permanent and much cheaper to construct than conventional high-tension systems. Baiting with peanut butter flags, described earlier, is essential to make this fence effective. Properly maintained, this fence has a life expectancy of about ten to twelve years.

Some Fencing Sources

Before becoming involved with ordering heavy-duty fence supplies from across country, look in your Yellow Pages and check for fence dealers in your area. The following companies sell all sorts of protective fences.

Deer Fence Direct (www.deer-fence-direct.com) sells a number of deer fences made of a patented ultraviolet-light-resistant polypropylene that can be fixed to posts yet wrapped around or drawn between trees in wooded areas. Its sister company, Deer Fencers, has installation crews based in New York, New Jersey, Connecticut, Pennsylvania, Delaware, Maryland, Virginia, Illinois, Wisconsin, North Carolina, Massachusetts, Maine, and Rhode Island. They also have California-based crews that cover areas from Monterey to the Napa Valley, including the Bay Area and the Sierra Foothills. Deer Fencers can be reached by dialing 1-800-BIG-DEER. If your property is located in another region, they most likely can still provide you with the names and numbers of contractors who are experienced with installing the fencing. Please call Benner's Gardens at 1-800-753-4660.

Gallagher Power Fence (www.gallagherusa.com) system enables the control of animals by giving them a short, sharp but safe shock which is sufficiently memorable that they never forget it. Today, the most powerful Gallagher Energizer has the capacity to power long distances of multi-wire fence. This has spread the use of electrical fencing on to large properties and enabled the control of all animals, including naturally wild ones. Their website has the following information that is frankly impressive. Gallagher Power Fences have kept elk off of golf courses in Montana and Oregon, blue herons out of crayfish ponds in Louisiana, raccoons out of sweet corn patches all over the Midwest, bears out of beehives from Montana to Maine, sea lions off boat docks in California, moose off of railroad tracks in Alaska, squirrels out of pecan orchards in California, deer out of flowerbeds and vineyards from Vermont to Virginia, and coyotes and mountain lions out of calving pastures across the USA.

Gardener's Supply Company (www.gardeners.com) markets an Easy-Up Fence that can be attached to posts or stakes to create a quick, temporary fence. At season's end simply roll it back up. Once in place, the black five-eight by three-quarter-inch mesh netting is almost invisible and seven feet high. The mesh is constructed of tough, UV-stabilized polypropylene for years of seasonal use. Can be cut in half easily with scissors for a shorter fence, and can also be wrapped around shrubs for deer protection.

Havahart Electronic Repellent (www.havahart.com) for deer attracts deer to posts with a lure scent—harmlessly repelling deer from your yard or garden. The system includes three posts covering approximately 1,000 sq. ft. total area. It is easy to assemble and install. Natural garden colors allow this product to blend into your garden or yard. Electronics are impervious to cold, heat, and rain for year round control. Extensive field testing backed by research has proven this product to be effective. Repellent delivers 400 volts (substantially less volts than a static shock) and with virtually no amps (0.1 joules). This will harmlessly repel deer and is completely safe for pets and people. Two AA batteries (not included) have a life of over one year. Havahart reports this method is: Very effective in suburban areas where deer density is low; damage is mild, infrequent, and unpredictable. These repellers are effective in suburban areas where deer density is medium and damage is moderate, frequent, and predictable. They are also effective if the repellent is moved as the deer travel pattern changes. They are not effective in rural, non-residential, agricultural areas where deer density is high; damage is extreme, frequent, and unpredictable.

Premier 1 Fence Equipment Company (www. premier1supplies.com) maintain that the only 100 percent deer barrier is an eight-foot-tall woven wire fence or solid wall but that's very expensive and very permanent. An alternative is the electrified fence. These fences rely upon a painful electric shock (not deadly) to persuade deer to forget about jumping or trying to penetrate a fence. Because these are not physical barriers, electric deer fences rely upon some key deer behavior principles. These include that deer are creatures of habit, that deer make risk-benefit decisions when feeding time comes around, and that electric fences work when deer are given a chance to avoid them.

Romancing the Woods, Inc. (www.rtw-inc.com) is a corporation up in Saugerties, New York (where the original festival was supposed to be), who designs and sells various gates, pergolas, and fences for keeping deer out. The styles are researched and finished in the grand manner of the nineteenth century parks and gardens, not to mention the marvels of the Adirondack Great Camps style. Everything they create is custom designed and constructed to your specific requirements, and available in any length and height. Indestructible eastern red cedar is used throughout.

Tree Shelters

I first ran across tree shelters while walking in a meadow adjacent to the Pink Beds, a glorious place to walk maintained by the U.S. Forest Service, not far from the Blue Ridge Highway. It's the sort of place where the deer roam free and with impunity.

And finally, for an isolated or precious specimen tree or conifer don't forget making a simple wire cage. A good size would be about four feet tall and one and one-half feet in diameter; using thin posts or imitation bamboo plastic stakes to hold the wire erect, you will prevent damage for a modest investment.

Wire cages four feet tall and one and one-half feet in diameter can be erected around individual plants and usually prevent browsing and antler rubbing damage by deer. But individual tree shelters and wire cages are often considered unattractive, especially for many show gardens, so sometimes the only solution is an outside fence.

Plastic netting, usually called bird netting, is another material that can be used to keep deer from trespassing and will often reduce deer damage to many plantings. Plastic netting is especially valuable for providing temporary protection for seasonal harvests like berries, fruit, and some flowers.

Tubex® Tree-shelters (www.treessentials.com) surround saplings encasing each plant within a plastic tube. Tree shelters are transparent, corrugated polypropylene tubes placed around seedlings at the time of planting. Tubex tubes are each supported by a one-by-one-inch wooden stake pounded into the ground right next to the shelter. An ultraviolet inhibitor is added to the polypropylene to prevent it from breaking down too rapidly when exposed to sunlight. Shelters normally disintegrate after seven to ten years.

A four-foot shelter is generally used and prevents deer from browsing on the seedlings. A five-foot shelter may be needed in areas with excessive browsing or snowfall. In addition, this also acts like a miniature greenhouse and promotes fast growth of the protected plant. These shelters are used mostly in forestry applications to protect hardwood tree seedlings, with up to one hundred shelters per acre. Larger shelters are also available. The shelters also make it easy to apply herbicides for weed control. Tubes are available in increments of two, three, four, and five feet.

Tree Armor (www.mytreearmor.com) manufactures spring-loaded plastic strips that are made to protect trees up to four feet high and trunks that are from one to four inches in diameter. The perforated spirals protect against mold and mildew and they are certified to be lead free and non toxic.

CHAPTER FIVE

Solutions on Your Own

We've covered the threat and the option of fencing in chapter 4, but there are other ways to control deer. Here are some of the various mechanical methods available for today's gardens.

Scaring Devices

Deer can be frightened just as easily as you. They hate unexpected loud noise, there are many smells they find offensive, flashing lights—but frankly unless far from your home, in order to be effective, these will probably annoy you, too. And they do not like roaming dogs or the smell of dogs.

Dogs in the Garden and Feeding the Deer

As long as we lived in Sullivan County, we had a dog. We began with a Vishlu, a great animal, esthetic as can be, a bit flaky, but fun to have around. If Zoltan walked the property in the early morning, noon, late afternoon, and evening, we had few problems.

But in the winter with a lot of snow on the ground, Zoltan was not perfect, especially as he was well-trained and not allowed to run the deer. And they soon learned that here was one dog who barked but never chased. That meant the garden around the house was pretty safe but the out-lying sections were still under threat.

Now here I must interject something that Jean and I did to protect our Sullivan County garden:

By the beginning of the 1980s I was earning the majority of our living by writing garden books and I tried to grow many of the plants I wrote about. But we had no way of fencing thirty-three acres, and our house and garden sat about a tenth of a mile back from the main road. So the entire front area, totaling about six acres, was free for the deer to roam. Zoltan did a good job around the house but beyond local perimeters, he failed.

We played radios (apparently works for some), with music from rock to Bach, but it never deterred the deer (possibly, the volume wasn't loud enough, but we lived there, too).

We tried tin cans and hanging spirals of shiny aluminum, to no avail.

So we decided to feed the deer during the worst of the winter. After making arrangements with a local hunting club (they provided the cracked corn), Jean went out every day to an area down from the house, and spilled a pail-full of corn (sometimes two) upon the ground.

The feeding of the deer ritual was an amazing thing to watch as moms, yearlings, and some stags stood around and pawed the snow as they followed what appeared to be a precise pecking order. And it didn't take long for the deer to accept Jean and soon, following a precise pecking order, they ate the corn and never wandered up to the garden not far away, so my dwarf conifers and roses were left alone.

Of course we had arguments with the NYDEC and only older members of the corps knew that as soon as the world greened up in the spring, the deer would go back to young bark, new leaves, choice bulbs, and the rest, but during the worst of the winter they ate on the hoof.

If you decide to provide food do not use hay, as it's bad for deer in the wintertime; their stomachs are not adapted for such digestion. And remember, in many states, feeding deer is against the law. So consult your local Department of Environmental Conservation, or a better bet is to enquire of your local hunting clubs.

When Zoltan died at the age of fourteen years, we went a year without a dog and were punished for it by an increase in the number of plant invasions.

So our next dog was a stray, a beautiful German Shorthair Pointer named Bismarck, and he (in conjunction with feeding the deer) kept the damage to a reasonable level until we left the farm for Asheville in 1989.

If you can have a dog in conjunction with the garden you are way ahead. But I must make it clear that the dog must be trained not to run deer in the winter, especially when they are hungry, possibly starved.

One method of using a dog as a deer deterrent depends on the so-called invisible fence, an electronic system with the dog wearing a radio receiver in his collar that administers an electric shock if the dog gets too close to a perimeter wire attached to a transmitter.

An Interview with Tom Nunnenkamp

Now we jump ahead to today and the concept of feeding the deer during the winter using cracked corn.

One of the more pleasant jobs I have is to be the Contributing Editor to *Carolina Gardener* magazine, a great source of gardening information published nine times a year, reporting on all things horticultural from both North and South Carolina.

In the November/December issue of 2014, I read an article by John Viccellio entitled: "Artists in the Garden." Among the gardens featured was a photo of a deer-feeding trough in the much-visited Charlotte garden of Tom Nunnenkamp and Lib Jones, Maplewalk.

So I called Tom for the story.

"We live," he said, "in the SouthPark section of Charlotte in an area dominated by half-acre residential lots. We are lucky to have two and a quarter acres for both home and garden. Now back in 1990, when we moved in, deer were not an issue. There were woods within a mile of our home and plenty of space for deer to roam and not threaten local gardens. But things changed.

"Development accelerated around Charlotte and with the push of population, the deer lost their end of the battle and began showing up in neighborhood gardens. We tried everything we could think of including our homeowners' association going to the city inquiring about allowing bow-hunters to thin the herd. This request fell on deaf ears.

"The deer got to be a bigger problem and during the rutting season the trees lost branches—especially Japanese maples and conifers—from the antlers rubbing on the bark.

"So it was my wife who suggested that we try to feed the deer using cracked corn purchased from a local farm and garden store. We feed 25 pounds of corn per night in troughs next to our driveway and away from most of our most precious plants. While not totally solving the problem, the expense is justified by the reduction in overall damage. Lib is particularly sensitive to the deer's plight of reduced habitat. I'm not quite so understanding and would love to see a herd reduction.

"Until the city comes to us with a better solution, we will continue to use cracked corn as one of our deer deterrent strategies."

Renting Out Your Land

If you live in the country or near a park where hunting is allowed and own a substantial amount of land, you might consider combining deer population control and recreational hunting.

You can invite hunters who are knowledgeable and trustworthy to use your land for the hunt.

Or you can decide yourself to become a recreational hunter.

Consider leasing your land to a local hunting club and develop a contract with clearly defined responsibilities. You might even barter the use of your land in return for some venison down the line.

The Rube Goldberg Method

Rube Goldberg (1883–1970) was a Pulitzer Prize–winning cartoonist, sculptor, and writer who over the years developed a number of fantastic inventions in order to get something done on a comic level.

He was the man who would draw the solution to a problem using all sorts of bells, whistles, gears, wires, weights, gadgets, and even live animals that would all work together in an imaginative way to wake somebody up without an alarm clock or feed a canary when you are out of town or start the car on a cold morning.

Today, the average home store stocks an incredible number of electronic devices that will turn lights on when somebody passes your house either walking or in a car, in fact I suspect that a sensor would react to even a mouse walking by, not to mention sensors reacting to the rising or setting sun.

There are electric eyes that if properly set in the garden would not only give you an accurate pest count but again, turn on lights, whistles, recorded barking dogs, or even explosions.

Be creative!

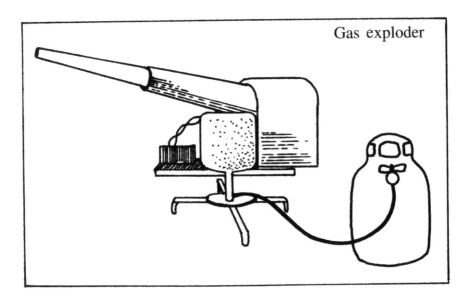

Gas exploder

Gas Exploders

An article published in the University of Nebraska at Lincoln, by the USDA National Wildlife Research Center in September of 2003, reported on all sorts of devices to repel deer including gas exploders and strobe light blinkers. These devices could be set around the garden's perimeter and electronic triggers would set them off and scare the deer away. But such devices are not cheap and the deer soon learn what to expect—and so these devices are only a short-term solution. Remember to get the most out of this product, you must move the appliance and stagger the firing sequence. Outside of moving in a flock of llamas or a herd of donkeys or a collection of Chinese guard geese,* most experts maintain that deer, being intelligent creatures, soon learn the routine.

Water Machines for Wetting the Fur

Deer have no problem with using water for their health but do have objections to getting their fur wet by natural means like heavy rains (I assume) or artificial means (I'm sure) like the following two appliances sold for garden protection.

The Scarecrow Water Spray Animal Repeller by Contech manufacturers is described as a humane method of repelling animals and uses a motion sensor to spray water when it detects an intruder. The harmless blast of water is said to deter even stubborn pests and is simple to use by connecting to an ordinary garden hose. There is a thirty-five foot range for flexibilty in placement of the apparatus, the spray head being adjustable from 10°–360°. This allows the spray head to be adjustable from covering your entire yard or just a small area.

Spray Away by the Havahart Corporation made their industrial name by developing and then selling specialized traps for humanely capturing animals like rabbits and woodchucks. Now they have

---

* Yes, as reported in the July, 2013, issue of *National Geographic* magazine, police in rural parts of China's Xinjiang Province are no longer turning to dogs for standing guard at police stations at night. They're using geese instead. And it works. Many readers will remember the experience of being attacked by a goose when visiting a farm as children and that's because a guard goose is very territorial and ready to sound the alarm when man or beast invades the compound, or in our case the garden.

produced the Havahart 5266 Spray Away Motion Activated Sprinkler Animal Repellent 2.0. The machines are described as being motion-activated sprinklers designed to protect yards from nuisance animals, detecting animal movement with infrared detectors that hunt out heat rays and movement which in turn activates a sprinkler. The sprinkler then shoots short, startling bursts of water to scare the animal off your property. Nine sensitivity settings allow the gardener to target specific animals at specific distances. And this machine actually defends an area up to 1,900 square feet. There is a step-in stake design for and easy setup.

ScareCrow Sprinkler Repellent (www.petstreetmall.com/Scarecrow-Outdoor-Animal-Deterrent) is versatile enough to keep deer, rabbits, and other foragers from snacking on plants and bulbs, to prevent dogs from digging up newly seeded lawns, to keep the cat from using your garden as a litter box, and to scare predators like herons and raccoons away from your fish pond. The ScareCrow's motion detector is powerful enough to guard an area up to 1,000 square feet of coverage with a single sprinkler. For added coverage, ScareCrow Sprinklers can be linked in series to guard larger spaces.

Trident Enterprises International (http://www.tridentcorp.com) offers a number of deer and animal repelling products. They include deer repellents; deer fencing (electric or non-electric invisible mesh barriers, and netting); scare devices that feature motion-activated ultrasonic animal repellents; sonic animal repellers including a motion-activated scarecrow that surprises deer (not to mention the neighbor's cat) with a blast of cold water when they trip the switch. Trident suggests this is an excellent repellent and a great way to move them out without having to reapply repellents; mole and gopher controls, featuring sonic repellers, mole and gopher repellents, or smoke bombs, and if you're out of sorts, they have poison baits, too; squirrel controls; and animal detection devices, these last being cameras that photograph the invaders as they set off the secret trips, so you know exactly who is out to get you.

Non-commercial Repellents

The number of deer repellents on the market today continues to grow as marketers keep up with the burgeoning deer populations. They are covered in chapter 6.

Here we deal with solutions that gardeners have devised using their own experiences and their own methods. But, lay off the mothballs because they are very detrimental to the environment, and that includes your own.

Human Hair

Human hair is one of those off-again, on-again methods of repelling deer that many gardeners swear by and others write off as an urban legend. The suggestions are to obtain hair from a local beauty salon or barber shop, storing it in plastic bags until ready for use. Then place the hair in small mesh bags, the kind used for packing small cheeses, etc., or nylon stockings or panty hose. The bags should contain at least two hefty fistfuls of hair and be attached to plants at a height of twenty-eight inches to three feet, no more than three feet apart. Start hanging bags in early spring and replace the used hair with fresh at least once a month. Some gardeners report increased success when occasionally spraying the bags with cologne or aftershave.

Tankage

Various extension agents mention tankage as a deer repellent so I include it here, although if faced with using this method, I would rather hire a watchman or build a high wall.

Tankage is a slaughterhouse byproduct traditionally used as a deer repellent in orchards where it repels deer by the smell which, unfortunately, would be readily apparent to anybody entering the garden. To prepare containers for tankage, remove the tops from aluminum pop cans, puncture the sides in the middle of the cans to allow for drainage, and attach cans to the ends of four-foot stakes. Drive the stakes into the ground one foot from every tree you want to protect or at six-foot intervals around the perimeter of a block. Place one cup of tankage in each can.

Soap

I'll bet you never thought when watching a bar soap commercial on TV that such a product might be used to repel deer. It's possible that again, this might be an urban legend, but many gardeners swear that it works. Do not use expensive soap from a cosmetics counter but rather the kind that comes in plastic bags at discount stores. Drill a hole in each bar (you can carefully use an electric drill or simply a Phillips-head screwdriver), then suspend the soap with a stout length of cord, and hang it from a nearby branch. Each bar appears to protect a radius of about one yard. Any inexpensive tallow-based brand of bar soap will work. In addition to being odor-based repellents, soap may reduce deer browsing as a visual cue because gardeners do report that empty soap-bar wrappers alone have sometimes reduced damage.

Meat-Eater's Urine

Now I once did a mental chuckle when I heard about this prevention method but now realize that if properly managed, it really seems to work. But in a so-called free society this is one of those subjects that is greeted with gentle amusement by some and shocks the sensibilities of others.

An article entitled "The smell of a meat-eater" by Nicola Nosengo, published in the June 20, 2011, issue *Nature,* discusses the reactions of animals that are preyed upon when they smell the urine produced by a meat-eater looking for a meal. The chemical is *2-phenylethylamine* and scientists think that it's a by-product of digesting the proteins found in meat. Carnivores, including lions and tigers, had the highest concentration, with herbivores ranging from mice to rabbits to, of all things, deer exhibiting some three thousand times lower.

Now the problem with many sophisticated New Yorkers can be summed up by having curtains in the bathroom window. Our old farmhouse was situated at the end of a driveway a tenth of a mile long and in the midst of some thirty-three acres of land. The window in the master bathroom was on the second floor and by day looked out on distant hills and by night, unless there was a moon, pitch blackness. There was no curtain.

Eventually, my wife was approached by a couple of lady visitors who asked if it was OK to put a towel in the window when they were using the facilities. Naturally, Jean agreed, but later on we installed some louvered blinds. But trust me: in that location the only living things that would be looking up at the activities in the bathroom were bobcats, an occasional bear, any number of smaller mammals, and marauding deer.

So the only guests who were asked to participate were males who cared naught about a curtain in the bathroom and were not vegetarians and myself, who at that time would do anything to find a way to herd the deer.

The procedure seemed to work during the summer months but when the weather was warm and balmy, the deer were usually kept in tow by the knowledge that the dog lived there too.

However, it was the winter that was always the problem, especially after December when the snow began to fall and on to April when the snow melted.

Today, our Asheville garden has been spared one major threat and that is the presence of a hungry deer herd; they never get over our way because most deer are wandering the vast acres of the Biltmore Estate and the mountains beyond, and if one or two get this close to town, they are immediately hit with semis on the two Interstates or trucks on city streets.

So if you wish to try the urine method remember that today there are a number of Critter Pees, and for basic vegetable and reasonable small flower gardens look for keeping deer at bay with CoyotePee. The manufacturers say: "Deer are the number one wildlife pest in America and CoyotePee is the solution. Create a 'pee-rimeter' by using CoyotePee liquid with ScentTags, 33 Day Dispensers or *Scent-Wraps* or hang *ScentTags* or 33 Day Dispensers right on shrubs or ornamentals."

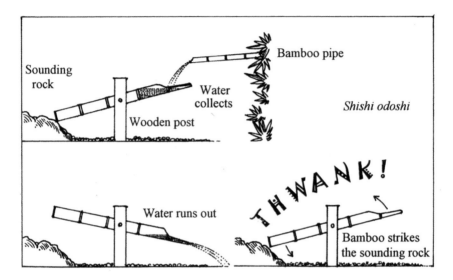

Deer Scares from Japanese Gardens

And you think you've got problems. Back in the days when Japanese farmers battled the elements (and the animals) without the aid of electric fences and contemporary deer repellents, they fashioned the *shishi odoshi*, or the "deer scare," to frighten not only deer but wild boars, too.

Water travels through a thin bamboo pipe into a longer, and larger, bamboo pipe, which is set on an axil, with the first bamboo joint of the front end being cut away as a type of spout and the bottom of the larger bamboo sealed.

The water collects in the bamboo and the weight forces the back end to tip to the ground. Then the continuing stream of water tips the pipe the opposite way, and the water runs out the front. Now the back end is heavier than the front, and the pipe falls back to strike a large rock giving a loud "Clack!" In terms of Japanese garden philosophy, the flow of the water and the regular movement of the *shishi odoshi* provide an effective counterpoint to the quiet permanence of the rest of the garden.

CHAPTER SIX

A Product Roundup of Chemical Deer Repellents—and a Few Others That Annoy or Shoot!

Years ago, when calling a corporation repellant, the reaction would have at least led to ruffled feathers—if only on the board level. Today, with marketing now revolving around the web and newspapers on a decline, it seems that many commercial successes continue to delight in hitting the big time (some continue to flaunt Global Warming), and care little for protecting the environment. But gardeners have persevered and with every commercial shove to ignore the rules of nature, gardeners organize and go out to their back forties or their backyard and still try to follow the rules. With that change in attitude, the garden world has traded buckshot and poisoning for products that are repellent to the animals involved.

The first time I consulted the web about chemicals to keep deer out of the garden there were a reasonable number of products. But today the numbers have multiplied to such an extent that if putting together a complete list—without comment—an impossible number of pages would be needed. So here are a few to research on your own.

The following chemical repellents are on today's market. Whenever possible I've given a description of their actions plus a web address. Again, it should be noted that most of the manufacturers note that their products work under most normal circumstances but when deer are starving, they will often eat things even they would find offensive when things were normal.

As to the efficiency of the various appliances listed below, unlike plants and garden utensils, there's no way I could test one or all of them. So it's up to you, the gardener, to check them out and make a decision as to their practical uses.

Out Out Deer® (www.outoutdeer.com) is the first entry because it's a complete deer repellent shopping guide with the following message: Don't buy a deer deterrent product based on label claims or advertising limericks. Be an informed consumer. All commercial deer repellents on the market are covered here. These deer repellent product reviews feature: Actual User Feedback; Application Information; Duration of effectiveness; Area of coverage; and Cost of use. If you go to http://outoutdeer.com/deer-repellent-reviews/ you will find over forty deer-repellent products rated as to use.

Bobbex Inc. (www.bobbex.com) manufactures all-natural deer repellents, organic plant growth stimulants, and chemicals for lawn treatments. Bobbex Deer Repellents coat foliage with a safe non-chemical residue which they claim deer, smaller four-legged pests, and those horrors of the bird world, Canada geese, avoid like the plague. The active ingredients are a series of proteins making the product extremely safe for use on the most sensitive plantings and are harmless to all wildlife including humans, pets, birds, and aquatic life.

Bonide (www.bonide.com) was founded back in the 1920s and sells a wide range of pest repellents including Go Away Deer and Rabbit Repellent Granules that are effective in all seasons. Bonide repellent is made with natural ingredients including white pepper, putrescent egg solids, garlic, and cloves and does not harm plants or animals. Not for sale in IN or NM.

Carnivore Urines (www.predatorpee.com) or predator pees are a new branch of protective gardening featuring urines collected from bobcats, coyotes, foxes, and wolves. They work by sending a signal to all those animals out in your garden that a vicious, meat-eating animal is out there roaming the vegetable rows or that great display of bountiful flowers. The vented dispensers last for about thirty days and are filled with the solution that represents the urine of your choice. To get it right, consult the following:

Coyote urine packs a wallop of a chemical punch and if prey animals such as deer detect it in on their turf, they are immediately warned to move on. This product is 100 percent real coyote urine and creates the illusion that coyotes are present. Deer, raccoon, and possum react instinctively to the fear of this predator.

Fox urine repels woodchucks (groundhogs), rabbit, skunks, squirrel, and chipmunks.

Bobcat urine stops moles, mice, and other small rodents (and it would certainly call a halt to my garden activities).

Deer Away® (www.treehelp.com) is a repellent that contains 37 percent putrescent egg solid. This contact (odor/taste) repellent has been used in conifer and hardwood plantations and is reported to be 85 to 100 percent effective in field studies. It is registered for use on fruit trees prior to flowering and ornamental and Christmas trees.

Deer No No® (www.deernono.com) is an all-natural product that uses a proprietary scent developed to keep deer away without resorting to poisons or harsh chemicals. Best of all, Deer No No's potency doesn't diminish over days or weeks like regular spray repellents. A single Deer No No packet delivers ten to twelve months of continuous deer protection! And its potency and long lifespan make Deer No No highly affordable and cost effective.

Deer-Off® (www.havahart.com) was acquired by the Woodstream Corporation (they make Havahart Traps) which goes to show you that fighting deer is a growing industry. Deer-Off is made of biodegradable food products that contain no harmful chemicals, are harmless to people, but deer, rabbits, and squirrels hate it. A single application lasts up to three months although back home at the kitchen sink, it can be washed off fruits and vegetables. It won't become dissipated from exposure to rain and snow, will not change the color or texture of plants, and does not leave a filmy residue. It should be noted that in a four-year study conducted by Rutgers' department of animal sciences, Deer-Off kept deer away from vegetation up to three times longer than the next most effective material.

Deer Out™ (www.DeerOut.com) is the deer repellent of choice for thousands of professional and hobbyist gardeners nationwide. A single application of Deer Out™ can keep deer away from your garden for up to three to four months.

Gempler's (www.Gemplers.com) protects your property from deer damage with non-toxic granular deer repellent and deer repellent spray. Easy and effective solutions are available to deter deer. Choose from deer repellents like Garlic Barrier®, Deer Off® Liquid Fence®, Shake Away® and more. Shop here for your liquid and granular deer repellents of choice.

Hinder® **Deer Repellent** (www.amvac-chemical.com) contains ammonium soaps of higher fatty acids. Hinder protects plants by forming a mild odor barrier that is inoffensive to humans. For use on apples, pears, soybeans, peanuts, carrots, nursery stock, ornamental trees, shrubs, and flowers. Hinder is the most cost-effective product for deer and rabbit management.

Hot Pepper Wax (www.hotpepperwax.com) is a secret, patented formula that stops animals like tree squirrels and rabbits from turning your garden and shrubs into their salad bar.

The product contains no chemicals or poisons, and it's biodegradable so it won't harm the animals or your soil! It is listed here because sometimes it's sold as a deer repellent that the manufacturers claim it is not. Such honesty deserves this short report.

Liquid Fence Deer & Rabbit Repellent (www.liquidfence. com) should be applied liberally to plants and their perimeter during a dry period, with the process repeated one week later and then approximately once per month thereafter. In areas where feeding pressure from deer and rabbits is intense, spray Liquid Fence Deer & Rabbit Repellent once a week for three weeks and then approximately once per month thereafter. According to the manufacturer, this product is member tested and recommended by The National Home Gardening Club and The American Rose Society! Two of America's most revered garden associations have tested and awarded Liquid Fence Deer & Rabbit Repellent with their prestigious endorsements.

Miller's Hot Sauce Animal Repellent (www.deerbusters. com) is a contact (taste) repellent and registered for use on ornamental, Christmas, and fruit trees. Apply it with a backpack or trigger sprayer to all susceptible new growth, such as leaders and young leaves. Do not apply to fruit-bearing plants after fruit set. Vegetable crops also can be protected if sprayed before the development of edible parts. Mixing this product with an anti-mixing transpirant such as Wilt-Pruf or Vapor Gard improves its use with various weather conditions.

Not Tonight Deer Repellent (www.nottonight.com) is the result of the right formula for halting the unwanted advances of our four-legged neighbors. It's natural, non-toxic and it safely and effectively keeps deer from turning your garden into an all-you-can-eat deer buffet.

Plant Pro-Tec® (www.plantprotec.com) manufactures clip-on capsules holding repellents that discourage deer from browsing trees, shrubs, flowers, and garden plants. They are effective and long-lasting, with a formulation based on long-known data that the garlic odor repels deer, elk, and rabbits. They emit deer-repelling garlic odor for six to eight months.

Plantskydd® is an Organic Animal Repellent considered the most cost-effective and environmentally safe animal repellent available. Plantskydd® is accepted and used by leading forest companies, agriculture, nurseries, private woodlot owners, landscapers, and home gardeners, as well as State/Provincial and National Conservation agencies.

Repellex® (www.repellex.com) is recommended as a safe and natural deer deterrent. Their state-of-the-art formulas are made from natural ingredients that do not harm or kill animals and are safe for the environment. Repellex® offers simply the best deer and rabbit repellent products you can possible find because they are so effective.

Ro-Pel® (www.nixalite.com) is called one of the worst-tasting substances ever known by the manufacturers. It tastes so foul—well you know the old joke. Applications are said to be effective against raccoons, rats, deer, beaver, cats, rabbits, and woodpeckers (yellow-bellied sapsuckers) when sprayed on the target plants. You are warned not to taste it lest it change your outlook on food forever.

Tree Guard® (http://www.conservationservicesinc.com/treeguard.html) is a pre-mixed, ready-to-use deer repellent that sprays on milky and dries clear. The active ingredient, Bitrex™, makes the coated plant taste bad. A detection agent lets deer know the plant has been treated. This product leaves a clear sheen, which resists washing off from rain and snow, may be used on any non-food plant, and poses minimal risk to deer, plants, people, and the environment.

Application of Commercial Repellents

First there are a few rules of thumb:

1. Repellents do not eliminate browsing, only reduce it. Success with repellents is measured by your success in keeping the

browsing down to an acceptable level. If you cannot abide any damage, you must fence.

2. Some repellents stand up to weather better than others, and rainfall (or compacted snow) will wash off many repellents, so they must be continually reapplied.

3. Rarely will repellents stop deer from rubbing antlers.

4. Just like with teaching children, it's important to start early, before the deer's feeding habits are established.

5. The availability of other food often determines the success of repellents.

6. One gardener's successful repellent is another gardener's failure, as the season, the time of application, the weather, and many other factors can affect success or failure.

7. Stay informed, as new repellents and new formulas are appearing in astonishing numbers.

Application methods for commercial repellents range easily from pressure sprayers available from most garden centers and nurseries on to machine sprayers and manual backpack sprayers, the type used by most nursery operations.

When applying contact repellents, common sense rules. Pick dry days (especially without any rains in the weather reports) and when temperatures are above freezing. Young trees should be completely treated. The cost of treating older trees can be reduced by limiting your applications to only the growth within reach of the deer, remembering more protection is needed if you live in areas with heavy snow cover. Remember, too, that any new growth is unprotected.

Then applications of most of these repellents are based on the time of year they are applied: the summer season or the winter season.

Finally, your first application for the summer period should take place at least two weeks before the leaves break bud. Then once the season has begun, apply repellents as a preventive measure, the first repellent every three to four weeks.

Other Deer Deterrents

There are a number of deer-repelling products on the market that do not resort to chemicals for shooing the deer away, but instead use a more physical approach to keep the foe at bay. I suspect this is an area of continued exploration that is a bit like the turnover in the restaurant trade: some ideas make it and some ideas do not!

Critter Blaster Pro (www.pestproducts.com) doesn't make repeating cannons because they claim that repeating cannons and pyrotechnics do not work—animals and birds quickly get used to the same sound. But Critter Blaster Pro features sounds that can be programmed in hundreds of different combinations so pests can't acclimate to a fixed pattern. Choose any or all of eight harassment sounds, then set the volume, mute time between sounds, and finally random play for hours of operation.

Deer-Departed® (www.deer-departed.com) manufactures an appliance called "The Gardener," that's equipped with two ways to deter deer. First, it issues an ultrasonic alarm which can only be heard by the animals, and a pressurized water jet that will scare the deer. The device uses a motion sensor to detect the presence of nearby animals. You can set the detecting area by adjusting the sensitivity knob. Detection range can be adjusted from 15 to 25 feet. Different weather conditions may slightly alter ranges. A unique feature of The Guardener is that it uses both ultrasound and water blast to repel animals. The sprinkler can rotate up to 170 degrees and shooting pressurized water as far as 17 to 22 feet. It has a built-in tank that can hold about 3.5 gallons of water. It is solar powered so there is no need for electricity or batteries.

Deer Gard (www.bird-x.com/deer-gard-products-46.php?page_id=146) safely keeps deer away from your outdoor space without chemicals or traps. Instead try a machine that emits high-frequency sound waves that irritate deer, forcing them to flee your garden in search of calmer, untreated areas. These transmitters are water and weather resistant, protect up to 4,000 sq. ft., and are easy to use or move.

Heartland Outdoor Animal Repeller www.heartlandamerica.com/outdoor-animal-repeller-65035.html is a motion-activated ultrasonic yard and garden protector that makes deer, dogs, cats, raccoons, squirrels, and other pests scram! As pesky deer and rabbits draw near to your garden or a stray animal starts prowling around, the infrared motion sensor on this repeller activates an ultrasonic pulse that's inaudible to humans, but makes animals head for the hills. It's easy to use and requires no harsh chemicals that can harm the environment. Waterproof design mounts in minutes. There is a thirty-foot range. Four AA batteries are required.

Scare-Away LP Gas Cannons (www.reedjoseph.com/lp_gas_cannons.htm) are responsible for multiple shots set off at irregular intervals during a short period of time, and such shots have proven to be an extremely effective means of dispersing bird and wildlife pests. Scare-Away LP Gas Cannons can protect your investment from bird and wildlife infestation. These cannons can automatically produce harmless thunderclap bangs to disperse birds and wildlife from areas such as crops, orchards, vineyards, campuses, golf courses, fish ponds, parks, airfields, and landfills.

Nite Guard Solar® (www.niteguard.com) consists of four lights mounted four feet high on a single post with each light facing a different direction (cluster mount). Place the post in the center of the area to be protected. Unlike other night animals, deer get used to seeing something in the same location so it is best to relocate the cluster mount about every one to two weeks to break the pattern.

CHAPTER SEVEN

Lions and Tigers and Moles

Some gardeners might think that linking two big-time carnivores with a lowly mole might be considered a salute to hubris, but let me quickly state that in many years of gardening, next to deer damage the mole is the big second feature. And never has a poor creature suffered from so much bad press.

Good Times Underground!

Last year when the snows of winter melted, the gardeners of the colder parts of the country were confronted by a wealth of damage to plants caused by voles—that's right, voles not moles.

This year there was another loud cry of despair heard echoing from hill to hill as everyone went out to the front or back yard and were suddenly aware that their once even lawn was now traversed with tunnels dug by moles—along with an occasional shrew— and now resembles the B & O Railroad Yards without a swath of peaceful green.

The last few years have certainly been called some of the worst mole years on record. One way you can tell is by those tunnels, but the other is from various garden writers who attack these poor creatures in print as though they were furry drones sent over from one of the enemy states to pillage the American way of life. Instead of trying for a little understanding, we get bumper crops of mole death machines ranging from irritating them to a fast demise with dollops of Tabasco Sauce and chili powder, to hooking up a hose to the exhaust of a car and gassing them to death with carbon monoxide—messy to the lawn and dangerous to everybody.

But the surfeit of moles is always tied to a bumper crop of grubs, especially Japanese beetles.

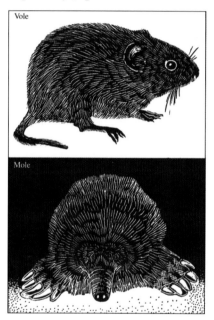

Top, a common vole that lives above ground and bottom the common mole that tunnels below.

Moles are little mammals with tiny eyes, small and virtually concealed ears, and very pretty, soft iridescent fur. They live almost entirely underground, feeding on smaller animal life, especially earthworms and grubs. I repeat: moles do not eat bulbs or roots. They will chew through them if the plants are in the way but they do not ingest the results of their chewing. They are generally beneficial to gardens, especially when it comes to consuming vast numbers of vociferous grubs. I do admit that in their zeal to devour they often do some damage by heaving up the soil, causing the grass to dry out quickly and creating unsightly ridges or tunnel-tops: a sight that irritates some people more than paying taxes.

Now there are many methods advised or sold to be used in the death and destruction of moles, but outside of cyanide gas—dangerous not only to both the mole recipient and the man or woman provider—nothing else is sure.

Catalogs sell windmills that feature spikes pushed deep into the ground that make rumbling noises in the earth, thus scaring them away, but I've never seen these appliances actually work: the moles still dig tunnels and hunt for food and only move out when the food source has been devoured.

Recently a garden writer told me of two workable suggestions, consisting of putting a dead mole back in the tunnels or a hunk of odiferous cheese, but he has no proof that works either. And there was no hint given on how to obtain a dead mole to begin with, although steel traps are also offered for sale by some catalogs.

Poison bait isn't such a good idea especially if you have a cat, dog, or child that is valuable to you. But there is an effective biological control called Milky Spore Disease that inoculates your soil with a fungal species that infects the grubs but bothers nothing else. The problem with this solution is the time it takes to effect the cure: at least a year.

So before going out and putting a toxic waste dump in your back yard to do away with the little pests, or driving up the family car to gas them out, how about thinking ahead to next July and the damage done by the beetles to the garden and the favors the moles have done for you. It should be remembered that the number of moles is in direct proportion to the food supply, and if your back yard and garden has a surfeit of moles, it probably needs them.

Instead of becoming involved with solutions guaranteed to cause you problems, how about buying a pair of those plastic shoes with spikes used to aerate the lawn (not, as someone thought, to kill the moles) and walk over those tunnels, then plant some grass seed, rake it up a bit, and by mid-May you'll never know they were there.

Voles: On to the Big Time

Next to deer, your worst garden enemy remains the vole. A few years ago I went out into the garden on one of the colder days of 2012 to check on the damages wrought by the past few weeks of ice and chill, coupled with the wind's bitter blasts.

Most garden perennials were surviving but when I spotted damaged goods, by far the worst chlorophyllic assault was perpetrated by our little furry friend, the vole. Everywhere I turned, the litter on the ground, the hay mulches, the backyard lawn, and forgotten piles of leaves were tunneled through and through. Where grasses touched the trunks of small trees and bushes like my arctic willow or my Himalayan honeysuckle, the bark was chewed unmercifully. My entire line of lavender was eaten right down to soil level—and blast them, they had taken all the leaves of the lambs tongue and ripped them up for nesting material.

The Complete Guide to American Wildlife has this to say about the vole: "Voles are best known to many readers by the popular name of 'meadow mice.' Voles have long, grayish brown fur, short ears and tails, and beady eyes. Their tails are more than an inch long, and are not brightly colored. They live on the ground usually in grassy terrain, where they make inch-wide runways, leaving behind cut grass stems and are active at all hours. They can swim and dive. In winter they make round holes to the surface through the snow. Their voice is a high-pitched squeak. They eat grass, roots, bark, and seeds. They construct a nest of plant material on the ground, and there are usually five to seven young.

There are a number of vole species but the meadow vole (*Microtus pennsylvanicus*) covers the country out to the area of Mountain Time, skipping the Deep South, while the long-tailed vole (*M. longicaudus*) goes from the Rockies to the Pacific, and the prairie vole (*M. ochrogaster*) joins these two areas in the center. For the South we get the pine vole (*M. pinetorum*).

The vole that did the damage to our gardens this year is the meadow vole, North Carolina being the southernmost state of their rein. They are between three and five inches long with an average two-inch tail and were known as Danny Meadow Mouse in the "Burgess

Bedtime Stories." A population of fifteen to an acre can increase to 250 voles in four years, and obviously that kind of growth explosion has occurred in the land about our home.

Our garden cat, Miss Jekyll, had tried to do her bit with the vole menace: Every afternoon, a freshly killed subject was left on the door mat in front of the back door and I'm sure there are many more that she has dispatched out in the garden and the years beyond.

Gardening in the mountains is never that easy but the first trip to the garden this spring was the worst I've yet experienced. But on the other side of the coin, the snowdrops are truly beautiful and the crocus the best yet. And by mid-June and the exuberance of summer, the vole will be a faint remembrance of things past.

Fighting Voles

Like the previous suggestions dealing with mole destruction, do not stick a garden hose or any hose hooked up to an engine's exhaust system in an attempt to suffocate the beasts because it's futile. Unless you live alone with no friends, no family, no pets, and no neighborhood attachments, do not use poison baits, not matter how attractive they appear to be.

Probably the safest method is to protect valuable bulbs and expensive cultivars is to enclose bulb or root within a hardware cloth cage.

Other easy things to do for the war on voles include the elimination of weeds, tall grasses (alive or dead), or all sorts of plant litter from the garden proper. Also protect young trees by encircling the trunks with quarter-inch hardware cloth of plastic guards made especially for such protection. For voles make sure the barriers extend below the ground at least three inches and eighteen inches above the surface.

You can help your lawn by close mowing in the fall before snows arrive, then raking up the cut grass.

Remember to be on friendly terms with local predators including shrews (they are carnivores and always hungry), foxes, owls, bobcats (if lucky enough to have them), and, of course, snakes of all kinds. These are more reasons never to use poison in the garden.

Next you can try and install a barrier between the voles and their targets. There is a product on the market called VoleBloc, advertised as being safe, non-toxic, lightweight, and permanent. It's made from a kiln-fired lightweight aggregate.

According to Chuck Friedrich, RLA, the inventor of VoleBloc, to protect existing plants, using a garden fork or spade dig a four-inch wide, one-foot deep "moat" around the drip-line of the plant. The drip-line is where drops of water would hit the ground from the most extended leaves. After the "moat" is dug, fill it with the VoleBloc to the top. Voles also like to tunnel under mulch so it's best to reduce the mulch around the plant and use VoleBloc to mulch inside the moat instead.

For new plantings, after tilling the beds, make the planting hole twelve inches wider and two inches deeper than the root ball. Place two inches of VoleBloc in the hole. Then set the root ball on top of the VoleBloc and backfill around the roots with 100 percent VoleBloc, completely surrounding the roots. Mulch with VoleBloc around the stem.

For bulbs, place two inches of VoleBloc in the hole and place the bulbs, then surround the bulbs with VoleBloc leaving just the tips exposed. Finally, place a 50 percent VoleBloc/soil mix over the bulbs to the desired depth. Don't worry about daffodils because they are poisonous to voles.

For more information, seek the website: www.volebloc.com.

Vole Repellents

As mentioned before, I generally stay away from poisons but there are a few repellents you might try.

Capsaicin is a topical, harmless hot sauce used to protect ornamental trees and shrubs, fruit trees, fruit bushes, grape vines, and nursery stock from vole damage. Don't use it directly on food to be harvested.

Some of the predator odors made from the urine of foxes and coyotes may be effective vole repellents. They are listed in chapter 6.

Get a garden cat. Cats are effective vole hunters and often leave them as gifts at the doorsteps of appreciated owners.

Finally, you can use mouse snap traps for getting small vole populations, baiting the traps with peanut butter (it's amazing how peanut butter is a favorite of almost all living things.)

The Lowly Cottontail

There are hares and rabbits. They both belong to the genus *Lepus* but species differ, and as a rule hares and jackrabbits are larger and have longer ears and hind legs than cottontails.

Hares, for example, do not make a nest. After about a thirty-day gestation period, three to eight young are born, furred, eyes open, and able to move about within minutes.

We will overlook the Arctic hare and just pause to mention the white-tailed jack rabbit (*Lepus townsendii*), an inhabitant of the far mid west; the snowshoe rabbit (*L. americanus*), found in most of Canada and just the most northern part of the states; the European hare (*L. europaeus*), making the area around the Great Lakes their home; and the black-tailed jack rabbit (*L. californicus*), a resident of the Southwest.

But when it comes to the cottontail, we enter the more populous areas of Pest City.

Cottontails are smaller than hares, have shorter ears and hind legs, and usually hide when threatened. Female cottontails breed at nine months of age and produce several litters a year. After about a thirty-day gestation period, about four or five helpless, naked, and blind young are born in a fur-lined nest in the ground. In less than three weeks they are weaned.

These rabbits are small with a sixteen-inch body and three-inch ears. Their fur is a grayish-brown with the underside of the tail cotton white, along with whitish feet. They live to be about five years old.

Cottontails are found in many places near farms, fencerows, junk-piles, thickets, woodlands, or just about anyplace they can find that great combination of food and cover. They will even live in abandoned woodchuck holes. In spring and fall they make a home called a form, a nest-like cavity made of grassy humps on the top of the ground.

In our neighborhood in Asheville proper, some of the cottontails are so brazen as to chow down in the middle of a driveway while the folks who live there are out shopping. They can dine in early morning, early afternoon, or on into the night. They eat a lot of green plant material including damage to annuals, perennials, vegetables, and trees and shrubs. The last two succumb to a process called girdling where the rabbits gnaw around the trunk, successfully killing the tree by preventing the flow of water and nutrients from the roots to the plant proper. Rabbit damage consists of gnawing or cleanly severed stems, plus their distinctive round droppings, and of course, in winter, their obvious tracks.

Rabbit Control

For all the reasons mentioned before, do not try to poison rabbits.

Instead, protect tree and shrub trunks from rabbits encircling the trunks with quarter-inch hardware cloth of plastic guards made especially for such protection. I also stack up proper-sized plastic planting pots with the bottoms removed, then cut down the sides. I always make sure at least a couple of inches are under the ground and the tops are at least eighteen inches up the trunk.

Some people recommend mothballs but I suspect the cure is worse than the disease.

A groundhog surveys his local kingdom before he starts eating the grasses again.
Photo credit: April King.

Instead try removing all those thickets where rabbits can hide. Clean up brush heaps, infested weed patches, litter piles, in fact anyplace a rabbit can hide.

Think about getting a dog, too—or a cat.

Check chapter 6 for repellents that are effective against rabbits, including the predator urines.

Small mesh chicken wire fencing can be very effective around a garden plot, or eighteen to twenty-four-inch cylinders to protect young trunks. Small units can be set around precious perennials.

Havahart traps are very effective when used to trap rabbits. Bait them with fresh greens, oats, apple chunks, even cat kibble. If traps are not used, move them around to different locations.

How Much Wood Can a Woodchuck Chuck?

Woodchucks (*Marmota monax*), or the common groundhog, are familiar animals of the roadside. There, all summer long, they can be seen eating greens in preparation for the coming winter. Amazingly they are members of the squirrel family, and count among close relatives prairie dogs, flying squirrels, and chipmunks.

They are large animals, up to two feet in length (sometimes a bit larger), with little ears, short powerful legs, and a medium-long, bushy, and somewhat flattened tail. The fur color is dark brown to yellowish brown above and a paler, sometimes rusty color below. Older woodchucks get gray hairs, too. They can weigh up to fourteen pounds, especially after eating all summer. They usually waddle rather than actually walking but they can move very fast. They can also climb and swim. And when disturbed they make their presence known with a sharp whistle.

Woodchucks choose to live along the edges of open land or along fencerows, grass-covered gullies, or stream banks. Here in the sides of banks or under existing walls, they dig their burrows. The main entrance is usually located near a tree stump and is not hard to miss because of the pile of freshly excavated earth (in our case under a wall with the soil helping the woodchucks to clamber over the top of the wall). Side entrances are smaller and better concealed. The total amount of subsoil removed in the course of digging one burrow can average up to 700 pounds.

By the end of October, most woodchucks are hibernating in their underground nests. They usually sleep all winter, although during longer periods of mild weather, some chucks may awaken and go outside.

Breeding begins in early spring and from a single litter, two to nine naked, blind, and helpless kits are born.

As a builder of other animal homes, the role of the woodchuck is significant. Because of this, the woodchuck occupies an important niche in the wildlife community. Skunks, foxes, weasels, opossums and rabbits all use woodchuck burrows for their dens. Also, because tremendous quantities of subsoil are moved in the course of burrow construction, the countless generations of woodchucks have contributed much to the aeration and mixing of the soil. Wood-chucks are one of the few large mammals abroad in daylight, and many people get enjoyment from seeing them.

When we lived in Sullivan County we found that along with deer and rabbits, the woodchuck was a popular pest. They are almost complete vegetarians, enjoying leaves, flowers, grasses, and of all things dahlias. When living near farms they enjoy alfalfa, clover, and all sorts of truck-garden veggies.

We were especially amazed the year we learned they can climb trees or fences. So never place your vegetable garden close to a tree and if fenced, electrify. So, being an excellent shot, up in the mountains I dispatched any that got too close.

But I did this only as a last resort, as these animals occupy an important niche in the natural world. All sorts of animals have used abandoned woodchuck dens for their own homes and over the eons, when building their underground burrows, woodchucks literally move around tons of soil.

I never thought I would be confronted with woodchucks in Asheville but this past spring, I was not only host to a bonded pair, but two small (and cute) kits as well.

Once I spent a great deal of time down in the garden, accompanied by a friend's BB gun, within a week I only had the elder male to confront as the rest of the family dispersed.

A neighbor told me that this particular woodchuck had been seen in the neighborhood for years and judging by his many gray hairs was certainly not a young sprout. He usually lived back along an abandoned road just down the street from our yard and garden, but with the drought, I had the best greens around.

Here in the city we cannot shoot, poison is an absolute no, so the answer was a Havahart trap. Once trapped, we took the captured animal to a nearby wildlife center, which, in turn, carried the animal out to the hills beyond.

The common chipmunk stops for a few minutes before beginning to search for more food. Photo credit: Gilles Gonthier.

The Wonderful Chipmunk

There are two chipmunk species: The eastern chipmunk (*Tamias striatus*) and the western or least chipmunk (*Eutamias minimus*). Between them they take care of most of the Eastern United States and much of the West, and on up into Canada. Chipmunks are marvelous creatures, intelligent, clever, and well-groomed (they rarely have fleas or parasites). They can live eight years, probably a bit longer when raised as pets.

The eastern chipmunk is about five or six inches long, reddish-brown above, white below, with stripes on its back and sides, ending at the reddish rump. They have internal cheek pouches they can stuff with nuts, etc.

Chippers not only live at the forest's edge but around rock piles, under or next to stone walls, outbuildings, and even abandoned drain holes left over from tumbling walls. They are at home throughout the suburbs. They are not social and except for mating, live happily alone in their tidy boroughs. They are often seen sitting upright, looking over the lay of the land, giving out with a clear, repeated *chip* or a soft *chuck*. When startled, they sound out with several chips in a row, followed by a trill, then raise their tail in the air and quickly run to safety.

The least chipmunk is smaller, with yellowish or reddish fur, with stripes on their backs and sides, extending to the base of the tail.

Chipmunks eat nuts, berries, seeds, and insects, including earthworms, slugs, and grubs. They do not attack gardens with a vengeance but many people think they do. They do not eat bulbs and pick them from your garden. Outside of some documentation of their eating (or storing) wild trout lilies (*Erythronium* spp.), the reports of chipmunk bulb vandalism are apocryphal. Chipmunk problems revolve entirely around the digging of boroughs and movement of dirt.

If you feel threatened by chipmunks, the easiest solution is to get a cat.

I, on the other hand, have learned to fight back. Whenever I find the beginnings of a hole, I quickly fill it in, packing the dirt as tightly as I can. When the hole is renewed, I fill it again. Because chipmunks are intelligent, and quite willing at a certain point to take their ease, if prodded by you, they eventually move.

If you are interested in making a garden friend out of a garden foe, then read *Eastern Chipmunks: Secrets of Their Solitary Lives* by Lawrence Wishner (Smithsonian Press, Washington, DC, 1982).

CHAPTER EIGHT

Stone Gardens, Container Gardens, and Moss Gardens

In this chapter I present three off-the-wall solutions for gardening in those situations when you imagine that the deer represent a consortium of developers and your property becomes a symbol for the last area that could support a small garden in an area the size of Texas (or another large state). A fourth suggestion revolves around a number of ornamental grasses, featured in chapter 9.

It begins with some basic deer knowledge about the resilience of the white-tailed deer and the availability of grass. These deer do not graze in the manner of bison wandering the plains or a few of the other deer species. They do not stand for hours chewing a cud and lack both the teeth and the endless stomachs that can grind up grass and zero in on what food value is left. They lack those special teeth and stomachs that can efficiently grind up and digest the tough fibers in grasses. Just like your jaw. the deer have incisor teeth but only on their bottom jaw, while there is a cartilage pad on the front of the upper jaw. Also like you, they have both upper and lower molars.

A boulder too massive to be threatened by deer is surrounded by a bed of ground-hugging juniper at the Bonsai Pavilion of the North Carolina Arboretum.

Because of this tooth arrangement, deer pull out blades of grass instead of shearing them like specialized grazers do. So the deer are able to nibble grasses in the lawn and tender leaves of many garden plants but find it difficult to work with some of the tougher leaves and stems that nature often provides. And when confronted with stones and rocks, they are literally between rocks and hard places. So here are some great gardens that stress the beauties of stones in the garden and the marvels of concrete and pottery containers.

Japanese Stone and Stream Gardens

The rivers of stone
Move naught yet silently run
With ripplets stilled.

This is the only time I've ever written about Japanese garden designs that I've featured the use of stones not only to emulate water—and around the country water is getting to be in short supply—but to landscape a garden so the odd deer-proof plant located here and there is surrounded by an inhospitable landscape that has both practical and philosophical beauty to human eyes but nothing except pain to a deer. And it's the first time I start a piece of writing with a *haiku* poem.

Until I took the proper time to look at the Japanese-inspired River of Stone that flows silently down from the upper terrace of the Bonsai Pavilion at the North Carolina Arboretum, I never realized that here was a case where water vanished from the garden scene with nothing lost in the transition except, perhaps, the sound.

Luckily, I know the great garden designer who master-minded the design and construction of the gardens surrounding this wonderfully built pavilion dedicated to the Arboretum's collection of bonsai trees—and his name is Mike Oshita. Mike is a man who not only designed the gardens surrounding the pavilion but actually went out on the road looking for, then choosing, and finally supervising the installation of rocks and stone used in the construction of this natural wonder.

There, except for the depth of winter, visitors walk along pathways and wonder at trees carefully shaped by this Japanese process of miniaturization and marvel that such a craft can produce such living beauty.

And when walking through this tiered garden you are immediately aware that visitors, who when out in the open would normally talk in an outspoken manner, here hush their voices in the same manner often found when people walk through a forest.

But in addition to the living trees on display, the visitor will walk on mostly level paved bridges that cross a mountain stream not of water but of rock that runs through the garden beginning at the top and fading away at the bottom.

Being an island nation, Japan generally has plenty of rainfall and, of course, is surrounded by great seas and oceans. But such

In the garden of the New England Wildflower Society a marvelous portable fence made of wire filled with autumn leaves can be moved around the garden with reasonable ease.

gardens also salute the use of sand and stone in their construction and there are many ways for such inanimate materials to be used as stand-ins for water. Flat or upright stones often symbolize a rushing mountain stream, and in Western North Carolina what better way to create a unique design element for a design that salutes the process, unique to Japan, of controlling the growth of trees?

Some Japanese-inspired tea gardens use sand that is carefully raked to represent the tides and flows of rivers or streams, and remember that sand is but finely crushed stone.

Mike Oshita's personal book of style advises gardeners to follow nature and study the materials that nature provides but never just copy nature—that is often not as interesting as using one's imagination to create your own style.

For example, when he creates a creek bed garden he makes sure that the beginning of the creek bed is narrow and deep compared with the end of the creek. Imagine a creek which begins in a deep mountain gorge, so he might add a small waterfall or a cascading terrace, the stone in the creek bed always made of rough-looking mountain stone.

The rivers that Mike creates are not the only such rivers I've found in the exploration of gardens. It turns out to be a great solution when the gardener is presented with stones large and small that might remain when clearing land. The careful placing of rocks both large and small

A river of stone.

can be used for pathways to be walked upon, or places where stones suggest to the visitor that water abounds where there's no water to be had.

If you live in a part of the country where large stones are in short supply then search for replacements that could be used for garden architecture. The following materials are often mentioned: polished pebbles, seaside beach pebbles, Mexican beach pebbles, beach lava pebbles, eroded beach glass pebbles, beach glass epoxy aggregates, pebble tiles, stone aggregate, shipped or shredded bark, bricks or brick chips, ceramic tile, cobblestones, concrete paving blocks, fieldstone, flagstone, granite blocks, grass, gravel (large bits or small bits), millstones (if you can find them), interlocking

A meandering river of stone in a coastal Virgina garden makes a great boundary.

pavers, pine needles, crushed seashells, oyster shells, terra-cotta tile, wooden rounds, wooden squares, and even a controlled installation of mulching material, often called "Nature's Helper" at garden store outlets.

First take paper and pencil and sketch a simple map of the area to be developed and planted. The map need not be complicated or artistic, and need not stifle your creativity; it just helps the gardener to arrive at the starting gate with some idea of what's coming down the line. Large-scale or small potatoes, planning it out beforehand saves time, energy, and money.

On your map indicate the presence of natural wind-breaks, existing trees, and all structures—whether already there or planned for the future. Then sketch in a meandering stream or a straight run, remembering that this is decorative, and allow it to bend around any existing boulders or trees.

Now in amongst the stones in the garden you can plan on adding a few dwarf conifers or small shrubs or trees (make them deer-resistant choices) and in the end have a very pleasant garden with pathways to walk upon and dry rivers that require no upkeep.

A Japanese Dry Stream Garden

As we have learned from the Japanese gardeners above, this garden only suggests the presence of water. A small creek or stream is constructed but it is filled with gravel or small stones instead of water. With the addition of a bamboo fence or a screen, it takes on a very oriental character. Many suburban lots have drainage ditches in the rear of the property. By filling the ditch with river stones and planting small conifers and ornamental grasses along the edge, it becomes an attractive addition to the garden instead of a liability. The illusion is heightened by placing flat stepping stones that wander across the gravel "water."

Among the plants to be considered for such a garden are the bamboos, including the beautiful Kamuro-zasa bamboo (*Arundinaria viridistriata*), with its beautiful colors of chartreuse, yellow, and pale green. The striking

An aging juniper grows in a river of stone at the Bonsai Pavilion.

Another river of stone at North Carolina Arboretum.

A constructed course to bring water to a garden at the North Carolina Arboretum would be a great planter if water is turned off.

green-and-tan Kuma bamboo (*Sasa veitchii*) and the larger ornamental grasses are perfect for this garden scheme. They include the various cultivars of *Miscanthus*; variegated prairie cordgrass (*Spartina pectinata* 'Aureomarginata') with five- to seven-foot sweeping blades edged with a pale brownish-yellow; and the common but still desirable Ohwi Japanese sedge grass (*Carex morrowii* var. *expallida*), which bears variegated leaves edged with white. The newer cultivars of Ohwi sedge—including

Budd Myer's container gardens are easily protected from deer.

This Chris Mello bottle tree withstands anything.

'Aureo-marginata,' with golden-yellow striping or 'Old Gold,' with green and gold stripes—are also excellent additions.

If All Else Fails, Try Pots

You would be amazed at what will hold a plant. There are vases and jardinières, urns and pots, troughs and tubs, window boxes for window ledges, pots to hang on walls or from trees, just plain hanging baskets, not to mention discarded sinks, old wheelbarrows, abandoned tires, abandoned super-market carts, and even a toilet (or two).

Believe it or not, an antique toilet bowl (especially from the nineteenth century), in good condition, makes a very effective pot. And while purists bemoan the use of old car and truck tires, I do not. Anything that helps to relieve the increasing monotony of both our urban and suburban scene is welcome—at least to me.

Tires, for example, can be stacked (you can glue them

Chris Mello uses a large moon for garden decoration.

Chris Mello's garden in West Asheville includes his own pet deer.

together if you fear they might come apart), but remember to break up the interior soil they sit upon, thus improving drainage.

Today, considering the demands made upon my time and my energy, if given a choice between having the backyard become an ample garden or provided with a terrace and a grand collection of pots with plants within, I'd take the containers, hands down.

Why? Containers provide so many choices for gardeners, choices from dressing up the front entrance to your home, to taking advantage of hanging plants from the limbs of trees that might be around your yard, to changing a bare deck from a lineup of uninteresting wooden planks or ceramic tile or concrete blocks, to actually hiding an ugly foundation without digging up the existing soil.

Want to change the look of your garden? Bring in some new containers with some new plants and take the old to a secret place on your property—well screened by a fence or hedge—and replant them at your ease.

Tired of the general look of your perennial border but not willing to take the time to redesign or replant? Move in some great containers holding, for example, a small Japanese maple or a beautifully planted mix of perennials and annuals that will bloom all summer, well into the fall.

New Zealand flax at home in a container on my Asheville garden.

Want to experiment with some plants that usually give in to the extremes of your climate? Try growing these beauties in pots. You'll have ample control of your environment, using mobility to your best advantage as you move plants from place to place, taking advantage of weather protection where you find it.

Thinking of a new color combo that even the trendiest magazines say is a bit too much? You might be right and they might be wrong and by using a pot, you can experiment without digging everything up if you're wrong.

Containers offer a short-term solution to growing a number of plants, like many bulbs, that come into bloom, then blooms fade and a clump of uninteresting foliage is left that must ripen before the bulbs go into storage. When the plants become unsightly, you simply move them out of sight.

Finally, if you're not as young as you once were and either your garden or your physical prowess is limited, containers can be placed at many levels and can be moved about with ease, remembering that

Garden containers are easy to protect with just a bit of netting.

larger pots can go on wheels or be lugged about on a dolly.

A Short History of Containers

According to ancient garden records, the Egyptians loved the rose and actually grew roses to supply the other countries around the Mediterranean, even shipping roses to Rome. Cut flowers were also beloved by all and anemones, thistles, papyrus leaves, reeds, and cornflowers were all available to buy at a bazaar and take home to brighten a room or two.

Marco Polo once claimed that the great Kublai Khan commanded that choice trees from the Asian Plains be dug up and carried to his palace gardens in China by a team of hardy elephants.

Flower pots from Ancient Greece were amazingly like many of today's more elegant designs and held everything from rooted tree cuttings to clumps of blooming poppies.

In her book of pot history *Pots and Pot Gardens* (London: Abelard-Schuman, 1969), Mary Grant White wrote, ". . . Greeks do not seem to have made gardens as we understand them, being hampered, no doubt, by the rocky nature of their soil. Such ornamental gardening as did exist had great religious significance, often taking the form of sacred groves dedicated to some god or goddess. Among their religious practices, none makes more delightful reading than the cult of Adonis which was thought to have originated in Phoenicia, and spread to Greece by way of Cyprus. In these particular rites, Adonis, a beautiful youth beloved by Aphrodite, was worshipped as the spirit of Nature and plant life. In the autumn he was believed to die and disappear into the underworld, to be rescued by Aphrodite and brought back to Earth again in the spring. The Greeks made great play of this myth and each midsummer held festivals during which they would place a number of earthenware pots around a figure of the god. These were sown

Deer-protected roses at the gardens of the University of Tennessee at Knoxville.

with quick-growing seeds such as fennel, lettuce, and barley, and when they sprouted, the people rejoiced to think that Adonis had come back to them."

Soon the pots planted for the Adonis festivals were in every home and became such a popular item of outdoor decoration that although Adonis faded, pot gardening continued.

The Adonis festivals spread until the Greeks developed the roof garden and in time Roman gardeners planted flowers, then bushes, then flowers and bushes in tubs and set them in courtyards and along garden pathways. In fact, it was Rome that began the custom of the window box.

Today all over Europe and the Mediterranean, earthenware pots remain in vogue and in continual use, and by the early 1900s had

At left is a garden generally ignored by deer and at right, it's too high to reach.

made their way to Mediterranean-style gardens found in Florida and California. Any great house in a Hollywood movie of the 1930s always sported pots of flowers carefully positioned on the tops of walls, adorning terraces, around tiled swimming pools, and here and there along the perennial border.

Esthetics of Pots

Unfortunately, there are two words associated with the pots of today: clay and plastic. Clay is a time-honored material with a long horticultural history and plastic is a Frankenstein monster, conceived in the 1930s and now out of control. Oh, sure, there are well-designed plastic pots out there but they remain at the dawn of the twenty-first century few and far between.

When our descendents search the rubbish piles of our time for clues to their ancestry, they will find not only a plethora of beer cans and disposable diapers, but also millions of non-disintegrating plastic flower pots (some with golden edges).

These plastic and Styrofoam pots work well for the commercial grower who must balance continuing rising costs and deadlines for seasonal markets (as hectic as the fashion industry) with demands for cheap transportation. He has an excuse to use such pots because they are cheaper. But you, the buyer, upon reaching home can easily remove the plant from its truly artificial container and replace it with one that actually functions as a plant container.

There are more than esthetic reasons for using clay containers. Clay breathes, allowing air and water to pass through the walls. It's much more difficult to over-water when using clay. I'm convinced that more damage is done by the lethal use of water than any other mistreatment known.

Furthermore, clay is much heavier and keeps larger plants from toppling over in a mild breeze or falling over because the cat bumped into a plastic container on its way to the water dish.

Clay will last much longer (as long as you don't continually drop the pots) than plastic, which becomes brittle with age. Finally, by looking at the algae and salt deposits forming on the clay, you have an early warning system that predicts problems long before the plant itself shows signs of trouble.

Clay Pots

Clay pots are made in many different sizes and shapes. They start at two inches, measured by the diameter across the top, and go up to sixteen inches or more. Their height is about the same as the diameter. Many have names long associated with English gardens. The two-inch pot is called the "thimble," the two-and-a-half-inch pot the "thumb."

When the height exceeds the diameter they're called "long Toms"; when shorter than they are wide they're called "dwarfs" (or dwarves, depending on your age and education). You'll also find azalea pots that are three quarters of the standard depth, allowing for shallower root systems.

I rarely find a use for the thimble or thumb pots because they are so small the soil dries out too quickly, but they're fun to have around for an extra small cactus or a tiny vine seedling.

Before peat pots and Jiffy-7's were developed, these small pots were extensively used for seedlings. Now we transplant the beginning seedlings and their peat pots into three-inch clay pots when plants are large enough for the move. Remember, depending on the age of the pot and the manufacturing process, you will find minor variations in the thickness of the clay walls and the top measurements.

New clay pots should be soaked in water before use, or they'll quickly draw most of the water from the soil. Old and reused pots must be cleaned and scrubbed. Steel wool will easily remove an accumulation of mineral salts.

Drainage holes are found in the bottom. These should be covered with a few shards of broken pot to keep soil from escaping and, if your plants are outside or in a greenhouse, a small piece of screening to guard against wandering slugs and other undesirables.

Unless you have the reputation of a Picasso, never paint pots. If you want to make an attractive display for a beautiful plant, find a suitable jardinière or other container and place the clay pot within.

Learning from the Experts

When it comes to gardening with containers, I temporarily push aside my predilections for native plants (although I often use them as subjects), and turn to English gardeners and those glorious photographs in English garden magazines.

High on my list of readable authorities is Gertrude Jekyll, who wrote many books on design for home gardens (not to mention grand estate gardens), and found that plants growing in pots were noteworthy additions to any garden scheme.

Miss Jekyll writes about the beauty of Italian gardens where most views include quantities of plants in pots standing at various levels and in interesting groupings. These are usually in addition to the larger pot containing oranges, lemons, oleanders, etc., that, in their immense and often richly decorated earthenware receptacles, form an important part of the garden design.

In our mountain climate the citrus fruits are out, but even here we can grow Japanese maples, conifers, most native shrubs, and many plants with winter interest, as long as the pots are over a foot in diameter.

Native red honeysuckle and clambering native geraniums grow too high for pests to reach them.

In her classic book, *Colour Schemes for the Flower Garden* (London: Country Life, Ltd, 1936), Miss Jekyll writes, "Good groupings of smaller plants in pots is a form of ornament that might he made more use of in our own gardens, especially where there are paved spaces near a house or in connection with a tank or fountain, so that there is convenient access to means of daily watering. I have such a space in a cool court nearly square in shape. A middle circle is paved, and all next the house is paved, on a level of one shallow step higher. It is on the sides of this raised step that the pot plants are grouped, leaving free access to a wooden seat in the middle, and a clear way to a door on the left."

Succulents hang high.

She goes on to describe terracotta pots lush with hostas, particularly *Hosta plantaginea* and *H. sieboldii*, standing in front of and hiding from view, the bottom part of common pots full of blooming annuals. Early in June *Clematis montana* is still in bloom, and near the side of the house are pots of cast-iron plants (*Aspidistra elatior*), not to mention all sorts of ferns. And, of course, there are pots of lilies including *Lilium superbum* and pots of Spanish irises and various cultivars of the gladiolus tribe, backed up by a trellis of the tropical cup-and-saucer vine (*Cobaea scandens*), either in the traditional purple or pure white.

"There are seldom more," she continues, "than two kinds of flowering plants placed here at a time; the two or three sorts of beautiful foliage are in themselves delightful to the eye; often there is nothing with them but Lilies, and one hardly desires to have more. There is an ample filling of the green plants, so that no pots are seen."

She chooses geraniums for their color, in one part of the garden linking white and soft pink, while elsewhere she has many pots of rosy-scarlet or salmon-reds. She takes great pleasure in grouping the palest salmon-pink next to a good and pure scarlet cultivar.

She suggests that when designing gardens that include areas of flagstones, many of the pots look their best when standing slightly above ground level, perhaps having the pots on clay feet, now available at most garden centers.

One of her favorites is the maiden's wreath (*Francoa racemosa*), a plant for many uses. The distinctive foliage is quite attractive, and the long flower-stems are flung out in all directions, much like the tapestry strands thrown out by in William Holman Hunt's marvelous painting, "The Lady of Shallot," which hearkens from the same time that Miss Jekyll was designing top gardens in England. At summer's end the flowering stems become so heavy that in a stiff breeze, there's danger of their snapping off or pulling some of the plant's roots right out of the pots. She suggests that short pieces of wood be used to sturdy the stems.

She espouses the use of potting, noting that a well-blooming plant will give life and interest to any uninteresting corner. After all, the bloom is long-lasting, and the fall color of many blooms and leaves is beautiful to see.

Finally, she notes that it's rare to see, at least in England, plant-tubs that are painted a pleasant color. In nearly every garden she describes, the tubs are painted a strong raw green with the hoops a contrasting black, whereas any green that is not bright and raw would be much better. And, I might add, it's much the same in the America of the twenty-first century.

Miss Jekyll advises that the matter of coloring most garden accessories deserves more attention than it commonly receives. Doors in garden walls, trellises, wooden railings, and hand-gates and seats—all these and any other items of woodwork that stand out in the garden and are seen among its flowers and foliage should, if painted green, should be of a green that is not too bright so that it immediately is seen as competition to the green of the surrounding plants. With tubs, it's the plant that should be in the limelight, not the tub. And there is no reason to paint the hoops of any tub black, either with a shiny or dull finish.

A good quiet green can be made with black, chrome No. 1 and white lead, enough white being mixed to give the depth or lightness desired. A pretty color of paint is much used in France that approximates to the decorator's malachite green. This is not the bright color of malachite as we know the polished stone, but a pale, opaque bluish-green approaching the turquoise tints. In the bright, clear climate of France, and in connection with the higher type of French architecture, also in more southern countries, the color looks very well, though it is not becoming to some foliage; but something quieter and more sober is better suited for England.

A Protected Garden of Containers

There is a map of our garden in chapter 11 on page 286 and that map illustrates the wandering woodland trails winding about extensive plantings of very old rhododendrons, hollies, azaleas, and various bushes, shrubs, and conifers that deer resent. The only other plants throughout are spring-and fall-blooming bulbs. The area below the terrace is an open meadow of wild grasses and a mix of annual and perennial wildflowers.

The Garden Room that is close to the house and the terrace (itself resting on a wall that is fourteen feet high) is protected by a high stone wall to the north, a ten-foot high wooden wall to the east, and another wall to the west. The plants that grow there are mostly in container, like my collection of small Japanese maples, various rock garden plants, and the open area is edged with American wildflowers native to the area.

I'll return to this subject in chapter 11.

The Ease of Moss Gardens

Back in 1907, Nina L. Marshall wrote the following tribute to mosses in her delightful book entitled *Mosses and Lichens*: "The blackened embers of the picnic fire are hidden with golden cord-mosses and the roadsides in the woods and the slopes to the lake are carpeted with sturdy hairy-caps. The crumbling roofs of deserted cottages and the unused well-sweep and old oaken bucket are decorated with soft tufts of green."

John Cram's pest-proof moss garden in Asheville.

I hesitate to mention this particular Japanese approach to gardening because so many Americans, when confronted with growing mosses either in their garden or, heaven forbid, in the lawn immediately call their County Extension agent and attempt to kill the invader. They should not, especially if they are now sharing much of their garden with a herd of deer.

There is a beautiful moss garden next door. It was created over many years by the late Doan Ogden, a brilliant landscape architect who, with his wife Rosemary, brought moss plugs from the nearby woods and slowly turned a thirty-by-fifty-foot area, consisting of sparse grass and some large white oaks and smaller maple trees, into a garden of contemplation that inspires the visitor at all times of the year. The only maintenance needed is removing fallen leaves so that the moss does not go into dormancy from lack of light.

But not all moss gardens must be big; they can also be a world in miniature. Small rocks become mountains, and the mosses change from tiny plants to thickets of impenetrable green. The yellow blossom of a tiny star grass (*Hypoxis hirsuta*) assumes the proportions of the Liberty Bell.

Friends in the mountains of North Carolina created such a garden by collecting all the rocks from nearby walking tours and the mosses from an area eventually to be cleared for a pond and small botanical garden. There are a number of small native plants, pinks (*Dianthus* spp.) and bluets (*Hedyotis purpurea*), but by far the largest number of plants in the garden are the mosses.

Most mosses need shade because they have poorly developed water distribution systems and the hot sun can dry them out before water reaches thirsty cells. Haircap moss (*Polytrichum commune*) will grow in open fields, but in that environment the grass provides some protection and helps to collect and channel the morning dew to the mosses below. When mosses become dry, they fold up their leaves, an action which markedly changes their appearance. But once the plants have water again, the individual cells quickly swell and the mosses revert to their normal size.

Advice from an Expert

Being a lover of the bryophytes or the members of the great moss kingdom, the first person I contacted about deer and moss was my old garden friend Mossin' Annie, who has a marvelous nursery in Brevard, North Carolina (www.mountainmoss.com).

"Thankfully," said Annie, "for moss gardeners, deer do not like the taste of moss. For that matter, no critter or typical garden insect pest likes to eat mosses due to their cellular content of phenolic compounds that make bryophytes taste unpalatable.

"The main damage concerns to mosses due to deer visitation are the "scuff" marks left behind as they stomp around eating other plants such as hostas. These impacted moss areas can be easily repaired by replacing the dislodged colonies or scooching and stretching the scrunched section back into place.

"Deer may do their business while enjoying their hosta dinner and leave behind an unwanted gift. If feces are removed in a timely fashion, then mosses don't seem to suffer. Pooper scooper duty solves this problem. However, deer urine may cause discolored yellow areas that will take months to recover, if at all. Personally, I usually remove the yellowed section and replant with a new moss colony. Occasionally, I just give the moss in question a heavy hand fluffing to rejuvenate the colony.

"The use of netting in a moss garden is primarily an act of maintenance or troubleshooting technique related to small critter damage, but usually not from deer. Squirrels, raccoons, even armadillos disturb mosses when digging vigorously for their preferred nuts or grubs. Black netting would be of little advantage if deer are the only critter visitors. It's easy to fix the occasional deer paw scuff. Additionally, netting may be used for leaf and litter control. Finally, netting can be beneficial during the establishment phase of mosses when employing the fragmentation planting method."

Next, while very hungry deer have been known to nibble at mosses, even when under the snow, here's a case where protection is easy to find.

Mosses need shade because they have poorly developed water distribution systems and the hot sun can dry them out before water reaches thirsty cells. Haircap moss (*Polytrichum commune*) will grow in open fields, but in that environment the grass provides some protection and helps to collect and channel the morning dew to the mosses below. When mosses become dry, they fold up their leaves, an act that markedly changes their appearance. But once the plants have water again, the individual cells quickly swell and the mosses revert to their normal size.

Mosses reproduce by releasing spores from little containers called peristomes. Looking at different peristomes—for each genus has a design all its own—is like looking at a Paul Klee etching of Turkish minarets. These fanciful capsules are edged with teeth that vary in number from four to sixty-four, always being in multiples of four. When the weather is damp, the teeth are closed tightly together; when it is dry, they open up and the spores are shaken to the winds like salt cast from a saltcellar.

Finally, mosses can easily exist on bare rock. By threading their rhizoids, or tiny roots, into microscopic pores in the rock's surface, they can remove elements for nutrition and eventually create soil. Even airborne dust is trapped by the leaves of the mosses and eventually combines with pieces of old and dehydrated plants to form dirt.

Woodland Mosses for the Garden

The following mosses are common to most temperate woods and not in any danger of extinction.

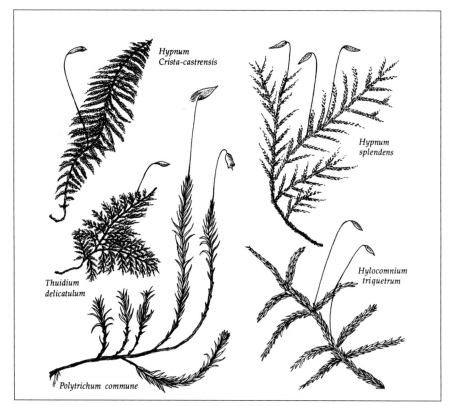

Some deer-resistant native mosses that can find a home in a shady garden.

Andreaea petrophila, the stone-loving andreaea, was named in honor of the German botanist, G. R. Andreae. The species is from *petra* or roc. This plant grows best on granite or slate rocks in shady, damp places. They are among the first colonizers to settle on these inhospitable surfaces.

Bartramia pomiformis, or apple moss, gets its species name, *pomum* (apple) and *form* (form) from the plant's tiny spore cases, which look like little apples. The genus was named in honor of John Bartram, the great botanist from Pennsylvania. There are thirteen known species of apple moss in North America, most of which are found growing in rock clefts.

Dicranum longifolium, the fork moss, gets its generic name from the Greek word for flesh-hook or fork, referring to the unusual formation of the teeth on its spore case. The species refers to the very long leaves. It is among sixty-five species in North America; at the turn of the century, six were found within the limits of New York City. The plants grow only in high-altitude rocky regions and are sometimes found at the base of trees.

Hylocomium triquetrum, the triangular wood-reveller, makes an excellent plant for a moss garden. The common name is the English translation of the Greek generic name. Triangular refers to the shape of the stems. This particular moss grows only on wood with a luxuriant delight. This moss was placed on the rock in a crevice that holds its wooden base.

Hypnum crista-castrensis, the ostrich-plume feather moss, is so called because the plants are plume-like and a bright yellow green. The Greek term *hypnum* suggests that these mosses were once helpful in promoting sleep; the species name refers to the shape of the branches. The spore capsules are large, curved, and held horizontally. This moss is common in mountainous regions and grows on soil or rotten wood.

Hypnum splendens, the arched feather moss, is a beautiful combination of gold and green leaves on reddish stems. This splendid plant is common on rocks in the deep woods and on nearby fallen stumps or rotten logs. Miss Marshall wrote of them:

"Glittering with yellow, red and green,

As o'er the moss, with playful glide,

The sunbeams dance from side to side."

Leucobryum longifolium, the pincushion moss, looks so much like a pincushion that little imagination was needed for the name. The generic name is Greek for white moss, which refers to the unusual pallid green color. Plants look pale because the cells with green chlorophyll are surrounded by larger transparent cells that carry water and protect smaller cells from heat.

Polytrichum commune, the haircap moss, gets its generic name from *poly*, many, and *trichum*, hair. Pliny called this plant "golden maiden-hair" because of the golden gloss the leaves exhibit when dry. The fringed edge on the spore-caps are said to resemble a lady's tresses—hence the common name. Hair-cap moss has been used in lieu of expensive feathers to stuff pillows. It was the first plant to be recognized by early botanists as not having true flowers.

Thuidium delicatulum, the tiny cedar moss, was named for its close resemblance to a miniature cedar tree (*Thuidium* is an ancient name for a resinous-bearing evergreen). This moss was well known to Linnaeus, the great Swedish botanist who devised the binomial system for naming plants. He called it *delicatulum* because of its dainty appearance. Tiny cedar moss enjoys damp shady places and runs over stones, earth, and rotten logs.

Moss gardens are not for everyone. They require a delight in the small, in fact a complete shunning of the bravado—not to mention a shady spot beneath some tall trees. But for those gardeners who have the inclination for creating a world in miniature, the moss garden is the answer.

CHAPTER NINE

Plants Unpopular with Deer

This book is basically about gardening and caring for gardens, whether in pots or in the ground. After all, if you had no interest in protecting plants then why would you pursue a book that offers some help in keeping deer at their distance? They are, after all, beautiful creatures, full of surprise, with antics equal to or better than TV programs featuring most of the activities of humankind—so the only good reason for keeping them at bay is their ability to ravage gardens.

But I wrote it before and I'll write it again (and if the technology were available, I would stress this over and over by printing it in all capitals, boldface, headline type, and accompanying music of a dirge-like tune): deer are intelligent living creatures programmed by their genes and their history to survive over all survivable odds. If starving, they will eat almost anything. An old garden friend said it best when joking about the deer diet: "They will eat anything except oleander—although I'm not convinced of that—and antique brick!"

When you glance through the following collection of plants, I suspect even many seasoned gardeners will be surprised by the number of species ignored, shunned, or disliked by deer, always remembering the disclaimer in the last paragraph. Of course, there will be exceptions but generally it's a safe bet that choosing plants from the following list will at least give you a fighting chance at having a garden. And any gardener who had to choose to garden with only the following plants would soon find they had a garden of great beauty and should be reasonably happy with their lot.

It's also interesting to note just how many of the following plants are listed in various herbal and medicinal guides for their use in treating an incredible number of diseases and bodily discomforts. From the American Indians to the early settlers and the pharmaceadical houses of today, many of our Native American plants and wildflowers were collected for use as drugs, poultices, herbal teas, disinfectants, and stimulators of bile, and the like. A number of these plants are bitter or have unpleasant textures or are highly purgative when eaten. Unfortunately, smaller pests do not necessarily ignore a number of the following plants.

Since this chapter deals with gardens allow me to remind you that any great garden always has a nursery bed providing impressive plants to replace any lost to weather, disease, or living threats. Such beds are out-of-the-way spots, behind a fence (not only for protection but as a screening aid) where you grow a number of plants, ready to be moved into the garden for replacements, after damage has been done.

As to USDA Zones, now that global warming is no longer a propagated myth, most gardeners have already noted that winters still fluctuate on a local level, but average temperatures continue to climb so it's now possible to grow Zone 7 plants in many Zone 6 gardens, especially when such zones can often always be moderated by gardeners experimenting gardens as protected places, or what are often called micro-climates. These are spots where temperatures are somewhat moderated by wind screens, out-buildings, or even below-ground septic tanks or sewer lines.

The soil descriptions rely on some knowledge. Poor soil means rocky, heavy clay, surface shale, etc. Good soil is garden soil that can be worked without a pickax, and has a reasonable amount of humus and other soil conditioners. Excellent soil has high fertility, good drainage, and you can plunge a shovel into the ground up to the top of the digging part without using a sledgehammer.

Annuals and Biennials

Annuals are plants that germinate, grow, flower, and go to seed in one season. Of course it's not that easy because there are many annuals happy with their lot and like to hang around for more than a few weeks. Then there are many plants that, although termed annuals,\ are truly perennials in disguise, usually hailing from tropical countries but will bloom the first year from seed.

Then we have a few biennial plants, one of the most noteworthy being Queen Anne's lace, which produces small leafy rosettes the first year after germination but never bloom until the second season.

Before going through this section again please be warned that deer have a penchant for hollyhocks (*Alcea rosea*), all sorts of impatiens (*Impatiens* spp.). and Mexican sunflowers (*Tithonia rotundifolia*). If you want these plants, provide heavy protection.

Floss-flowers (*Ageratum houstonianum*) are tender annuals that bloom with small balls of fluffy flowers, usually in many shades of blue and pink to white, and useful in borders or massed for color. Plants are short, usually under a foot high. Originally imported from Mexico, they are killed with the first frosts of fall.

Calico plant (*Alternanthera ficoidea*) is another tropical perennial hardy to USDA Zone 10 and grown for the great leaf color featuring basic greens splotched with yellow, orange, copper, or purple shades, sometimes with colored leaf veins. If growing from seed pick only the brightest seedlings for planning on.

Forget-me-not (*Anchusa capensis*), is a biennial treated as an annual, originally from Africa and bearing flowers of, that's right, forget-me-not blue (but sometimes pink or white). Best used in mass plantings, they are also very fine growing in pots.

Snapdragons (*Antirrhinum majus*) rank at the top as favorite garden flowers and are especially valuable because the flowers open from the bottom up instead of the top down. Thanks to Global Warming, many snaps will over-winter in a warmer Zone 6 climate zones but for most gardeners in Zone 5 and below, they are still grown as annuals. Cultivars are legion, with single and double flowers blooming on stems that range from dwarf to about a foot-high, to some over two feet in height. Unlike most plants that are treated as annuals, snapdragons do not like heavy clay soil so mix in some additional compost when planting out.

Wax begonias (*Begonia* x *semperflorens-cultorum*) are usually grown as edging plants and will bloom all summer long until cut down by frost. They adapt to full sun but prefer some afternoon shade, especially down South. Unless you are interested in the newest of the new, don't bother growing these from seed, as garden centers always have a good selection.

Three yuccas surrounded by beds of annual begonias are deer resistant and withstand the hot suns of summer.

Swan River daisy (*Brachycome iberidifolia*) is another great annual plant sporting daisy-like flowers having with blue, violet, or white rays surrounding center disks that are almost black blooming on foot-high stalks. Flowers bloom for three to four weeks and can be had for a long-term summer by sowing seeds on alternate dates.

Calendula (*Calendula officinalis*) are annuals of long standing, native to the Mediterranean region, with large flower heads up to four inches across and blooming in colors ranging from pale yellow to deep orange. Deadhead to prolong the blooms, in times past a yellow dye was made from the petals to both color and flavor custard dishes.

Calendulas bloom as summer annuals.

Million bells (*Calibrachoa* spp.) are attractive relatives of the petunia family and also known as the trailing petunia. The flowers are rarely eaten by deer because they have a bitter taste in addition to a strong fragrance. Plants reach a height of four to six inches and produce hundreds of pink, red, purple, or blue flowers for the entire summer to late fall season. They prefer a lot of sun and work especially well in containers.

Madagascar periwinkle (*Catharanthus roseus*) is a trailing perennial that is treated as an annual below USDA Zone 8. This plant generates a crystalline alkaloid called *vinca-leuko-blastine*, abbreviated to VLB, and is found to have promise as a cancer therapy. It's perfect for hanging baskets.

Cockscombs (*Celosia* spp.) were popular plants back in Thomas Jefferson's garden and their decidedly odd flowers grow and bloom on stems up to three feet tall with one type of blossom resembling a cock's comb (or a tasteful caricature of a flowering alien species). Colors range from bright red down to pink and there are now a number of cultivars on the market.

Celosias bloom above dusty millers.

Basket flowers (*Centaurea Americana*) are annual native plants from the Midwest where each stem bears a single flower, with a base that resembles a little woven basket. The stems are between three and four feet tall. The blossoms close at night. Bachelor's button (*C. cyanus*), or cornflower, are familiar annuals that flower in white, pink, rose, purple, red, and blue.

Cornflowers (*Centaurea cyanus*) are also called bachelor's button, bluebottle, the boutonniere flower, and cyani flower, the last in a salute to the grand blue color. It is not to be confused with chicory, a blue-toned perennial that often blooms along the roadsides of much of America.

Because of their tall habit, spider flowers or cleomes (*Cleome hassleriana*) look like perennials but are really annuals of great beauty. From the gardener's point of view, it's wonderful that cleomes are deer resistant. They reach six feet and when massed in large groupings make a great statement, especially because they adapt to most soil conditions. The stems and leaves have a slight stickiness and there are very small thorns here and there. Colors range from white to deep violet and many cultivars are available.

Coleus (*Coleus* spp.) are tropical perennials usually treated as annual and bearing amazingly colorful foliage, decking the garden with great colorations from red to yellow to maroon to marvelous shades of green. There are two types: sun-lovers and shade-lovers, and

Fountain grass and spider flowers are both disliked by deer.

marketed as such. When grown in bunches they are sometimes eaten by deer (or at least ravaged) and I have often wondered if the color perception of deer plays a part in acceptance or rejection?*

---

* According to an article published in the November 22, 2009, issue of *The Pittsburgh Post Gazette* by reporter Ben Moyer, continued scientific research points out that deer have traded a high color sense for the ability to see well in low-light conditions. But that doesn't mean they are color blind. "What we discovered is that deer are not color blind, although they do see color differently than we do," said Brian Murphy, CEO of the Quality Deer Management Association and a wildlife biologist who participated in the University of Georgia research. "Deer are essentially red-green color blind like some humans. Their color vision is limited to the short [blue] and middle [green] wavelength colors. As a result, deer likely can distinguish blue from red, but not green from red, or orange from red."

Coleus and horsetails, the top protected by the bottom.

Larkspurs (*Consolida ambigua*) are most attractive plants growing up to two feet tall and bearing spurred flowers resembling small delphiniums blooming over fern-like leaves of dark green. These plants are easily grown from seed and should be sown in the fall using a fertile, well-drained soil. The seeds are poisonous.

Cosmos (*Cosmos bipinnatus*) are tall branching annuals with strong stems bearing attractive ferny foliage and petalled blossoms of white, pink, or crimson especially fine for the back of the border. There are a number of great cultivars including 'Sensation' which won the 1936 All-American Selection Award for the great flowers blooming on three-to four-foot stems. A fairly new cultivar called 'Sea Shells' curved petals and is truly beautiful. The Sonata Series cultivars are dwarf plants only growing to about a foot or two tall. And plants are tough and bloom with abandon unhindered by drought, poor soil, and, of course, browsing deer, not to mention the act of self-sowing.

Cigar plants (*Cuphea ignea*) are tropical perennials or subshrubs that bear one-inch slim tubular red flowers with bright yellow lips, hence the common name referring to miniature tools of smoking. They reach a height of three feet and develop brittle semi-woody stems. They are reasonably hardy in Zone 10.

Woodchucks (or groundhogs) love young dahlias (*Dahlia* spp.) but deer seem to dislike the taste. These are tender perennials from

Mexico, grown as annuals in most gardens, they produce plants ranging from small to stately, blooming all summer, with many-petalled flowers. If dug up in the fall, the tubers can be used year after year. Dahlias will grow the first year from seed but if set out in the border, remember the smaller pests like them, especially the red-leafed varieties. Dahlias need a good garden soil, plenty of water, and full sun.

Datura or angel's trumpets (*Datura inoxia* and *D. metel*) are the annual form of a deadly family of plants, best known as the source of the drug scopolamine, a fact apparent to the majority of deer. The trumpet-shaped flowers are large, white, or sometimes purple, sweet-smelling but the plants themselves have an unpleasant, foxy odor. Single- and double-flowered cultivars are available. Another member of the tribe is jimson weed (*D. stramonium*), with off-white flowers but ill-smelling foliage. Remember, while beautiful, these are very dangerous plants, as all plant parts are poisonous, with the seeds being the worst. The perennial form of this plant is *Brugsmansia* spp., a tropical-perennial that is used on an annual basis for a special accent for a summer garden. All of it, like those above, is poisonous.

Queen Anne's lace (*Daucus carota*) is a champion wildflower that is capable of surviving long periods of drought, making do with woeful soil, enduring the hot, baking sun, yet blooming with hundreds of small white florets packed in the center of a three-inch diameter circle of lace with each blossom exhibiting one purple or light violet floret smack dab in the disk's center. This salute to the Good Queen Anne is a member of the carrot family, a fact quite evident when you smell the carroty fragrance of the root. These are biennial plants but once in the garden should continue year after year and they remain unpopular food where deer are concerned.

Queen Anne's lace is a great flower for the wild garden. Photo credit: Dee Holladay.

Sweet Williams (*Dianthus barbatus*) are old-fashioned biennials that will often bloom the first year if seed is started in late winter or very early spring. As members of the pink family, they are pleasantly fragrant and great as cut flowers. There are many cultivars available and plants do well started from seed.

Foxgloves (*Digitalis purpurea*) are famous biennials that bloom on three-foot-tall stems, crowded with dozens of white, pink, or cerise pouch-like flowers of great beauty. Once in your garden they reseed with ease. These plants are the source of the heart stimulant digitalis and apparently, the drug is just as dangerous for deer as it is for humans, so they give this plant a wide berth.

Wallflowers (*Erysimum* spp., formerly *Cheiranthus* spp.) grow as perennials in warmer gardens but here in Asheville they are usually treated as annuals or biennials, because rarely is it balmy enough

Little yellow foxgloves are very poisonous plants.

in the spring for using the word perennial. They are four-petalled, fragrant blossoms blooming in many colors but chiefly orange, yellow, white, with shades in between. The fragrance is worth the effort in the growing. Wallflowers care not about soil fertility but only need great drainage, which is the reason they seem to succeed; their plot consists of the crevices between stones in walls. In warmer climes they are great in window boxes. Generally deer avoid them.

Wallflowers bloom in late winter.

The California poppy (*Eschscholzia californica*) bears beautiful golden flowers that once were so thick along the coastline that early explorers shouted: "Gold! Gold!" when they first saw the blooms. Perennials in warmer climates, they are usually treated as annuals in most of the country. These native wildflower bears up to dry weather (although its usefulness fades in very hot climates) and mixes quite beautiful satiny-petalled flowers that come in great shades of orange and yellow, especially when they grow in well-drained sandy soils, because if the soil is too good or had too much water, they do poorly, if at all. Plant them from seed in the fall or very early spring. Although these poppies prefer moist soil when sown, they are drought-tolerant when established. And like all poppies, they dislike transplanting. Sow seeds again in the fall, especially in warmer-climate areas. And the best news is, of course, deer do not like these salutes to California and have been known to nibble, but usually pass these flowers by.

Blanket flowers (*Gaillardia pulchella*) are native annuals, named in honor of colorful Indian blankets, and originally from the Southeast and Mexico. They produce daisy-like blossoms of yellow, orange, red, or yellow with reddish bands on stems up to twenty inches high. They are great for the bed or border, tolerating a number of conditions.

Amaranth flowering in Jefferson's Monticello garden.

Globe amaranth (*Gomphrena globosa*) is an annual plant that grows up to two feet tall with globular flowers in shades of purple, red, pink, lilac, and white on twenty-four-inch stems. This annual plant is a native of Brazil and Guatemala. The pom-pom flowers are great butterfly magnets and at year's end make marvelous additions to winter bouquets. Deer find them objectionable, too. They are not fussy plants so they also do well in containers.

Licorice plant or vine (*Helichrysum petiolare*) bears insignificant umbels of white flowers but does sport elegant, silvery leaves that are great in containers—especially because they spill over the container edge like lazy vines inclined to flop rather than climb—and as edgings for borders. 'Lemon Licorice' has leaves colored chartreuse. It's not a true annual but a tropical shrub that blooms the first year from seed. The common name refers to the leaves emitting a faint odor of licorice.

Straw flowers (*Helichrysum bracteatum*) bloom with round, two-inch-wide daisy-like flowers whose petals make rustling sounds when rubbed together and feel as if they are made of pressed straw. The colors are brilliant and obviously not the most pleasant thing to chew that's produced in the garden. They are great in dried flower bouquets.

Heliotropes (*Heliotropium arborescens*) are sweet-smelling tropical perennials from Peru, usually grown as annuals. Often used for perfumes, they have been popular in summer gardens for centuries. Plants up to two feet high bear myriads of small, intensely fragrant flowers, usually violet or purple, but there are pastels and whites available. Plants need good soil and plenty of sun.

Polka-dot plants (*Hypoestes phyllostachya*) are tropical plants from Madagascar, long popular as houseplants, not because of their small purple flowers but because of the large oval leaves liberally spotted with tiny pink dots (in cultivars, the dots are sometimes white). It's a cute plant and it's amazing that deer are not attracted to their leafy display. They do well in average but well-drained garden soil and can be dug up in the fall and moved indoors to bring some color to a gray winter.

The morning glories (*Ipomoea purpurea*) that deer resent are annual, rarely perennial twiners that bear three-parted leaves and very showy flowers, four inches wide (or more), in colors ranging

Polka-dot plants have a most attractive foliage.

from purple and white to red, blue, and pink, not to mention being streaked and striped. The Imperial Japanese morning glories are included in this genus. Plants will also do well in pots and only ask for strings to climb.

Burning bush (*Kochia scoparia*) is a fascinating member of the annual plant family, especially because it looks too complex to be just a one-summer wonder. Also called the summer cypress, the plants resemble dwarf conifers and are perfect for a temporary summer hedge, along borders, or as a single garden accent in the ground or in a pot. With fall's arrival, the foliage turns scarlet red, hence the name of burning bush. 'Acapulco Silver' has light green leaves dusted on the tips with silver.

Lantanas (*Lantana camara*) are small, perennial shrubs in warmer parts of the U.S. that bloom in their first year. At the same time, they are viewed as invasive pests in the Deep South. The flowers bloom in flat-topped clusters on a long stalk, each flower being small, tubular blossoms in shades of white, pink, or yellow, changing to orange or red as they age. Newly planted lantanas need frequent watering but once established are tolerant of dry conditions. To keep them in bloom deadhead when needed and overgrown plants can be pushed into new elegance by cutting back by one third. As to deer, their dislike of this plant is probably because the small green berries that follow each flower are poisonous, and because of contact dermatitis some gardeners can be allergic to the touch of the leaves.

Sweet peas (*Lathyrus odoratus*) have been garden favorites in England since the first seeds landed on those shores back in 1699. The English have doted on them ever since. Why deer usually leave them alone is not understood, but a number of gardeners told me that is the case. Sweet peas need a deep, moist, cool, and well-prepared soil and should be started in the garden as soon as the soil can be worked. They do not do well in very warm climates.

Limoniums (*Limonium* spp.) are a large family of plants, also called sea lavenders, bearing clusters of tiny flowers, each surrounded with bright, papery wraps on two-foot stems. Those papery wraps are a clue to deer dislikes. Sea lavenders are fine in bouquets and in dried arrangements. Three species are usually sold—often interchanged—and usually billed as annuals, so it's best just to look for statice. Colors range the gauntlet, with red and orange very popular.

Flax (*Linum usitatissimum*) originally came from Asia and has escaped in much of North America. Early settlers and the textile industry used the plant as a source of fibers for cloth in addition to a seed crop for the manufacture of linseed oil. Plants contain a cyanide-like compound, and the oil is thought to be emetic and a purgative, hence deer refuse garden offers.

Edging lobelias (*Lobelia erinus*) have to be one of the most popular plants for edgings, groundcovers, planters, and window-boxes. Their cheery little blue flowers bloom all summer long and feature a number of attractive cultivars. The plants contain a poisonous alkaloid called lobelic acid and should not be eaten. Obviously deer know all about it, too.

Sweet alyssum (*Lobularia maritima*) is an old garden favorite that, while an annual plant, blooms over a long season and is best planted as a groundcover. Sometimes in warmer climates plants become short-lived perennials. Closely packed tiny flowers bloom in small racemes with stems that grow longer as the lower flowers fade. White is the usual color but look for shades of pink, lavender, and violet. When in active growth it will produce more flowers if old flowers are removed. This is a plant that's very happy when growing in cracks in a sidewalk or between paving stones. Some references suggest that flowers and leaves are edible but I've found that anything deer question, people should do the same; gardeners with sensitive skin may develop a rash when handling the plant. Remember this plant is in the mustard family (*Brassicaceae*).

Evening stocks (*Matthiola incana*) bloom at night and are best grown for their wonderful scent of jasmine that wafts across the evening garden. The small pink or purple four-petalled flowers look like windswept, rain-washed scraps of tissue paper that have been pasted onto stems. In England, the common name is melancholy gilli-flower because the plants look so sad during the day. To be sure of having enough in bloom for fragrance, set out new seed every ten days or so, at least to the middle of July. Having written a book on night-blooming plants, I found that over ten or more years, these members of the great mustard family were left along.

Four O'clock (*Mirabilis jalapa*), or in older books, the miracle of Peru, are tender tropical perennials that bloom the first year from seed. The three- to four-foot plants sport nocturnal, sweet-smelling flowers of attractive colors including red, pink, white, crimson, and yellow. The plants spring from potato-sized black tubers that can be dug up in the fall and stored over winter in a cool, dry place. Four O'clock roots are the source for a fast-acting purgative drug known as jalap which might explain the deer's aversion to this plant.

Bells-of-Ireland (*Moluccella laevis*) hail from the Molucca Islands west of New Guinea. The shamrock-green bell-like flowers are really enlarged calyxes, the small leaves that in most plants wrap around an unopened blossom. The tiny white flowers sit within. Three-foot stems are ringed with these green bells, making them among the most beautiful of everlasting flowers for the garden and especially attractive in winter bouquets. Bunch the plants at the back of the border. I suspect that deer find them just too tough of a chew.

Flowering nicotine (*Nicotiana* spp.) is represented by a number of species but my favorite is *N. alata*, the jasmine tobacco, a true perennial from the tropics that's grown as an annual. There are a number of cultivars available that range in height from one to three feet and bear two-inch flowers that bloom throughout the day (older varieties only bloom at night) and have marvelously scented flowers. The plants are poisonous and I guess the deer know about this because I've never been bothered in the garden. For those with a historical bent to their gardens, for a spectacular plant and wondrous display of flowers try growing *N. tabacum*, the true tobacco of commerce, often reaching a height of seven feet in one season and bearing pinkish blossoms one and a half inches long. Unless you are a smoker avoid handling the leaves too much or you will truly get a nicotine buzz.

African daisies (*Osteospermum* spp.) are tender perennials but usually found in the listing of annual flowers. Over the summer they produce many daisy-like flowers in shades of white, apricot, orange, and yellow, blossoms that look great in pots or in rock gardens. I first encountered these beauties in English gardens south of London.

Opium poppies (*Papaver somniferum*), are the source of opium and, except for the seeds, full of toxic alkaloids. The production of the drug is, of course, illegal in the United States. It's also illegal to grow these flowers so the nursery industry now calls them peony-flowered poppies and ducks the issue. Plants can grow to a five-foot height, and bear blossoms up to five inches wide. There are all sorts of cultivars leading to many single and double blossoms of great color combinations. And by planting seeds every few weeks over the summer, flowers will be available until frost cuts them down.

Zonal geraniums (*Pelargonium* x *hortorum*) are the very popular summer bedding plants with the large, usually red blossoms on stout stems, produced by plants with various zones of color on the leaves, and having a very strong scent. They like hot weather, plenty of sun, and should be dead headed as the flowers fade. Also included in this collection, the scented geraniums (some smell of apples, some of pineapple, some of mint, etc.)

Beefsteak plants (*Perilla frutescens*) are annual members of the mint family having square stems. In the world of foliage plants it has been called beefsteak mint, Japanese basil, and wild coleus. Perilla does well in partial sun or some shade and is drought tolerant. Flowers are small and not particularily important but the leaves can be green, purple, or variegated. In warmer areas this annual reseeds with enthusiasm, but being short rooted, young plants are easy to remove if unwanted. Perilla is deer resistant because it's toxic to cattle and contains perilla ketone, which causes pulmonary edema in some animals. All plant parts are toxic.

Petunias (*Petunia* x *hybrida*) are closely related to tobacco and, as such, have moderately sticky stems and a bitter taste. They are one of the most popular bedding annuals for gardens across the country. Flowers come in most colors, including striped, and are great in baskets or in the border. Again, the selection of plants at garden centers precludes starting them from seed.

Petunias are disliked by deer.

Castor bean plants (*Ricinus communis*) are among the most poisonous of plants and are listed as such in the danger plants listed by Homeland Security. These are fast-growing annuals with huge, cut leaves often with up to eleven lobes, and usually in colors of dark purple, deep green, or bronzed green. Small flowers turn into prickly fruits that contain the shiny beans. These tropical-looking beauties come in many cultivars and are still available from the more adventurous seed companies. All parts of the plant are poisonous. Frequently, American nurseries have dropped castor bean plants from their catalogs, due to worries about lawsuits. But they are easily obtained from the more adventurous seed houses, not to mention Canada and England.

Blue salvia (*Salvia farinacea*) is a tender native perennial of Texas and New Mexico, not reliably hardy in most of the U.S. and thus treated as an annual. The violet-blue flowers are an inch long and grow in spikes up to three feet high. The calyx, the cupped part of the flower that holds the petals, is dusted with a white powder, hence the other common name of mealy-cup sage. I suspect the deer dislike the powder. Provide good garden soil and plenty of sun.

Castor bean plants have great leaves and interesting flowers.

Strawberry begonia plants (*Saxifraga stolonifera*) are a good choice for the indoor gardener who wants a compact and rapidly growing houseplant and outdoor gardeners in USDA Zone 7 and above, who are looking for a deer-resistant groundcover of great charm that is not a strawberry or a begonia but instead is a saxifrage. They root with ease so are easy to get established.

Dusty millers (*Senecio cineraria*, syn.: *Cineraria maritima*) comprise a number of sun-loving annuals that like well-drained soils and full sun. Flowers are small and insignificant but the silvery-gray, feathered foliage is often brushed with powdered silver. They are excellent seaside plants. Look for 'Silverdust."

St. Mary's thistle (*Silybum marianum*) is a member of the thistle family, having basal leaves up to fourteen inches long and very lobed and very spiny. The surface is decorated with a fine network of veins and spots of silvery-white. Towards late summer, light-purple thistle-like flowers, about two inches across, appear on tall stems. These plants can exist on poor and dry soil.

Marigolds (*Tagetes* spp.) are strong-smelling annuals, well-known in the nursery trade as one of the most popular of summer bedding plants. In case you remember color photos of the pageantry involved with an Indian funeral or wedding during the hot summers of India, all of those bright yellow and orange flowers are marigolds. Today there are hundreds of cultivars, usually in shades of yellow, orange, tan, and almost white. They are great in beds, borders, for edging, in containers, baskets, and even in the vegetable garden, as the roots produce a chemical that repels nematodes.

Verbena (*Verbena* x *hybrida*) is a perennial hybrid that freely blooms from seed the first year. The flowers are attractive and bloom in a number of colors, looking especially pretty when massed together. Provide a good garden soil and plenty of sun.

Herbs, Vegetables, and Fruits

Deer love flowers in general, and anything that holds up a flower, but do draw the line at a number of vegetable offerings especially plants known to have a smelly and strong taste, usually exemplified by chives, dill, mint, fennel, garlic, and leeks, but never forget that deer love basil and parsley. However, in general, deer resent fuzzy leaves and prickly plants, including squash and cucumbers. I cannot speak to melons, as these have always been easier to buy than to grow, but other gardeners have told me lots of animals like melons so be warned. When it comes to root vegetables, deer usually avoid anything that has to be dug up to be eaten but when hungry they have been reported to actually hoof up carrots and beets. While the tops of many root veggies are considered to be less palatable to deer, they do revel in sweet potatoes, beet foliage, and radish leaves.

When it comes to poisonous plants such as members of the nightshade family, plants that can grow wild like Jimsonweeds (*Datura* spp.) are recognized as being bad for the system and avoided like the plague. Among those harvests listed as being deer resistant are tomatoes, tomatillos, potatoes, eggplants, and most peppers. Eggplants, by the by, make great ornamental plants for the garden. Rhubarb leaves are toxic to humans and also to deer. Because of the alkaloids present in asparagus, deer will avoid mature plants but do like new shoots.

The following plants make up a smaller list that includes some herbs and vegetables, in general, plants either famous for flavor, texture, or both. I didn't list turnips because they are not my favorite root vegetable, but Patryk Battle, a fellow organic gardener (he is interviewed on pages 71–72 for his experience with fences) here in Asheville, advised me that deer do not disturb turnips.

The onion species (*Allium* spp.) in general are passed over by deer and the ornamental plants are listed under bulbs. Chives (*Allium schoenoprasum*) serve two duties in the garden: They bear attractive flowers most of the summer, and the hollow leaves, when cut into small sections, give an incredible zest to cottage cheese. Garlic chives (*A. tuberosum*) bear leaves with more of a garlic flavor and the white flowers are great sprinkled on a salad.

Common dill (*Anethum graveolens*) is an annual herb belonging in the celery family and is the sole species in the genus. The fernlike leaves of Dill are very aromatic, hence their use to flavor many foods ranging from salmon to borscht to soup to pickles and is revered around the world of cooking as such. Dill is best when used fresh because it loses its flavor rapidly if dried. The oil from the seeds is distilled and used in the manufacturing of soap. Deer do not like dill but you as a gardener should have some every year, if only for the kitchen aspects.

Deer resent the smell of dill, here in bloom.

Angelicas (*Angelica archangelica*), also known as wild parsnips, are biennials, blooming the second year. They prefer a cool, moist spot in the garden and produce grapefruit-sized round umbels of attractive yellow-green flowers in early summer. The stems are candied and the plant is also used to flavor liqueurs.

Horseradish (*Armoracia rusticana*, syn. *Cochlearia armoracia*) is a perennial belonging to the cabbage family and is native to south-eastern Europe and western Asia and now popular around the world. Leaves can grow up to five feet tall and it's primarily used for the root which can be an incredibly intense trip with sharp flavor. As a plant there is little odor, but once that root is grated, enzymes go into action producing mustard oil which irritates the mucous membranes of the eyes and the sinuses. Deer avoid the plant but it's not the most attractive perennial on the farm. But look for the spectacular variegated horseradish 'Variegata' for it's a splendid-looking plant.

The variegated horseradish is a stellar plant.

Wormwoods (*Artemisia absinthium*) are extremely bitter perennial herbs, native to Europe but now naturalized in the Northeast. If tasted, all parts of the plant are unforgettable. Wormwood prefers dry soil and full sun, the silvery leaves are very attractive, and small yellow flowers appear in late summer. This is the additive that once made the liquor absinthe illegal because it's a habit-forming drink that leads to delirium, hallucinations, and permanent mental decline. No wonder deer leave it alone. Russian tarragon (*A. dracunculus*) is an erbaceous perennial, with two-foot stems and aromatic leaves often found in kitchen gardens.

The papaw (*Asimina triloba*) is a deciduous shrub that can, in the wild, reach a thirty-foot height and bears a five-inch edible fruit beloved by some and ignored by others. Luckily for landscaping, deer usually ignore the plant.

Borage (*Borago officinalis*) is an beautiful annual herb that looks like it should be a a perennial, having drooping sprays of attractive light-blue flowers. The entire plant is covered by delicate short silky hairs that glow in the afternoon light of the garden. Young leaves have a cucumber-like fragrance and make great additions to summer drinks, ciders, and wines. Try freezing borage flowers in ice cubes for a great garnish. Deer resent the silky hairs.

Ornamental peppers (*Capsicum annuum*) are perennials that are used as annuals growing up to twenty inches high, and in addition to being at home in the garden, make great pot plants. These plants bring forth colorful little peppers from mid-May right up to frost. They are one of the best bedding plants for hot-weather climates, and are great as a groundcover or mixed flower borders or in containers. The flowers are to be ignored but the fruits are brightly beautiful in a wide range of colors ranging from red to purple to yellow and even white. These peppers look edible but most palates (including mine) find them much too hot. Look for a new cultivar 'Pepper on a Stick', a plant that produces little one-inch mini-peppers that when plants are mature you strip away the foliage and leave colorful pepper beads. These peppers are truly hot and deer—at least in my experience—prefer milder salad additions.

Caraway (*Carum carvi*) is an erect biennial with an overwintering tap root. The seeds are used as a great flavoring for breads, meats, and cheeses, and are the basis for the liqueur kümmel, a drink that isn't bad to salute success (or failure) in fighting deer.

Pyrethrum (*Chrysanthemum parthenium*) is a perennial member of the great chrysanthemum family, native to Yugoslavia, and the source of the pyrethrum used to fight a number of insects and mites. Prolonged contact with the plant can cause human skin irritations and other possible allergies. Having long, gray, finely divided leaves and clusters of small white daisy-like flowers, pyrethrum looks great in the border.

Lots of people dislike the pungent flavor of coriander or Chinese parsley (*Coriandrum sativum*), and deer seem to agree. Small, pinkish-white flowers bloom in composite umbels followed by round, yellow-brown seeds, blooming in May and June. The seeds smell of lemon or orange peel with an overlay of sage. It's a staple in Indian cuisine.

Globe artichoke and cardoons (*Cynara scolymus*) are very large border plants with heavily cut, silvery foliage of great beauty; artichokes are grown for their fruit and cardoons for flowers and general habit (although Italian cooks often cut the stems in sections and deep-fry them). These perennials are hardy, with protection, to USDA Zone 6. Now I never had problems but my gardens have always included many deer-resistant plants, but recent Internet chat has suggested that contrary to present beliefs deer will chew away at the leaves, even though they are loaded with fiber. But it's such a beautiful plant, give it the old college try.

Cardoon leaves sharing the garden with violas. Photo credit: Pam Beck.

Persimmons (*Diospyros virginiana*) are large shrubs or small trees grown for their interesting foliage and picturesque habit, not to mention their edible fruits. They need sun, good drainage, and a decent soil, and withstand city conditions. Persimmons are difficult to transplant so buy it as a potted plant or a professionally balled-and-burlap-bound tree.

While not reliably hardy throughout the United States, the edible fig (*Ficus carica*) is easily grown in a pot below USDA Zones 7 and 8. The cultivars 'Brown Turkey' and 'Celeste' are hardy to Zone 7 and are self-pollinating, a necessity with figs in our climates because back in the Old World this action was done by small insects called fig wasps. In Zone 6, gardeners often bend the soft trunks slowly to the ground then cover the plants and mulch well with straw or leaves. The figs usually survive.

Fennel (*Foeniculum vulgare*) is a favorite perennial herb, used for flavorings and often welcome as a hot tea to relieve tension, including nervous problems resulting from deer rampages. The leaves are finely dissected with threadlike segments, like dill leaves but thinner. Stems are hollow. The flowers bloom in terminal compound umbels and are quite beautiful in the garden. The plants are food for swallowtail caterpillars and should be grown for that reason alone. Leaves contribute an anise flavor to foods and salads.

Sweet Woodruff (*Galium odoratum*) is a perennial that lives in woodlands of central Europe. A creeping rhizome sends up erect stems about ten inches high, with whorls of dark-green leaves and clusters of white, small, star-like flowers.

Dog fennel is an attractive roadside weed, here at the Atlanta Botanical Garden.

The leaves contain coumarin, a chemical that smells like new-mown hay or vanilla. Coumarin is actually a blood thinner and is used as the rat poison known as Warfarin. Now, thanks to better living through chemistry, Warfarin has moved up the line to be patented as Coumarin, for use as a blood-thinning chemical for humans. Perhaps the deer know something?

Jerusalem artichokes (*Helianthus tuberosus*) are tall members of the sunflower clan with up to twelve-foot stems, blooming with bright yellow flowers like small sunflowers, and produce edible potato-like tubers especially good for diabetics. They were an important food for the American Indians. Plant them in full sun at the back of the border. Because the leaves have a rough and hairy texture, deer do not approve.

Walnuts (*Juglans nigra*) are stately native trees known for their ability to cause the death of many plants when grown in their vicinity because the roots produce a chemical called juglens. That said, they are great shade trees; initially they grow quickly, and when a certain height are usually left alone. Younger trees should be planted in tree tubes (see chapter 4) to prevent deer browsing.

English lavender (*Lavandula angustifolia*) is a beloved herb, with that special scent that's been formulaic since toiletries were employed in the Middle Ages. The entire plant is covered with short wooly hairs and in early summer, tall spikes topped with lavender to purple flowers appear, as do the bees and the butterflies. Spanish or French lavender (*L. stoechas*) also does well in a hot, dry spot in the garden but is not as hardy as the English variety. Remember the old adage about location that real estate agents use? When it comes to lavender, the word to use three times is location. So with lavender make sure the drainage is spot on and provide as much sun as possible.

Mint (*Mentha* spp.) is represented by a number of perennial plants all having square stems, and is easy to adapt when only poor soil and damp conditions are available. The plants spread far and wide using both surface and underground runners. It can be a pest but deer dislike mint, giving it an edge in the herb garden. Because they grow with such vigor, they have a tendency to exhaust the soil over a few year's time, so here's where crop rotation is a necessity.

Bee balm (*Monarda didyma*) or Oswego tea is a stout, very upright, aromatic perennial that grows to four feet, native to the East Coast (and inland), bearing red, tubular flowers that bloom in dense whorls, and are beloved by hummingbirds and nectar-seeking insects. It was first observed by the English in 1637 and was a hit in European gardens right from the beginning. Bee balm likes a good, moist soil in partial shade. Mature clumps should be divided. One of the oils derived from monardas is used to hide unpleasant-smelling chemicals.

Sweet cicely (*Myrrhis odorata*) is a gracefully growing perennial reaching a height of about three feet. The fernlike leaves have a strong scent of anise. Small, creamy-white flowers bloom in large umbels in late spring to early summer. The ripening seed pods are an inch long and shiny black. Early settlers brought this plant from Europe, using the stalks as flavorings and sweeteners for conserves.

Catnips (*Nepeta cataria*) are branched perennials about three feet high, originally from Eurasia. Catnip plants can attain a size of three by three feet. The stems and the leaves have a soft gray-hairy down, giving catnip the look of being dusted with light hoarfrost. In summer small purple-dotted white flowers bloom in dense whorls and from a distance look like a blue mist. Provide a good garden soil and sunlight. Generally, the words catnip and catmint are interchangeable unless you are describing *Nepeta mussinii*, the one and only catmint. This plant flops over and is only about a foot high and has bluer flowers. The odor of catnip is addictive to most cats and perhaps deer dislike the associations made if they eat these plants.

Sweet basil (*Ocimum basilicum*) is a marvelously flavored herb usually found in every good garden. Five thousand years ago basil was cultivated originally in India. Different cultivars provide for a change in leaf shape, scent, and color, ranging from green to deep purple, with white, blue, burgundy, or pink flowers. In addition to flavor, the leaves are a great addition to the garden. However, while they belong in every garden, if you have many deer, even though basils meet all the qualifications for a deer-hating plant, I'd keep it close to the house and try growing it in pots. It's used for both flavor and for the decorative leaves.

The biennial basil has a very strong scent which might be good reason for deer to dislike nibbling there.

Prickly pears (*Opuntia* spp.) have too many hair-like spines for deer to bother with eating the padded stems. These natives produce a profusion of beautiful yellow flowers in late spring to early summer. They are listed here not as garden perennials but as the source of seedpods and are when delicious when prepared for use in Tex-Mex dishes.

The majorams (*Origanum* spp.) are common names for a number of garden herbs that belong to the mint family and are grown for

Spiny prickly pear cactuses have beautiful blossoms in early summer bloom.

flavoring foods. They want full sun. Common oregano (*O. vulgare*) is especially useful as a groundcover and the cultivar 'Aureum' has leaves of golden-green.

Parsley (*Petroselinum crispum*) is grown in most gardens as a garnish on all sorts of foods but can also be utilized as a great edging plant, plus it looks great in pots. To guarantee a continual supply of leaves for summer meals, plant several sowings.

Rhubarb (*Rheum rhabarbarum*) is usually grown in the vegetable garden for its tall stalks, which are cooked in various ways and often mixed with fruits, like strawberries. It provides a noble aspect and is often used as a perennial. The leaves contain a toxic chemical (anthraquinone glycosides) and deer give it wide berth. Rhubarb does not grow well in very hot climates.

Rosemary (*Rosmarinus officinalis*) is a beautiful herbal treat from around the Mediterranean Sea and being quite piquant in flavor in spite of its beauty—and marvelous little flowers—it is disliked by deer. For gardeners in USDA Zone 6, there is a cultivar called 'Salem' that is fairly resistant to winter chills—as long as it gets perfect drainage.

Well-developed woody stems can be used as skewers for shish kebobs. In the landscape, use rosemary to make both topiaries and hedges or plant it against stone walls or along pathways; plus it's great in containers.

The annual sages (*Salvia officinalis*) are very aromatic herbs native to the Mediterranean region. The plants produce spikes and tubular flowers in passionate shades of red, purple, lavender, and white, best given some shade if you garden in the warmer parts of the Southeast. Cultivars provide various leaf colors, with 'Tricolor' being especially attractive in the garden.

Perennial soapwort (*Saponaria officinalis*) contains a frothing chemical called saponin that dissolves grease. Because of its gentle action on woolens, soapwort continues to be used for cleaning precious linens such as tapestries and canvases. The pink tubular flowers are very attractive, scented by night, and bloom for a long period in early summer. This is an unfussy plant that will survive in the garden for decades if left undisturbed.

Wild soapwort has a sudsy sap.

Potatoes (*Solanum tuberosum*) probably would be loved by deer if they found them suitably prepared for their table, but being members of the vastly poisonous tomato family, plants are shunned by deer.

Spanish broom or weaver's broom (*Spartium junceum*) is a small shrub from the south of Europe and used as an ornamental. There's only one species in the genus, related to the dyer's broom (*Genista* spp.), but has larger flowers. Fragrant, one-inch long flowers are a bright yellow and look like the typical pea flower. The flower is followed by a small, thin peapod. Leaves are few and simple in shape. At home in dry soil, this is an ideal plant for a xeriscape garden and, as such, is fairly common in California. A very strong fiber is obtained from this plant and used in the manufacture of rope. It also has some medicinal uses and was once used as a purgative, emetic, and diuretic. Provide full sun, well-drained and a slightly alkaline soil. They are hardy to USDA Zone 7. This one is worth growing in pots and keeping in a warm place where winters are severe. Prune to the ground if it gets scraggly.

Blueberries (*Vaccinium* spp.) are not only good to eat but they are an attractive shrub, up to eight feet tall with pleasant flowers and great fruit, and does well in acidic soil. The rabbit-eye blueberry (*V. ashei*) reaches a height of four to six feet with a five-foot spread with glossy-green foliage, turning a dull red in the fall, and bearing sky blue berries. These are great plants for a hedge or a border but remember, while deer ignore blueberries, birds love the fruits. My Sullivan County friend, Ben Wechsler, reminded me that for a time he noticed deer nosing around a big patch of blueberries and upon investigation he found that in the shade of the shrubs, some blackberry vines were growing along the ground and the deer were eating the blackberry leaves.

Perennials for the Garden and the Border

Before going ahead with the following list of plants, again be warned that deer have a fondness for daylilies (*Hemerocallis* spp.), hostas (*Hosta* spp.), cardinal flowers (*Lobelia cardinalis*), all sorts of phloxes (*Phlox* spp.), and roses (*Rosa* spp.) of almost any variety—and that includes those with thorns. Deer are able to purse their lips then clamp their teeth on stems allowing them to avoid thorn damage. They will sometimes eat wild geraniums or cranebills (*Geranium maculatum*).

Here's the major list for gardeners. These plants have a history of generally (note the word generally) being left alone by most deer. This does not mean that deer haven't attacked some of these plants in the past or might decide to do so in the future. But for all

Daylilies bloom amidst willow-leaf sunflowers.

practical purposes, deer leave the following plants alone. Whenever possible, I've given the reason for their dislikes.

Yarrows (*Achillea* spp.) are attractive plants grown in the garden proper, the rock garden, and the herb garden. Easy to grow, they prefer a lot of sun and the common yarrow (*A. millefolium*) produces a number of attractive cultivars with tightly bunched flower heads of unusual colors.

Monkshood (*Aconitum* spp.) bears unusual-looking flowers that resemble a monk's cowl. The reining color is dark

Garden phlox have a strong scent and bloom in late summer.

blue, and plants prefer partial shade and are very attractive when planted in groups. There are a number of cultivars and an introduction of new species and most bloom in the fall. Look for *A. carmichaelii* 'Autumn Indigo' and 'Pink Sensation.' The roots and most of the plant parts are poisonous to most mammals and are often used as a murder weapon in detective novels. They also prefer moist soil. You might have to stake the taller varieties.

Bishop's weed (*Aegopodium podagrara*) is one of the most despised weeds of gardening England and known there as ground elder. Here's a plant that the whole of the empire wishes were a deer favorite, but it isn't. While the species is somewhat attractive, its exuberant habits outweigh usefulness. But for an attractive groundcover with reasonably nice flowers, try the variegated form 'Variegatum' with leaves margined in white. When a leaf has areas of white that means there's no chlorophyll present in that area because food is only produced where the color is green.

The century plant (*Agave americana*) does not require a hundred years to produce bloom (more like thirty-five) but it's a great perennial for a desert garden in Zone 7 or in pots where the climate is too cold for a winter outdoors. They need full sun and well-drained soil.

Mescal (*Agave parryi*) is another succulent that even does well in Charlotte, North Carolina, and originally was grown at the JC Raulston Arboretum in Raleigh, having been introduced by one of America's great plantsmen (and his first name was actually JC) from a collecting trip he made to California in 1979. Growing as a rosette about two feet tall and three feet wide, thankfully, it's slow to bloom because when it does, it fades from the scene.

Carpet bugle weeds (*Ajuga reptans*) are attractive and tough groundcovers with pretty spring flowers resembling tiny snapdragons. There are many cultivars producing leaves with variegations or unusual shades of green. These plants have a tendency to invade lawns, a fact that I, who do not spend hours with a lawn, rather enjoy.

Amsonias (*Amsonia tabernaemontana*) are clump-forming native perennials with three-foot stems topped with powder-blue flowers blooming from spring into early summer—and longer, if dead-headed. The sap is milky and, I suspect, quite bitter. In the North, grow them as annuals.

Pearly everlastings (*Anaphalis margaritacea*) were often found in farmhouse bouquets, as the flowers have strawlike petals and last literally forever. American Indians used them for many medicinal treatments including diarrhea, dysentery, and bronchial coughs. They do well in poor, but well-drained soil in full sun.

Anemones or windflowers (*Anemone* spp.) belong to the buttercup family and produce very beautiful petalled flowers. The florist's anemone (*A. coronaria*) can be grown in pots, the beautiful Pasque flower (*A. patens*) for rock gardens in the spring, and the majority, including the Japanese anemone (*A.* x *hybrida*), for great autumn bloom. They need a good garden soil and partial shade.

Columbines (*Aquilegia* spp.) are time-honored native American wildflowers and the genus also includes a few great garden perennials, originally sired in Europe. The smaller types are perfect for the rock garden and the larger in the border. They benefit from deadheading. While seeds of the wild columbine (*A. canadensis*) were used by the American Indians as a cure for headaches; they are potentially poisonous.

Goatsbeard (*Aruncus dioicus*) is a native plant with good-looking leaves and crowned with pyramidal plumes of tiny white

Columbines are bloomers of early spring easily grown from seed.

flowers, making it an excellent plant for the wildflower or the proper garden. The roots were pounded into a poultice to treat bee stings and a root tea used to allay bleeding after childbirth.

Butterfly weed (*Asclepias tuberosa*) is a native plant of great beauty and should be in all American gardens. The plants are drought-resistant and the usually long-lasting, orange flowers, blooming in early summer, are especially attractive to butterflies. They do not transplant well so buy plants in pots or grow them from seed. There are a number of attractive cultivars. The spent flowers eventually form seed pods that burst when ripe and release seeds attached to silvery tufts of hair that fly in the wind. This silk was once used to stuff life jackets in WWII and named in honor of the movie star Mae West.

The native and wild butterfly weed is another plant easily grown from seed.

Known as asparagus fern (*Asparagus densiflorus* 'Myersii') here's a great looking ferny plant that is truly an asparagus but inedible, growing about two feet tall with plumes that gently arch with age. Unless in the Sahara, this plant will do well in full sun or partial shade, and is deer resistant, heat tolerant, drought tolerant, and very easy to care for, looking great in a pot. USDA Zone 9 or 10.

Originally from China, the cast-iron plant (*Aspidistra elatior*) is a humble plant with dark green and leathery leaves growing up to twenty inches in length and spreading in clumps. Some cultivars of aspidistra are variegated with streaks of white or dots like little stars. Their common name refers to their being one of the toughest houseplants ever cultivated, but many gardeners are not aware that it's a great deer-resistant plant in warmer gardens and a natural for the shade garden. Strange star-shaped purple flowers bloom close to the ground and must be looked for to be found. USDA Zone 7 and above.

Originally from Southern Europe and Turkey, basket-of-gold (*Aurinia saxatilis*) is a long favorite for early spring rock gardens because of its long panicles of pale yellow against a background of silvery-gray leaves. There are many cultivars in various shades of yellow, and the plants adapt to growing in walls with ease. Well-drained soil and full sun is preferred.

Astilbes (*Astilbe* spp.) are garden favorites because of attractive and deeply cut foliage and tall, spire-like blanches of tiny flowers. They are easy to grow but need good garden soil and plenty of moisture at the roots. Here's a perfect plant for waterside plantings. There are a number of cultivars with exceptional colors on today's market.

False indigo (*Baptisia* spp.) is an American native, growing as a three- to six-foot bush-like plant, almost a deciduous shrub. Strong stems

In USDA Zone 8 the houseplant Aspidistra does well, here surrounded by Algerian ivy.

bear blue-green oblong leaves and pea-like indigo-blue flowers in late spring. The spent flowers give way to inflated, brown pea pods that rattle with the enclosed seeds and were once used as children's toys. The entire plant turns black when hit by frost and is really a thing of beauty in the garden. Once settled in, this is a very-resistant plant. There is a beautiful species with heavy clusters of white flowers called *B. alba*.

The winter begonias (*Bergenia cordifolia*) bear clump-growing, stout cabbage-like leaves that, with time, can form large colonies. Nodding, bell-like flowers appear in early spring or late winter and south of USDA Zone 7, the leaves are usually evergreen. *B. x schmidtii* is the hybrid usually sold in nurseries. In the South they must have partial shade.

Cross vines (*Bignonia capreolata*) are evergreen climbers that ramble over stonewalls, fences, and random rocks. The common name refers to the visible cross revealed when you cut a cross-section of a stem. In winter leaves turn a deep burgundy and in late spring the vines burst forth with orange trumpet-shaped flowers. While somewhat aggressive, it can be controlled. Provide full sun.

Black-eyed Susans in full bloom.

Black-eyed Susans (*Rudbeckia* spp.) were well-known in wildflower gardens back in the 1800s and favorites of Henry Thoreau. Classified as an annual, biennial, or short-lived perennial, these great wildflowers have leaves that are bristly-hairy, making them a problem for highly allergic gardeners. The flower disks are bright yellow surrounded by drooping ray flowers. American Indians used the roots to treat many illnesses. They do well in poor but well-drained soil. There are reports of deer sometimes eating these plants but they have to be hungry to do so.

Boltonias (*Boltonia asteroides*) are white-flowered wildflower members of the aster family, sometimes reaching a six-foot height and covered with starry blossoms in late summer and early fall. When sited in a good spot, they eventually form a large group of plants.

Heathers (*Calluna vulgaris*) comprise one species of usually low-growing evergreen shrubs, originally from Europe, especially the hills of Scotland. An amazing number of cultivars have been developed, with many colors to the small, but many, flowers. Colors range from white to pink to red, and beyond. Since the Scots have almost as much trouble with deer as Americans, it's lucky that our hoofed friends generally ignore heathers. Heathers prefer very acidic soil and excellent drainage.

The bellflower (*Campanula glomerata*) is described as a rather coarse erect perennial to three feet bearing bell-like flowers of blue or white, arriving on our shores from Eurasia. There are a few cultivars available. Canterbury bells (*C. medium*) arrived from Europe and are biennials to three feet high and while seemingly ignored by deer, have been nibbled by woodchucks when they grew along one of our garden paths. The mountain harebell (*C. rotundifolia*) has flowers of white to a deep lavender blue.

Bluebeards (*Caryopteris* x *clandonensis*) are not reliably hardy below USDA Zone 7, but where the weather is warm enough they grow as low shrubs on stout stems and bear attractive flowers of blue, lavender, or white.

Bittersweet (*Celastrus* spp.) is a vine that is not only a killer of other trees and shrubs but one of the most invasive plants in the lexicon, at least east of the Mississippi. There are two garden species, the American (*C. scandens*), its gene pool now mostly corrupted by the invader, and the oriental bittersweet (*C. orbiculatus*). One of the continuing ironies about plants and animals is the fact that this invader, which can take over just about all in its path, is ignored by deer. If you do grow this plant—its berries dot the fall landscape with the brightest of oranges and reds—make sure you do not let it seed about in your yard.

Knapweeds (*Centaurea* spp.) are a large family of plants (between 400 and 500 species of annuals, biennials, and perennials), and in the perennial class, there is one particular species know as *C. macrocephala*, an erect plant to about three feet bearing golden yellow flowers of great charm, loved by bees, and described in botanical terms as being scabrous or rough to the touch with many small, annoying projections. Give average garden soil and full sun.

Snow-in-summer (*Cerastium tomentosum*) grows as a mat-forming perennial in well-drained soil and full sun. The white-wooly one-inch leaves on trailing stems bear one-inch-wide showy white flowers. The deer dislike the white-wooly part.

Shasta daisies (*Chrysanthemum* x *superbum*) were created by America's most famous botanist and plant breeder, Luther Burbank. They bear large daisy-like blossoms on top of three-foot stems and make great cutting flowers.

Green and gold (*Chrysogonum virginianum*) is a usually evergreen wildflower of great charm with creeping stems, scalloped leaves, and daisy-like flowers bearing five bright yellow petals. Use at least three plants spaced about a foot apart and if

Green and gold is a native plant with marvelous flowers.

you have an old garden wall, plant this beauty along the base, especially if you have acidic soil, as they love a bit of sweetness in their soil world.

The bugbanes (*Cimicifuga* spp.) are American native plants of great beauty, having very attractive foliage, doing well in partial shade, and bearing in early summer tall spires of tiny white, petal-less flowers that resemble white candles lighting the afternoon shade. There are many species available but my favorite is the summer cohosh (*C. americana*), usually topping out at six feet. Provide a good moist soil and, of course, partial shade. For this plant to be deer resistant is a blessing for gardeners interested in great plants and good gardening.

Cimicifuga americana, or bug bane.

For years I grew the wild clematis, old-man's beard, or virgin's bower (*Clematis virginiana*), not for the small white flowers but for the great silver-toned feathery seedpods that appear in late summer to early fall. Clematises like a cool root run with the rest of the vine in good light to full sun. They clamber through branches without any harm to the host plant or tree. The seed pods glistening on the autumn vines are alone worth the price of admission.

Turtleheads (*Chelone glabra*) are aptly named perennials with blossoms that look exactly like a turtle's (or perhaps a lizard's) head. The bunches of flowers bloom on top of a two- to three-foot stem and were used by early settlers to make an ointment to treat piles and painful ulcers, not to mention herpes. Turtleheads prefer partial shade and damp to moist soil, doing well when planted at the edge of a stream or small pond.

Lily-of-the-valley (*Convallaria majalis*) are beloved flowers of spring bearing drooping bell-shaped flowers with cut edges, blooming in mid-spring, and having a wonderful fragrance. Originally from Europe, they have naturalized in the United States since, being brought over by the colonists to remind them of home. The early settlers used a tea concocted from the roots to treat heart disease and as a substitute for digitalis, the well-known heart medicine. Over many years of walking the Appalachian Trail above Hot Springs, North Carolina, I noticed that although deer abound, the lily-of-the-valley never seem to be bothered so I assume, especially from their use as medicines, that the taste must not be pleasant.

The perennial coreopsis (*Coreopsis grandiflora*) reaches a two-foot height and bears yellow to orange daisies and is native to the Midwest and as far south as Florida. It needs full sun.

Turkey corn and wild bleeding heart (*Dicentra eximia*) are native perennial wildflowers grown, usually in the wildflower garden for their interesting flowers which resemble their namesakes. These plants need a good fertile soil in light shade.

Gas plant (*Dictamnus albus*) is one of those perennials that, unless grown, nobody knows what a great perennial it can be. The common names comes from the fact that gas plant seedpods, when squeezed, will produce a whiff of flammable liquid that burns, for only a moment, with a blue flame. They have a distinctive and heavy citrus smell that apparently deer dislike. Never transplant gas plant as they resent any disturbance to the roots. For the garden buy one in a pot.

Wild yam vine (*Dioscorea villosa*) is a marvelous native vine that in nature grows around lakes, streams, along roadsides, and in open forest areas. This is a perennial that can reach a length of ten feet in a season, and only wants a tripod of bamboo stakes to climb upon. There are insignificant dioecious flowers in late summer but the small pods that appear later are very attractive as they twist and turn on the stems. The beauty here is the heart-shaped leaves that turn a bright golden yellow in the fall (dioecious means flowers on any one plant are either male or female and for seed you need both male and female plants).

These vines do not produce edible tubers.

Over the past ten years, purple coneflowers (*Echinacea purpurea*) have achieved almost cult status for gardeners. These daisy-like flowers have a sharp and prickly central cone surrounded by weeping pink petals (really ray flowers) on strong two- to three-foot stems. They are especially valuable in the drug industry and that (plus the prickly flowers) could explain the average deer's reluctance to eat these blossoms. Provide a good soil and full sun.

Globe thistles (*Echinops* spp.) are tall plants with

Wild yam vines on bamboo poles.

Coneflowers need sun and well-drained soil.

interesting and beautiful cut leaves and round blossoms made up of many individual flowers, mostly of a striking metallic blue. They are not fussy as to soil but do like plenty of sunlight. In most of the species, the leaves have spiny-toothed margins.

Viper's bugloss (*Echium fastuosum*) hails from the Canary Islands where it produces purple panicles or dark blue flowers on six-foot stems that are botanically described as being scabrous or rough to the touch. They are greenhouse or pot plants except in warmer parts of the country as they succumb to freezing. That said, they are beautiful in the garden.

Barrenwort (*Epimedium* spp.) are great groundcovers that bear attractive compound leaves on wiry stems and, in spring, flowers that resemble a bishop's mitered cap. There are a number of species and in general, deer choose to ignore them. They do well in average garden soil with partial shade.

Horsetail or scouring rush (*Equisetum hyemale*) is a perennial plant closely related to the ferns and almost a living fossil because it's all that's left of the giant rushes that ruled the world in the

Horsetails grow along a backroad in Ohio.

Carboniferous Era. Back then these green spires grew up to twenty feet tall and formed much of what makes up today's coal deposits. They are adaptable plants, and as such, great runners and so are best when contained. The deeply buried rhizomes produce erect, green, ribbed, hollow-jointed stems resembling children's beads known as pop-its. Plant them either at the edge of a pond or in pots set directly in a pool or on the terrace. The stems are heavy with silica and their sandpapery stems were once used to scour greasy pots and pans. They have a special ability to concentrate gold in solution and are valuable for indicating the presence of this precious metal.

Heaths (*Erica* spp.) are generally thought of as being companions to heathers, except there are more than one species available. They are rock garden and alpine plants that flower, according to type, throughout the year but are best kept for the winter garden. They need acidic soil and perfect drainage to succeed.

Rattlesnake master (*Eryngium yuccifolium*) is a unique wildflower that bears yucca-like leaves and flowers over a long period of time with spreading branches bearing small round orbs, each loaded with tiny spikes, each spike being a small flower. One request is for soil that features excellent drainage. Native Americans brewed tea made from the dried roots and used the drink it as an antidote to rattlesnake venom.

Blooms of rattlesnake master.

Joe-Pye weed (*Eutrochium* spp.) was named for a white man who posed as an Indian medicine man in order to sell a folk remedy for the cure of scarlet

The cultivar known as white Joe-Pye weed is usually shorter than the species.

Joe-Pye is a great magnet for most any butterfly, here visited by swallowtails.

fever, made from the roots of this plant. In moist soil and full sun, plants often top fourteen feet with beautiful plumes of light lavender flowers at the top. They are beloved by butterflies.

Another member of this genus is the snakeroot (*E. rugosum*), a handsome fall-blooming plant with small fuzzy white aster-like flower heads entirely made of disk flowers. It loves a woodsy setting and is a great addition to the fall garden. Unfortunately, when eaten by cattle this plant can poison milk, in some cases leading to fatalities. Such milk caused the death of Abraham Lincoln's mother.

Queen-of-the-prairie (*Filipendula* spp.) is a handsome member of the rose family that blooms with pinkish-red blossoms in terminal clusters that look for all the world like cotton candy. This plant has a high tannin content (tannin was once used to cure leather), and astringent properties, too. It also contains chemical forerunners of aspirin, know as salicin. Provide good garden soil and good drainage.

Creeping wintergreen or teaberry (*Gaultheria procumbens*) is a popular wildflower of a crawling habit, being a low-growing evergreen shrub of small stature, bearing white, nodding bell-shaped flowers that mature as edible, bright red, pulpy berry-like capsules with a spicy flavor. The leaves have a distinct wintergreen flavor. The extract of teaberry is used to flavor many products including chewing gum.

Carolina jessamine (*Gelsemium sempervirens*) is an American native often seen growing up trees and over and under fences when driving the roadsides of the Southeast—hence a clue to its being a great screening material. The vine reaches a length of about twenty feet, with attractive pointed leaves and fragrant yellow tubular flowers blooming singly or in small bunches. Tolerant as to soil, but for healthy growth demanding as much sun as possible, this is a great plant for the home garden. There is a double-flowered cultivar 'Pride of Augusta.' Jessamines are hardy from USDA Zone 6 to 9.

Avens (*Geum* spp.) are great perennials with many species popular in gardens. One particular species, *G. Quellyon*, has produced a number of very colorful cultivars, including the famous 'Mrs. Bradshaw' with red flowers and 'Lady Stratheden' with yellow flowers. The stems and the leaves are hairy. Water avens (*G. rivale*) bears dull reddish nodding flowers and grows in bogs, water gardens, and moist soil. Here the roots are astringent, being used at one time as diuretics and producing a wash for skin diseases and boils.

Balloon cotton-bush, or *Gomphocarpus*, are poisonous. Photo credit: Susie Morrisey.

Balloon plant (Gomphocarpus *physocarpus*) is also known as balloon cotton-bush, swan plant, and in an irreverent manner, bishop's balls. Known as another tropical perennial it's usually treated as an annual blooming the first year from seed. This genus is another member of the great milkweed family. A native of southeast Africa, the plant has been widely naturalized and often used as an ornamental. The common name refers to the swelling bladder-like follicles which are full of seeds.

Baby's breath (*Gypsophila paniculata*) is often used in floral arrangements because of the large, airy profusion of tiny blossoms numbering in the hundreds on one stem. There are a number of cultivars available with colors ranging from pure white to those with a double number of petals.

English ivy (*Hedera helix*) is such a prolific spreader that even if some of your output is eaten by deer, in the end you'll probably applaud their efforts because ivy, once established, can take over everything within its reach. Some references claim that deer eat this plant with abandon while others suggest growing it. In my experience I've found that deer only eat this plant when nothing else is available. And there are a number of very attractive cultivars, so if this was all you could grow you would still have a chance at an interesting, if not beautiful garden. Algerian ivy (*Hedera canariensis* 'Gloire De

Regular English ivy with a variegated form and both disliked by deer.

Marengo') is another great cultivar of the ivy family, this time having great variegations with dark green playing against white. This ivy is resistant to: deer, disease, drought, heat, insects, mildew, foot traffic, and planted at the seaside, tolerates salt. USDA Zone 7.

Iris (*Iris* spp.) have never been touched by deer in any of my northern gardens, but then, I had so many other succulent things around that most deer would just ignore them. That said, old-fashioned flags (*I. X germanica*) and the majority of the bearded irises seem to escape the curse. Also in my many woods-wanderings, I've never seen our native American wildflower, the dwarf crested iris (*I. cristata*) ever nibbled at.

Lenten roses (*Helleborus orientalis*) bloom in late winter and early spring, producing flowers of great charm. Hellebore flowers last up to six weeks in the garden before turning to seed pods because what look like petals are really long-lasting sepals. They have very attractive palmate leaves with a serrated edge and not only provide blossoms, but also evergreen groundcover. The plants are also very poisonous.

Giant Solomon's-seal in autumn color with the small grape-like berries.

Hesperaloe parviflora is often called the red yucca. Leaves can reach a length of three feet and red to pink bell-like flowers appear on nodding four-foot stalks, hardy to USDA Zone 7. A native plant from Texas, the evergreen plants are beautiful as edgings but there are reports that when times are bad, deer will nibble at the flowers.

A bitter substance derived from glandular hairs on hops (*Humulus lupulus*) is used to give aroma and flavor to beer. Various disorders ranging from cramps to coughs to cancer are said to be treated by chemicals from this plant, not to mention jaundice, neuralgia, and worms. The plant and all its parts are bitter. It's also a

Perennial hops grow fantastic vines.

very fast-growing vine and quite useful when used as a living garden screen. The pollen can cause contact dermatitis. There is a very attractive yellow-leafed form called 'Aureus.'

Candytuft (*Iberis sempervirens*) is known as a flowering subshrub and is a favorite of rock gardens. Plants bloom in early spring with terminal clusters of small white flowers. The small leaves are usually evergreen except in cold climates.

Yellow waxbells (*Kirengeshoma palmata*) are Japanese natives of wooded mountains. Plants have attractive maple-like leaves emerging in early spring and later set off pendulous, waxy yellow flowers with glossy green calyxes. They prefer a moist, compost-rich soil. In my garden, these are among the top ten summer show-stoppers. Why Japanese temple bells are usually ignored by deer is anybody's guess.

Spotted dead nettles (*Lamium maculatum*) sport oval leaves often spotted with whitish blotches and bloom with small snapdragon-like flowers of pink, purple, purplish-brown, and sometimes white. They adapt to most any garden conditions and have a tendency to spread about.

Rough blazing star (*Liatris aspera*) and prairie gayfeather (*L. spicata*) are both disliked by deer. The first plant bears tall stalks, with about thirty rose-purple flowers per stalk, blooming in early summer and accustomed to dry but well-drained soil. The second is much the same only a bit shorter. A root tea was used as a folk remedy for bladder and kidney ailments as well as some social diseases.

Blue toadflax (*Linaria canadensis*) bears small, light blue-violet, spurred flowers like mini-snapdragons on plants about two feet high. They grow in open, dry, rocky sites, blooming in summer. Butter-and-eggs (*L. vulgaris*) have yellow, two-lipped, spurred flowers with an orange ridge. They grow in waste places, along the roadside, throughout the East and if they weren't so common, everybody would want them.

Perennial blue flax (*Linum perenne*) grows about two feet high, bearing pretty flowers of chicory-blue. It is related to common flax and the source of flax used in making linens and linseed oil.

Honeysuckles (*Lonicera* spp.) are fond favorites of the garden and our native species make great additions to the backyard. It's the Japanese *Lonicera japonica* that is the infamous Thuggee. With many varieties to choose from, some evergreen, some semi-evergreen, and a few deciduous, plus a large range of flower color, there's a species right for your garden—and deer almost never eat it! When they do, and occasionally they will browse on honeysuckle, you're dealing with a plant that responds with the fervor of a "*Star Wars*" devotee presented with a new chapter.

Loosestrife (*Lythrum salicaria*) is a plague on all our houses. The plant was brought to America for a special garden in Central Park, Manhattan, that was going to display all the flowers of Shakespeare.

That initial threat was loosestrife—and it escaped. Now it's a major environmental impact to both the Northeast and the Southeast; wherever there are bogs and wet meadows, loosestrife simply takes over. Garden cultivars are sterile and cause no problems; only the pure species is a problem. And wouldn't you know it? Deer dislike the plant.

Myrtle (*Myrtus communis*), or periwinkle, is a creeping evergreen groundcover of great beauty that originally came over from Europe with the original settlers. Five-petalled blue flowers appear in spring and then again in fall. Although a beautiful plant, myrtle is an aggressive spreader and can easily take over a large area, choking out other plants.

Evening primroses (*Oenothera* spp.) represent a large family of native American plants, principly the sundrops that bloom by day and the evening primroses that bloom at night. Sundrops stand about three feet high, are rampant spreaders, and bloom with bright yellow, four-petalled cheery flowers that close by night. Evening primroses have the same kind of flowers but open slowly at twilight. Evening primrose oil is a natural source of gamma-linolenic acid and the plants have been used for many medicinal purposes.

Prickly pears (*Opuntia* spp.) bring to mind the cactus family in general. Most gardeners ignore these fascinating and drought-resistant plants because of the spines. Well for the same reasons, most deer avoid them, too, especially those with the tiny hair-like thorns that get into the skin (or a nose) and are so difficult to remove. In spite of their threatening appearance, these cactuses have downright beautiful blossoms, with plenty of satiny petals, and feathery stamens that in many cases (prickly pears included), respond to touch and curl up before your eyes. Prickly pears are native plants as far north as New Jersey and the warmer parts of coastal Massachusetts and Connecticut. Once established, they grow on and on and even in drought years will thrill the gardener with their golden blooms.

Oregano 'Kent Beauty' is a hybrid ornamental oregano (*Oregano rotundifolium* x *O. scabrum*) that is usually grown for its attractive flowers and foliage. This is not an oregano meant for salads and seasoning, but a cascading ornamental plant that features everlasting, papery pink flowers nestled among gray-green leaves borne on fine branches. For a plant of such beauty it's amazingly hardy (USDA Zone 5b to 10).

There are two species of pachysandra used in American gardens, Japanese pachysandra (*Pachysandra terminalis*) and Allegheny spurge i(*Pachysandra procumbens*). Both are deer resistant but the first is a boring plant only to be grown if you are too far north to grow the other. Spurge, on the other hand, has more beautiful leaves, more elegant spring flow-

ers (white tinged with pink and twice as many per plant as its Japanese cvounterpart), and as fall approaches the foliage of Allegheny spurge becomes peppered with flecks of silver. Both are excellent groundcovers but, again, spurge, once it gets settled in does a better job all around. In USDA Zone 7 to 10, both are evergreen.

Believe it or not Russian sage (*Perovskia atriplicifolia*) originally came from Afghanistan and Pakistan. It's a

Oregano 'Kent Beauty' in a pot.

hardy perennial that reaches a height of four to five feet, blooming with tall spikes of lavender/blue flowers. Provide full sun and the plant is quite

happy in dry to average soil. The square stems reflect their belonging to the mint family and the plant's scent might be the reason that deer do not immediately attack this plant.

New Zealand flax (*Phormium* spp.) is a member of the agave family and hails from New Zealand.

Allegheny spurge in early spring bloom.

These plants are tender perennials and not reliably hardy below USDA Zone 7, although they will overwinter in pots when kept dry and about 40°F. The flowers, when they bloom, are interesting, but it's the leaves that make the display. The word Phormium is derived from phormos, a basket, and refers to the use of the leaf fiber for basket making, in addition to the commercial manufacture of rope and twine. There are many cultivars coming in a host of attractive colors plus variations of green, yellow, and white, to red-purples, tones of deep copper, and often striped with yellow, orange-red, or salmon pink. The height ranges from three to fifteen feet depending on the cultivar and the growing conditions. They make a great statement in my North Carolina garden and are especially suited for coastal gardens. I suspect that deer resent the fibers.

Balloon flowers (*Platycodon grandiflorus*) are a one-species genus, originally from Japan where they are often used as vegetables, and from China where the dried roots are staples of many Chinese herbal medicines. The unopened flowers look exactly like little hot air balloons. Plants often reach a height of three to four feet and after a rush of growth sometimes need to be tied up to prevent flopping. There

Balloon flowers are aptly named.

are a number of cultivars of various colors available from catalogs.

Mayapples (*Podophyllum peltatum*) first show up in early spring when their large umbrella-shaped leaves unfurl on top of a single stem poking through the forest floor. Usually in late April or early May, one pendulant bud per plant opens to a large, white, waxy flower, ultimately ripening into a plum-sized yellow-green "apple." All parts of this plant, excepting the fruit, are poisonous but even the fruit, though not fatal, can lead to unpleasant stomach problems.

Jacob's ladder (*Polemonium caeruleum*), or as it's sometimes called, Greek valerian, is a perennial wildflower from Europe and Asia with subspecies native to America, generally the far west. Paired leaves grow from stems to three feet tall, and bear loose clusters of violet-blue bells in late spring and early summer. Here is another plant utilized by the American Indians to treat all sorts of ailments from snakebite to complications with the bowels.

Solomon's-seal (*Polygonatum biflorum*) is a stunning wildflower addition to any garden or garden plot. Give it some shade and some decent soil, and you are in for the long haul. Underground, the plants have many-jointed rhizomes with oval seal-like scars left where the previous year's stem would grow. These scars resemble the wax impressions once used to ensure the authenticity of ancient documents, hence the common name. Solomon's-seal can reach a height of six feet. Beautiful fall foliage complete with little hanging dark blue berries.

Giant Solomon's-seal in autumn color with the small grape-like berries.

Potentillas or cinquefoils (*Potentilla* spp.) are named for the palmate leaves that number five. The flowers are five-petalled and usually yellow when blooming in spring. Most of the species have roots used by American Indians to treat diarrhea and are considered astringent. I suspect that's why deer avoid the plants.

Silver lace vine (*Polygonum aubertii*) is a rampant climber that bears fleecy bunches of small white flowers in the summer and when in full bloom looks like the froth on ocean waves. The stems are very strong and quickly encircle most any support. The leaves are usually so thick a growing vine can substitute for an overhead canopy for protection from the sun. They are not fussy as to soil and adapt to full Southern sun or partial shade.

Primroses (*Primula* spp.) are charming flowers of spring, with the common cowslip (*P. veris*) and the English primrose (*P. vulgaris*) being stars of the garden where there's shade and moist soil. The fragrant, five-petalled flowers come in many colors and arise from a tuft of leaves that resemble lettuce. There is a mealy texture to the stems and unopened buds that apparently deer do not relish.

Lungworts (*Pulmonaria* spp.) bear very pretty flowers of pink, white, or lavender in very early spring and as flowers fade, produce rosettes of slightly hairy but very attractive leaves usually spotted

The lungwort cultivar known as 'Samurai' is very deer-resistant.

with silver blotches. They like moist soil and light to medium shade and in areas with warm summers, often wilt. These are plants often mentioned in the Doctrine of Signatures, where a plant that resembled a human organ (in this case, thanks to the spots, lung tissue) was thought to cure a disease of afflicting that organ. While deer often leave these plants alone, my good garden friend Alison Arnold who is our local Extension Agent, reminded me that when times are hard, deer will even chew upon lungworts.

The hoary mountain mint (*Pycnanthemum incanum*) begins to bloom on hot days in July and goes on into mid-August before retiring from the scene—and it's always missed because the little flowers of this plant are hosts to some of the most beautiful and efficient pollinators, not to mention those great and beautiful predatory wasps. The flowers appear in small disks surrounded by leaves of a silvery-white, and these special leaves encircling the floral disks are adaptations to help the visitors find the little blooms. Grab a place to sit and just watch and be amazed by the visitations. Plants grow between two and three feet high.

Horse-mint, sometimes called mountain mint, has a very strong minty odor that is disliked by deer but is a great perennial for the garden in full sun.

Buttercups (*Ranunculus* spp.) are another one of those plants that if rare, everybody would want a few for the perennial border. The palmately divided leaves grow on two- to three-foot stems and in spring produce many shiny, golden-yellow flowers that gleam on cloudy days or in early twilight. The fresh leaves and the poulticed roots were used by many American Indians and the early settlers to treat diseases like gout or various skin abrasions. But be warned, as the saps can cause intense pain and burning of the mouth. Yellow water buttercups (*R. flabellaris*) are aquatic plants found in ponds having three-inch leaves divided into hair-like segments and bearing pretty, waxy-yellow blossoms about an inch wide.

Bloodroot (*Sanguinaria canadensis*) is a native American wildflower of great beauty, although the white fragile pristine flowers rarely last a week in the spring, especially with spring snows or rains. But after blooming, unlike many spring flowers, each bloodroot leaf can reach a height of a foot and that single leaf continues to grow, and with its scalloped edges, makes a most attractive edging on a pathway or along the margins of an old stone wall. The root sap was used by Native Americans as a dye for baskets, clothing, in addition to an insect repellent.

Bloodroot leaves have great garden interest.

Lizard's Tail (*Saururus cernuus*) is an aptly named plant usually found growing in marshes or along the edge of ponds and streams. The common name refers to the flower stalk which consists of a raceme of little white flowers, generally reaching a length of about

Lizard's Tails like a damp place in the garden.

six inches. The leaves are heart-shaped but the majority of the plant would prefer being under water, the plant usually reaching a height of five feet. Deer dislike it.

Hens and chicks (*Sempervivum* spp.) are mat-forming succulent plants with each individual plant forming clusters of rosettes, the parent rosettes being a hen and the offspring being chickens. Reaching a height of about four inches, the individual plants die when they flower but there are always scads of smaller plants to keep things going. Leaf color ranges from red to green and mixes in between. They are great in pots and do best in rock gardens, remembering that if denied good drainage, they soon vanish from the scene. Deer pretty much leave them alone but have been known to browse on the leaves.

The flowering potato vine (*Solanum jasminoides*) has slender oval leaves that are semi-evergreen and often blooms from mid-summer on into the fall, sporting small, white, star-shaped flowers that also waft sweet fragrances into the garden. The flowers are followed by an inedible purple-black berry. Prune back to a few feet high in the fall. It's USDA Zone 8.

Goldenrods (*Solidago* spp.) are popular garden perennials in Europe having been collected in America back in the 1700s. They are still thought to be the source of fall hay fever, although ragweed has long be known as the true culprit. The cultivars make great garden subjects especially as they bloom in the late summer and early fall. A few were used in folk medicine but some authorities believe that fungus-infected plants could be poisonous to the system. Regardless, their stiff stems are unpopular forage with our Bambies. And to fox the deer, try growing our tallest goldenrod (*S. altissima*), a magnificent plant that can top seven feet with golden spires.

The tall goldenrod *Solidago altissima* in bloom.

Lamb's ears (*Stachys byzantina*) are named in reference to the silver-gray, feel-like-felt leaves of the plants, a texture dependent on white-wooly hairs that give the leaves a decided tactile sense. Pink to lavender flowers are borne in whorls on leaved stalks up to eighteen inches high. They are great garden plants but dislike heavy clay soil and extended wet winters. In The Middle Ages, the leaves were used to bandage wounds.

Common tansies, or golden buttons (*Tanacetum vulgare*), are coarse, aromatic perennials that grow about three feet high and bear bunches of small tubular, golden-yellow flowers. The dried leaves are used medicinally and the leaves have insecticidal properties. The oil from this plant is lethal and a half-ounce can bring death within four hours. It's a charming wild plant.

Foam flower (*Tiarella cordifolia*) is a native American wildflower of great and long-lasting bloom. The common name comes from the delicate white flowers which are more stamens and pistils than petals and truly look like a wand of foam. They are also medicinal because the freshly gathered leaves were used on scalds and burns.

Foam flowers provide early spring bloom. Photo credit: Pam Beck.

Star jasmine or as it's sometimes called, Confederate jasmine (*Trachelospermum jasminoides*), is a twining vine or groundcover that reaches a length of up to twelve feet in a season. Confederate doesn't refer to the South but to the Confederated States of Malasia. Small clusters of very fragrant white star-like flowers bloom in May and June. While only hardy to USDA Zone 8 and 9, I grow these vines in large pots (backed by a trellis), and they are moved into an unheated potting shed with winter temperatures never below 40°F and they do beautifully year after year. There is a dwarf form called 'Nana.' These plants need a fertile, high-moisture soil and partial shade, for in nature they are protected by a high tree canopy.

For gardeners who wish to live dangerously, the American white or false hellebore (*Veratrum viride*) is a perennial native plant with pleated leaves up to six feet high, and small, star-like flowers opening as a yellow-brown but quickly turning green. Early settlers used it as a painkiller but all parts, especially the roots, are highly toxic, and ignored by deer.

In general, mulleins (*Verbascum* spp.) are plants that form basal rosettes consisting of gray-green leaves, usually having the texture of well-worn flannel, and tall stems with attractive yellow flowers of small stature. The wild biennial known as the common flannel plant (*V. thapsus*) is naturalized throughout the Northeast and most of the Southeast. Its flower stalks are covered with the same tiny hairs that adorn the leaves and I suspect the texture is not attractive to your hoofed friends. Although the common flannel has fewer flowers than the more cultivated types, it's a great plant for a desert or low-water garden and is quite attractive when planted in groups.

Hungarian speedwell (*Veronica latifolia*) is a pubescent or hairy perennial, up to eighteen inches high and blooming during the summer months. Spikes of sky-blue flowers bloom over a long period and if deadheaded, will repeat the flowering. They are very attractive plants and apparently deer dislike the hairs.

It's a shame that deer find wisterias (*Wisteria* spp.) an unattractive food as here's one vine that usually could benefit from some pruning. When left to their own devices, wisterias become rampant vines that, upon reaching a tree trunk of any girth, will wind around and around eventually choking the plant to death. I have seen these vines actually twist steel poles. So care must be used and vigilance is required when it comes to pruning. But when in bloom, they are spectacular plants.

Yuccas (*Yucca* spp.) are large-scale American desert plants found in most of the country. They produce stiff sword-shaped leaves up to four feet long, often tipped with a sharp needle-like spine. Some species produce trunks with clusters of leaves at the top. They are beautiful landscape plants, great as living fences to keep dogs (and children) out of the garden area. In late spring to mid-summer, they produce tall spikes of beautiful waxy-petalled flowers that open in the evening. The most common species for gardens are Adam's-needle (*Y. filamentosa*), soapweed (*Y. glauca*), for USDA Zone 7 and above, mound-lily yucca (*Y. gloriosa*), with the leaves growing from a short trunk, and for Zones 8 and 9, Spanish bayonet (*Y. aloifolia*), with a height to fifteen feet, a

Adam's-needle yucca has many forms with colored leaves.

five-foot spread, plus stiff and pointed leaves up to two-and-a-half feet long. It's interesting to note that American Indians once used yucca roots to make a powder which they sprinkled on still waters, thus putting the fish beneath to sleep, and they would rise to the surface.

Bulbs to Brighten Up Spring

The following bulbs are resented, ignored, or nibbled at by deer in order to twit gardeners. Remember, deer love crocuses (*Crocus* spp.), tulips (*Tulipa* spp.), and will sometimes eat wood hyacinths (*Endymion*

Adam's-needle yucca in early evening bloom.

spp.). Also, my own garden experiences show that although deer know that daffodils and narcissus (*Narcissus* spp.) are poisonous to consume, they have been known to nip off the blossoms then toss them aside. Whether or not this is a veiled threat to the gardener, one never knows.

Ornamental onions (*Allium* spp.) belong to the same genus that produces the common onion that serves as a garnish for hamburgers, additions to great stews, or by a few brave souls, eaten raw. Deer avoid all members of the onion family and luckily the following bulbs not

Golden garlic, a flowering onion.

only do beautifully in the average garden (as long as your clay soil is cut by enough humus to offer good drainage), and according to the species, begin blooming in late spring and on into summer. The leaves disappear a few weeks after bloom is over. They bloom in many colors including yellow, blue, pink, white, and purple, and with time increase in size. Provide full sun but they will tolerate some shade, especially down South. *Allium* 'Moly' blooms with an umbel of yellow star-like flowers on foot-high stems. *Allium christophii* or the Star of Persia is probably the most beautiful with enormous silver-purple flowerheads of hundreds of individual blossoms. *Allium* 'Ivory Queen' is a short plant under eight inches with wide leaves surrounding a white ball of small flowers. *Allium giganteum* is a dramatic star of the garden with round six-inch balls of deep purple blossoms on four-foot stems.

Lily-of-the-Nile (*Agapanthus africanus*) is the common name for tender bulbs only hardy to USDA Zone 7—and then they must be mulched. Tropical plants can endure more cold than people imagine

Blooms of lily-of-the-Nile, or *Agapanthus*.

but resent—to the death—damp, chilly temperatures, especially below 40°F. These lovely lilies boast many narrow, strap-like leaves and bear tall scapes topped with round umbels of funneled flowers, from twelve to thirty individuals, in colors of pale lavenders and light blues. Like with many potted plants, provide some fertilizer during the growing season, as continual watering will deplete the earth's fertility. Remove flowers before seeds form.

Jack-in-the-pulpit (*Arisaema triphyllum*) are woodland flowers of great interest thanks to the flowers which consist of a fleshy green to purple *spadex* (or Jack), enclosed by a hooded and striped *spathe* (or pulpit). The dried corms were used medicinally by American Indians and when boiled a number of times, a palatable food. Corms and other plant parts are rich in crystals of calcium oxalate and are known to cause intense irritation and burning in the mouth.

Mariposa lilies (*Calochortus gunnisonii*) demand perfect drainage whether in the garden or in pots. In areas below USDA Zone 8, they must be mulched in the winter and cannot stand alternate freezing and thawing. The three-petalled flowers are banded from white to purple and edged with glandular hairs. These are absolutely beautiful flowers.

Autumn crocuses (*Colchicum autumnale*), often called meadow saffron, are perennial flowers growing from corms native to Europe and North Africa. These are not to be confused with the regular spring crocus (*Crocus* spp.), a plant that deer are very fond of nibbling. In the US, these plants bloom in the fall, with lovely purple to white crocus-like flowers on short stems and without any leaves in attendance. The leaves appear in the spring. Autumn crocuses are highly

Autumn crocus blooming in the fall.

poisonous and used today for the manufacture of colchicine, a treatment for gout, and in the nursery industry where this chemical can shock plants like daylilies into doubling their chromosomes in order to increase blossom size. Obviously, deer know the dangers.

Winter aconites (*Eranthis hyemalis*) generally appear in late winter to early spring and carpet the ground with pretty, inch-wide buttercup-like flowers of a golden yellow. They warm a heart burdened by the cold and the snow. Attractive leaves persist as a groundcover until late spring when they disappear from the scene after building up food reserves for bloom the next year.

Fritillaria (*Fritillaria imperialis*), or frits as they are sometimes called, produce spring flowers consisting of whorls of lance-shaped, light green leaves and umbels of three to six, pendant bell-shaped flowers in orange, yellow, or red. The flowers have a foxy smell that deer don't like but it is not offensive to most people and you must put your nose up against the flowers to get more than just a hint. The other member of this tribe is called the checkered lily (*F. megaleris*), a smaller plant bearing single, nodding, bell-shaped flowers something like upside-down tulips, only

Snowdrops blooming in late February.

the petals are actually marked like part of a chess board. Provide full sun to partial shade, moist soil, and let them alone after planting.

Snowdrops (*Galanthus nivalis*) are very early blooming bulbs of great charm. Bulbs grow in bunches, each bulb sending up a one-flowered stem, the flower with three large petals and three that go almost unnoticed. When coming up thick and toughened leaves protect the bud when pushing through the soil. Flowers remain open for a long time. Eventually with the coming of spring, the leaves disappear until the following year. They are not reliable in areas warmer than USDA Zone 7.

Common hyacinths (*Hyacinthus orientalis*) or Dutch hyacinths are great spring flowers, reliably coming up year after year. Once the favored bulbs of the French, it was the Victorians who popularized growing the bulbs in special glasses using water as a medium. Dutch nurseries produced most of the colorful cultivars of today.

Plant these bulbs four inches deep and about three inches apart. Some people are allergic to hyacinths and get a skin reaction which might explain the deer not liking their noses involved.

Summer snowflakes (*Leucojum* spp.) are bulbous perennials with strap-like leaves and nodding dainty white flowers that, regardless of their name, usually bloom in late winter or early spring. The flowers consist of two to five nodding, bell-shaped, mildly fragrant flowers with six petals (really three sepals and three petals), each with a green spot at its tip. 'Gravetye Giant' is larger then most of the species and the one usually offered by bulb dealers. Plants should be set out in bunches for greater effect. They like a good, well-drained soil but will tolerate clay soil, too.

Tiger lilies (*Lilium lancifolium*) are tough and beautiful plants that grow for years in abandoned gardens. Originally from Asia, it arrived on our shores in the late 1700s. It's worth a try as it was never eaten in our New York garden but, again, that is no guarantee. Provide full sun and average garden soil.

Grape hyacinths (*Muscari* spp.) are among the most popular bulbs of early spring. A genus of over thirty species, some come from the Mediterranean region and others from Asia Minor. Depending on the species, they bloom from early to late spring. Muscari are small bulbs. Plant them four inches deep and use a lot of them to make a big display. Full sun and reasonably drained soil are needed. The flowers set seed and will naturalize without being invasive.

As noted above, daffodils (*Narcissus* spp.) are poison. And they like heavy soils, naturalize with ease, and are available in many different sizes and flower forms. By choosing the proper cultivars, you can have blossoms from early spring right up to the end of May. Some of the best larger cultivars are 'Fragrant Rose' with white petals and a rose-pink cup; 'Ice Follies' having white petals and a yellow cup; and 'Barrett Browning' with white petals and an orange-red cup. Three smaller cultivars are 'Thalia' with two to three white flowers on one stem; 'Chit Chat,' a later-blooming flower on a six-inch stem; and 'February Gold,' one of the best for late winter bloom.

Siberian squills (*Scilla siberica*) bloom in early spring with vibrantly blue flowers of great charm. They deserve greater popularity, especially because they are not liked by deer plus the fact they

Daffodils are poisonous plants.

naturalize over your lawn with ease, yet by the time you're ready to mow, the leaves have already disappeared until the next year. Squills bear up to ten star-shaped, blue-purple flowers, providing vibrant blues to your early spring grass. Pink and white cultivars are available.

The death camas (*Zigadenus nuttallii*) is a member of the lily family. Grass-like leaves grow from an onion-like bulb, followed by a leafless stem topped with a branching cluster of many greenish-white, star-like flowers, about a half-inch wide. It blooms in spring and is an attractive and interesting plant for the wildflower garden. A toxic substance is present in the entire plant, an alkaloid that in people causes breathing difficulties followed by a coma and also poisons grazing livestock, including deer.

Ferns for that Shady Glen

Ferns are great additions to the garden both as groundcovers or specimen plants. They prefer a good moist garden soil, usually partial shade (especially in the South), and plenty of water during hot and dry spells. If your space is limited, you might think about growing ferns in pots spread about the backyard. This gives the gardener more control over the fern's environment.

I suspect that many more than the following are not deer favorites, but those ferns listed below have documentation, both by extension services and talks to fellow gardeners. One reason for a deer's aversion to many ferns could be their various medicinal quali-ties leading to a bad taste and the generally dry texture of the fronds.

Maidenhair fern (*Andiatum pedatum*) is one of the most beautiful of the ferns with its fan-shaped, light greenleaflets set atop shiny, ebony-black stalks and the overall grace of the plant. Fronds grow between twelve and twenty-four inches tall and spread slowly in partial shade. Every so often a dwarf form listed as 'Nana' is offered by fern collectors and fern specialists.

Ebony spleenworts (*Asplenium platyneuron*) are usually evergreen ferns mostly with deeply cut or compound leaves and a

Maidenhair ferns are surprisingly tough when it comes to climate.

great choice for a spot in a shady rock garden. The blades are rarely over an inch long and their almost black stems are really visible when plants grow against a background of rocks and roots. If gardening in very acidic soil you will note that whenever rocks or even breaks in cement walkways or stairs are evident, you will find small ferns rooting there. They are one of the few plants that honestly can respond to being called charming.

Hay-scented fern or boulder fern (*Dennstaedtia punctilobula*) is a delicate creeping plant with graceful fronds of a pleasant yellow green. The broken fronds emit the fragrance of new-mown hay. They prefer a dry, shaded site and are often found in hillside pastures. They rapidly spread by crawling rootstocks and, once established, can invade many parts of the garden but are easily pulled up by hand. The fronds turn white when touched by frost. Plants are about sixteen inches tall. A great use of this fern is its ability to spread quickly with a carpet of deer-resistant foliage making an extremely valuable groundcover.

Lady fern (*Athyrium filix femina*) grows about two feet tall and appreciates a spot in moist soil under partial shade. The name is derived from the delicate structure of the leaflets. You will find its elegant form at home at the edge of meadows, in the woods, along stone walls, and under canopied trees.

Japanese painted fern (*Athyrium nipponicum* var. *pictum*) is another beauty. Its fronds are about twenty-four inches long and bend gracefully towards the ground. The general color is a rich gray-green lightly tinted with a brush dipped in maroon. The color is best achieved in partial shade. This fern needs water in hot summers to prevent leaflets turning brown. While it appears too delicate to be hardy in the cold, like many plants originally from Japan it is durable.

Autumn fern (*Dryopteris erythrosora*) is one of the best ferns for highlighting in the landscape, but when originally named, the botanist must have gotten his seasons mixed because this fern opens its fronds in colors ranging from a metallic red to an off pink, then as the summer advances, the colors fade to a bronze-green. In fall,

Because of their coloring, Japanese painted ferns often look artificial.

the fronds deepen in color to a mellow brownish-red. In frost-free gardens this is an evergreen fern.

Ostrich ferns (*Matteuccia struthiopteris*) are one of the largest ferns in North America, reaching heights in excess of five feet. The gracefully arching leaves resemble ostrich plumes of a rich dark green and bring an architectural quality to any garden. Although tropical in looks they are exceptionally hardy, surviving winters to USDA Zone 3. Found growing along streams and riverbeds, they prefer plenty of water and a lot of sun. They wither with the first frost. Deer do not like this fern at all. This fern is also not a good choice for hot sun in the Deep South.

Sword ferns (*Nephrolepis* spp.) are mostly tropical ferns from America, Africa, Malaysia, and the West Indies. The most popular variety of this fern is the well-known Boston fern (*N. exaltata bostoniensis*), with its long, drooping fronds and easy adaptation to a home environment. The most popular is *N. exalta*, found in Florida

Ostrich ferns can grow in large beds.

Sensitive ferns quickly burn with the lightest frosts.

and California gardens. These ferns need a minimum temperature of above 50°F. Deer do not like these ferns and if nothing else, grow some in pots for a dashing look to a backyard oasis.

Sensitive or bead fern (*Onoclea sensibilis*) reach a height of about two feet, with leaves unlike most other ferns because the component leaf blades are large and lack frilly indentations. There are prominent network-forming veins in the leaves. The common name of sensitive refers to their shriveling at the first frost. The second name of bead fern refers to the erect, beadlike, fertile spikes that over-winter and were often used in dried flower arrangements. They do well in damp or wet places, in full sun or shade, and are quite attractive groundcovers.

Cinnamon fern (*Osmunda cinnamomea*) is large, coarse, common, and described as being vigorous, with the arching fronds growing from a heavy rootstock covered with thickly matted horse hair–like roots. In late spring golden cinnamon club-like fertile leaves arise from the clumps, easily distinguishing it from any other type of

Interrupted ferns are named for the fertile leaflets that occur in the center of the leaf blades.

fern. It's the most common fern in the United States and found in almost every swamp where large colonies become fern jungles. Height is over three feet. The matted rootstocks of the osmunda genus are often used as a growing medium for orchids.

Royal fern (*Osmunda regalis*) reaches a height of over six feet, with translucent pale green foliage, but it's quite delicate in its overall appearance. Royal fern is an inhabitant of wetlands, the edges of streams, and will grow happily in a few feet of water, along the edge of a lake, and wet places in general. Because it grows from a crown rather than runners, this fern spreads slowly. Provide a cool, acidic soil. The leafelets turn golden-brown in the fall. Osmundas tolerate some sun if they have adequate moisture but do their best in light shade.

Interrupted fern (*Osmunda claytoniana*) is a reasonably large fern standing about four feet high. The arching blades have distinct interruptions in the center of the stem where sterile leaflets were. This makes them very easy to identify. One of the earliest ferns to appear in spring, they grow in most soils and prefer dry to wet spots.

Christmas fern (*Polystichum acrostichoides*) is a very attractive evergreen fern with spiny-toothed, holly-like leaflets, making it a popular holiday decoration. The fronds begin their first year growing erect but as the seasons pass, they fall back to the ground, persisting in place for another year or two while new fronds emerge. While preferring a rich limy soil, it will survive just about anywhere, sometimes in

The New York fern has white blades in early fall.

swamps and sometimes in rocky open spaces. This fern grows about three feet high. Christmas ferns make an effective erosion control. This is a great plant for massing on slopes.

Bracken fern (*Pteridium aquilinum*) is probably the most common fern in the U.S. From three to six feet tall, the fronds are divided into three parts, each bearing triangular leaves, growing on stout stems, making a very attractive groundcover. Although American Indians and early settlers used various bracken mixtures to treat stomach cramps, diarrhea, and smoked fronds for headaches, the plant is poisonous in large doses. White-tailed deer will only eat small amounts in the summer or the fall, and generally spurn this fern. Goats are the only livestock that normally eat bracken. The fronds are thought to release hydrogen cyanide when they are bruised and the basic taste is one of unadorned bitterness.

New York fern (*Thelypteris noveboracensis*) bears delicate yellow-green fronds with three (or sometimes more) leaves per tuft and grows in spreading colonies without ever being a threat to neighbors. The leaves are about eighteen to twenty inches high and are found naturally at the edges of woodlands in reasonably dry soil. Like the hay-scented ferns, the leaf blades bleach out with frost.

Ornamental Grasses and a Few Bamboos

For the money, not to mention the time, ornamental grasses fill a great deal of space without waiting for years to see the ultimate garden. If you

Variegated giant reed grass with elephant ears and a butterfly bush.

want the feeling of walking through a jungle, plant a thicket of eulalia grass or Revenna grass. By summer's end you will be amazed at their height.

Because most of the grasses depend on the wind for pollination, they have no need for large and brilliant floral displays, those garish petals necessary to attract bees, butterflies, moths, ants, beetles, and birds to ensure pollination. In the world of grasses their pollen drifts with the breeze to reach their intended target. Most of the grasses still produce flower clusters, but for these beauties the clusters are made up of subdivisions called spikelets and they are often quite beautiful. Because they dry well, save some for winter bouquets.

Soil for the grasses need not be better than average. If starting anew, remove the existing turf, then try to turn the earth to a depth of one foot. Add a mix of clean garden soil and some composted manure to make up for the lost dirt and give the roots a good start in life.

Another grassy plant that is linked to the ornamental grasses is the genus Carex, and I am adding three more plants to the bottom of the grass list because they are so attractive and easy to care for.

Giant reed grass in a Raleigh, NC, garden.

The only chore in dealing with grasses is the annual pruning for the larger types in early spring. Then you will cut the dead stems and leaves to within six inches of the ground, before the new growth appears.

Giant reed grass (*Arundo donax*) can reach a height of twelve to fourteen feet, putting it out of reach of most deer. It is also very invasive, eventually producing vast groves of bamboo-like stems (or culms). The variety 'Variegata' has attractive blades with white strips and is not as invasive as the parent species. The dried culms are used to make clarinet reeds. These grasses can grow up to twelve feet high.

Korean feather grass (*Calamagrostis brachytricha*) is a beauty that flowers in September with plumes tinted a rich purple-red tone, lasting well into winter. It also tolerates some shade. Clumps grow about four feet high and three feet wide.

Sea oats, a grass that likes a shady spot in the garden.

River oats (*Chasmanthium latifolium* [*Uniola latifolia*]) or as it's sometimes called upland sea oats or wild oats, is one of our most beautiful native grasses, long admired in the trade and at home in most any garden. It's a tall and graceful perennial with flat leaf blades and open, hanging panicles of compressed and flat spikelets that resemble oats, hence the common name. In moist soil they grow about five feet tall but lose a bit of height

Ravenna grass tops twelve feet in one summer and likes sun.

in dried conditions. They might seed about but are initially shallow rooted, so easy to pull up.

Pampas grass (*Cortaderia selloana*) is one of those ornamental grasses that became a cliché before its time. When driving in most of South Carolina and northern Florida, this is the grass that is planted on either side of a driveway, driveways that lead to homes, farms, or even motels. And, guess what? They are rarely damaged by deer so that every fall their plume-like blossoms stand tall on eight-foot stems, resembling the fans that Cleopatra's slaves used to cool her royal forehead. Provide a well-drained soil and full sun.

In one summer season Ravenna grass (*Erianthus ravennae*) will grow into a clump of plumes about twelve feet high and five feet wide. This grass is not only spectacular, but deer need ladders to get started on munching if they ever thought about it but like all the other grasses, the stems are dry and from a taste point of view leave much to be desired. Remember not to stint on space.

Japanese forest grass (*Hakonechloa macra*) is a classic woodland groundcover and it nits variegated form one beautiful deer-resistant grass for the garden. The most commonly used cultivar is 'Aureola' with the blades entirely striped with wide or narrowing variegations of yellow and green. 'All Gold' has golden-yellow blades.

Hakonechloa, a Japanese grass that deer dislike.

Muhly grass in bloom at the University of Tennessee.

Miscanthus grasses (*Miscanthus* spp.) represent a number of orna-mental grasses great for the garden, not only because of their attractive leaves that grow in a clump and resemble a fountain in aspect, but also for the plume-like flowers of autumn. 'Gracillimus' has a graceful form while 'Zebrinus' has leaves stripped with creamy-white. There are many cultivars, and all seem to be too tough for deer to enjoy the nibbling.

Pink muhly grass (*Muhlenbergia capillaris*) is originally a native plant from Georgia and one of the most beautiful and spectacular of the grasses. It's as fall bloomer that bears purple panicles, in a color best pirctured by imagining a purple haze on the horizon, with the Sons of the Pioneers humming a cowboy ballad in the background. The mist of blooms hovers about three feet above the ground. It's hardy to Zone 7 and up. Provide full sun.

Switch grass (*Panicum virgatum*) is a great native grass originally from the American prairies. It's great for mass plantings or when used as a low screen to block an unwanted view. The open panicles are especially attractive when viewed against a dark background. Plants can reach a height of seven feet and begin to flower in July. Switch grass will withstand poor drainage and flooding so it makes a great erosion control for banks prone to seasonal flooding.

Two beautiful grasses (*Pennisetum alopecuroides* and *P. orientale*) sport plumose bristles in spike-like panicles, and their flowers rank them in the top ranks of the grasses. If not hardy in your area, then plant and grow them as annuals. The first is called fountain grass and bears a fountain of weeping blades that soon support very showy flowers that last well into late summer each resembling graceful foxtails.

The second grass is called oriental fountain grass and it's another clumping grass with great flowers. For a pink effect to the plumes try 'Karley Rose.' There are a number of fountain grass cultivars, and new varieties continue to be developed.

Ribbon grass or whistle grass (*Phalaris arundinacea*) is often found growing around abandoned farmhouses, as it was once a staple perennial for the floral border. The attractive leaves are stripped with green and white. When a blade was held between joined thumbs and a kid blew, the result was a shrieking whistle-like noise. These grasses can be rampant when not held in check.

Little bluestem (*Schizachyrium scoparium*) grows about four by four feet in a clump and is the state grass of Nebraska. The flowering stems turn a golden reddish brown in the fall sparked with tiny white tufted blossoms along their edge. This species was a very popular grass used for erosion control back in the 1930s.

Indian grass (*Sorghastrum nutans*) is one of the big prairie grasses, named for the Native Americans of the area. It's a beautiful grass with roots so penetrating that plants easily survived flash first that often swept the prairies years ago (and thanks to Global Warming are starting up again). Usually plants are about three feet tall but they can reach five feet if the soil is moist and fertile. In late summer the showy yellowish-tan panicles appear, the spikelets bearing bright yellow anthers that turn golden-brown after the first autumn frost when the foliage starts to turn a bright orange.

Once called Morrow's sedge, *Carex morrowii* 'Variegata' was rare in cultivation but then about twenty years ago the plant hit the big time and the advance is well deserved. This has the broadest leaf of the clump-growing sedges and bears tough, glossy, variegated leaves up to eighteen inches that when planted at the edge of a wall or used in pots, the leaves drape over the edge in a typical fountain form.

The great weeping sedge, or as I prefer to call it (using its English name), the great pendulous wood sedge (*Carex pendula*) is one of the tallest of these grass-like plants. A well-grown specimen becomes a fountain of light green leaves, usually each over four feet in length. The spikelets consist of three- to five-inch catkin-like flowers, formed on very thin stems that are often up to six feet long, persisting well into the winter. If allowed to grow undisturbed—and the deer seem to walk on by—these plants can make a sizeable statement. Originally imported into England back in 1600, this sedge is easily grown from seed available from mail-order sources. Provide good moist soil, and along a small body of water this is a beauty.

Carex siderosticha began its plant existence growing in the mountain woods of Japan and on to Korea. The time-honored plant is not too exciting but the cultivar 'Variegata' has curved green leaves with a white edge on either side of the leaf. There is just a touch of pink at the base of each leaf. Peter Gentling gave me this plant a few years ago and it's done beautifully growing in a shallow space between an ascending stone wall and a descending stone wall. There, in a small basin full of sea oats and a mass of Lenten roses (*Helleborus orientalis*), broad blades of icy white and green (with just a touch of pink at the base) sport their colors to all passers-by.

Two Great Bamboos

Here are two great bamboos for the small garden. Bamboos are in a class by themselves but belong with the grass family. They are tropical-looking plants that are tough survivors once they are established in the garden. In addition they are truly unusual because when one species of bamboo comes into flower, all the members of the species—regardless of where they are—come into flower at the same time. Then in the process of flowering and setting seed, the original plant dies.

This is one of the continual problems that the Chinese government has with its panda protection programs. Remember, bamboos are the only food for pandas and if a species dies when flowering, there goes a major part of the panda food supply. The government must step in and take over the chores of feeding these animals until the new crop burgeons and can take on the responsibility.

Remember that bamboos spread, not all the time but generally three times a year their rhizomes will begin to wander and over time you suddenly find bamboos in the midst of your rose bed. So make sure where you plant them so that spreading will not be problem to you—or to your next-door neighbor.

Kamuro-zasa bamboo (*Pleioblastus viridistriata* or *Arundinaria viridistriata*) is a true beauty hardy to USDA Zone 7 (perhaps these days even 6). The leaves are hard to describe—their color often depends on the time of day and the heat of the summer, although colors seem to fade when summer temperatures reach into the high 80s). The leaves have a velvety look when new, and sport varying stripes of chartreuse and golden tones the meld together from a distance. In the South they really require some shade and, while not fussy as to soil, do need adequate water. The usual thirty-inch culms should be cut down to ground level in early spring when new growth appears.

Sasa veitchii probably ranks as my number one bamboo for both home and garden. Because of its late autumn leaf color it's sometimes called a variegated bamboo but it really isn't. True, the green leaves develop a light tan to off-white edge when cold weather appears, but that's just dead tissue, not a true color variation. The stems are between three and four feet high and during the summer it's just another green-leafed bamboo but it shines in the winter

Kuma-zasa bamboo is a lack-luster green during three seasons of the year but a spectacular addition to the winter garden.

garden, whether planted directly out-doors in a stone garden or in a pot on a terrace. A slow spreader, it's hardy to USDA Zone 6.

Shrubs and Trees

Once they have reached a certain height, shrubs and trees are fairly deer proof. It's getting them to that height that's rife with problems. So until a tree or shrub or bush (a bush is a low and thick shrub without a distinct trunk) exceeds the browsing height of a deer (from three to five feet high), it's a good idea to protect

Closeup of variegated bamboo leaves in winter.

it with a cage of chicken wire, snow-fencing, or when there is more trunk than growth, a plastic tube with ventilation holes.

We are writing here about shrubs and trees that have histories of being ignored by deer, but there are others that deer make a bee-line for. They include American arborvitae (*Thuja* spp.); balsam fir and Fraser fir (*Abies* spp.); Norway maple (*Acer* spp.); eastern redbuds (*Cercis* spp.); winged euonymus (*Euonymus alaus*), itself a weedy and invasive plant; golden rain tree (*Koelreuteria* spp.); apples; cherries; plums; many rhododendrons (*Rhododendron* spp.); shrub roses; European mountain ash (*Sorbus* spp.); and the yews (*Taxus* spp.), and when it comes to the yews, the only part of the plant that is not poisonous is the red berry or properly termed an aril, that represents the future cone, but, apparently, the deer have never been informed.

Catclaw (*Acacia greggii*), is a member of the mimosa family and also known as the Texas mimosa. It's a shrub that can reach the tree stature and a height of about twenty feet, blooming with yellow flowers in spikes over two inches long. It is a well-armed plant that can be daunting to deer and they only eat new growth so once you have a substantial plant started, you should be worry free. Plants need plenty of sun and water and are only hardy to USDA Zone 9 and above.

When it comes to Japanese maples (*Acer palmatum*), you confront one of my favorite trees. In my experience, deer always picked something closer to the beginning of my garden, because most of the Japanese maples I've grown have been cultured in pots and were on the terrace. Hence I needed a more direct knowledge of their eating habits with this particular plant. So I called Patricia Smyth of Mountain Maples located in Laytonville, California, and asked her about deer and a fondness for maples. "It's been our experience," she said, "that deer might take a leaf for a taste-test, but then immediately move on to better pickings. When they are starving, it's a different story but when given a choice they ignore Japanese maples."

Japanese maples are incredibly beautiful trees ranging in height from a few feet to upwards of forty. There are over 200 cultivars of *A. palmatum*, plus other Asian maple species in the same league. To begin collecting these trees is the beginning of truly a life-long pursuit. Japanese maples can easily be grown in pots and when pot diameter is over a foot, they can winter over outdoors in USDA Zone 7. There are Japanese maples that top out at a foot and all the way up to thirty feet or more. One of the most beautiful is the laceleaf Japanese maple (*A. palmatum dissectum*), with such finely cut leaves only a deer with 20/20 vision will ever spot them.

Unlike many shrubs, bottlebrush buckeye (*Aesculus parviflora*) is noted for blooming in the summer. This is a multi-stemmed, dense, suckering (meaning that it spreads when allowed), deciduous shrub usually growing between six and twelve feet height. Palmate green leaves (five to seven leaflets) surround showy, cylindrical panicles (to a foot long) that closely resemble the bottlebrushes used to clean test tubes in a lab. The foliage turns yellow in autumn. USDA Zone 6.

Bottlebrush buckeye in summer bloom.

The tree of heaven (*Ailanthus altissima*) is a prized tree in China, brought to American as a landscaping tree because it would grow just about anywhere a seed landed (Betty Smith's book, *"A Tree Grows in Brooklyn,"* saluted that tree. It has become an outstanding weed tree and has invaded many parts of the country, choking out native species. Well, irony of ironies, deer will not touch it. And when all is said and done, it's an attractive tree in the landscape. Trees can reach a height of sixty feet and are very attractive when covered in flowers but if choosing this tree, buy a female, as the male flowers emit a sweetish but fetid odor.

Allegheny serviceberries or June berries (*Amelanchier* spp.) are shrubs or small trees that live along the edges of woodlands in the Northeast, although *A. arborea* will do well down to northern Florida. I personally can vouch for this lovely tree because every spring up in the Catskills, just about when you were ready to give up any hope that spring would arrive, up at the crest of the hill behind our farmhouse, at the beginning of an old stone wall, there would be burst of white flowers like a galaxy of stars. We knew, then, that even if the blossoms were blown by snow-laden winds, the wildflowers of May were not too far away. And in all those years of living there, with the countless deer that walked the edge of that wall, the serviceberries were never touched. Now then if the blooms turned to berries, that was a different story: unless we were there when ripening occurred, thanks to the birds, there were no berries to find.

False indigo (*Amorpha fruticosa*) is a shrub that can reach twenty feet and resemble a small tree. The branches are woody and twigs are hairy and green. Palmate leaves have thirteen to twenty-five one-to two-inch leaflets that are dotted with resinous glands. The dark purple flowers are terminal, blooming in clustered spikes. Fruit is about a quarter-inch long and also bears resinous dots. Reliably hardy to the warmer parts of USDA Zone 5, false indigos are native plants that have become somewhat invasive in wetlands so care should be used in planting. While deer have been known to break branches, they apparently resent the resinous flavors. In spring, just remove the damaged wood. Provide full sun.

Depending on the age, Japanese angelica (*Aralia elata*) is a shrub or a tree reaching a height of forty-five feet with attractive feathery leaves and usually covered by spines. During spring, panicles of white flowers are followed by black fruits. In the Orient this plant, when properly cooked, is an edible mountain vegetable but it contains saponins and alkaloids. Angelica has a long history of use in Korean traditional medicine with the bark and roots used in treating cancer, diabetes, and gastritis. There is a cultivar bearing leaves with white margins called 'Variegata.' It's easy to grow and adapts to any well-drained soil in sun to light shade. This tree is also tolerant of city pollution and neglect.

Monkey-puzzle trees (*Araucaria araucana*) are only hardy south of USDA Zone 7, but everybody who ever read an Agatha Christie mystery story should recognize the name. No matter what library, manor home, or vicarage where a murder occurred, there was a monkey-puzzle tree in the garden. These evergreen coniferous trees originate in Chile where they are the most important coniferous timber crop. Monkey-puzzles are rather bizarre-looking trees, up to seventy feet high, growing in a loose, pyramidal shape, with stiff, scale-like leaves of dark green. The common name refers to an Englishman in the 1800s who, when he saw his first tree, remarked that it's a puzzle as to how a monkey could climb such a tree. They do well in pots.

For information about the hairy *manzanita* (*Arctostaphylos columbiana*), I spoke to Wallace W. Hansen of Native Plants of the Northwest in Salem, Oregon. According to Mr. Hansel, the hairy *manzanita* is one of the best native ornamental plants for the landscape in the Northwest. And the deer, unless times are egregious, ignore the plant. It's one of the first plants to colonize an open canopied forest. It's a small, slow-growing evergreen shrub, from three to ten feet in height, with reddish-brown bark, simple leaves of an attractive blue-green color and hairy on both sides, thus not that attractive to deer. Plants flower in spring with clusters of small pale pink to white urn-shaped blossoms, followed by small red fruits described as a tiny flattened apple. Manzanita means "little apple" in Spanish.

Ponytail palms (*Beaucarnea recurvata*) always had a place in all my gardens but only growing in pots. In nature they are only hardy in and south of USDA Zone 9. With age these plants can reach a height of fifteen feet and are easily spotted because of their greatly swollen

A barberry named for Darwin.

trunk base and the narrow and weeping light green leaves of narrow width. If your garden is warm enough, use these as specimen garden plants or grow them in a cunning pot. They like a well-drained sandy soil and full sun.

Except for garden interest, barberries (*Berberis* spp.) are not a great group of plants to get a good grip on. They have thorns up and down the bark, and would seem to be unpleasant plants to eat. Darwin's barberry (*Berberis darwinii*) is an evergreen barberry from Chile with shining green leaves and lovely orange-yellow flowers that usually bloom in March. Once established, it's drought-tolerant, easy to grow, and while not as prickly as the other barberry species, don't grab a handful unless wearing gloves. USDA Zone 7. Wintergreen barberries (*B. julianae*) are great-looking shrubs, about four feet high and three feet wide, and impenetrable because of thorns. The foliage is a glossy deep green and yellow flowers bloom in early April, followed by blue-black fruits. Mentor barberries (*B. x mentorensis*) are rounded and upright shrubs

Wild barberry has many thorns.

reaching a height of about six feet with a six-foot spread. The dark green leaves turn yellow to red in the fall. Yellow waxy-petalled flowers appear in early spring followed by a dull red fruit. When planted in a row they form an impenetrable barrier or hedge. Japanese barberry (*B. thunbergii*) is a beautiful plant, growing about five feet high with a five-foot spread. Leaves are medium green turning scarlet in the fall. Creamy-white flowers are followed by orange-red fruits. Does well in poor soil and once again, forms an impenetrable hedge.

Deer dislike at least three of the birch family (*Betula* spp.). The first is the paper birch (*B. papyrifera*), that tree of legend with bark was used by American Indians to make canoes; the second, the European white birch gray (*Betula pendula*), a smaller tree to forty feet, and short lived; and the third, the gray birch (*B. populifolia*), a tree of poor soil, short of stature, but with a very attractive chalky bark. All three of these trees dislike warm temperatures and are best below USDA Zone 7. But though they won't last long, while they do grace yard or garden, they are most beautiful to look at.

Butterfly bushes (*Buddleia* spp.) are so popular with butterfly lovers that it seems strange that nature didn't take a chance to be persnickety and make it a deer treat. This open and irregular-growing shrub can reach a height of seven to eight feet with a six-foot spread, and when in flower (usually most of the summer), it's a treat to both the eye and the nose; the fragrance of 'Black Knight' actually resembles an aged cherry cordial. They need full sun, good drainage, and a soil with good fertility, so it's necessary to fertilize every year or so. Most gardeners treat this shrub like a perennial and cut it to the ground in the fall.

The common boxwood (*Buxus sempervirens*) fits the description of a compact shrub to a T. After all, it takes hundreds of years to reach thirty feet; like the oak, this is not a tree to plant for instant gratification. Hardy to USDA Zone 6, these dense shrubs with their lustrous dark green foliage can be used in many landscapes, but perhaps the most important thing about this boxwood is its smell, especially on damp days. For boxwood leaves give off a strange fragrance, slightly foxy and penetrating, but quite distinctive—liked by some and abhorred by others. Apparently, deer dislike the smell along with some people.

The common catalpas or Indian bean trees (*Catalpa bignonioides*) are popular lawn and street trees, very showy when in bloom, and pendent with fifteen-inch-long bean pods in the fall. The common catalpa can reach a height of sixty feet and is often seen unmercifully cut back in many city yards. The tree is ill-smelling when bruised, hence its being disliked by deer.

Leatherleaf (*Chamaedaphne calyculata*) is a mostly perennial evergreen shrub with lily-of-the-valley type blossoms and very tough and leathery leaves, sometimes red, not green, on the undersides. Plants begin blossoming just as snow is melting. Flowers are similar to those of a lily-of-the-valley. A toxin called *andromedotoxin* can be released from the plant if leaves are infused in boiling water. Research on deer in New Jersey point out that leatherleaf was a minor part of white-tailed deer winter browse. Canadians reported that small amounts were consumed by caribou in Michigan and northern Canada. Leatherleaf does well in poorly drained sites or those with standing water, is acid tolerant, and needs such conditions to multiply. A great bog plant.

Bottlebrush (*Callistemon citrinus*) is a twelve-foot-high shrub, hardy north to USDA 8, consisting of three-inch-long leathery leaves with a distinct scent of lemons, hence the species name. It's grown primarily for the floral display that consists of many bright red, three-inch spikes full of one-inch stamens, like bottlebrushes for small glassware. It's tolerant of soil, withstands drought, and is a good plant for beachfront properties.

California lilacs (*Ceanothus* spp.), or redroots, first came to my attention when touring the gardens of Sissinghurst, in southern England. Deciduous or evergreen shrubs, growing to small trees, one cultivar of *C. arboreus* from the Catalina Mountains of California, has been reported as being reasonably deer proof: 'Mills Glory' grows about three feet tall and bears bright blue flowers and is—up to now—left alone in gardens.

Deodar cedar (*Cedrus deodara*) came to America from India, imported as a sterling addition to landscape planting. Reaching a height of about fifty feet, the tree exhibits a pyramidal shape with pendulous branches, decked with one-to two-inch bluish-green needles growing in dense bunches. Four-inch cones are rarely produced. Provide sun or partial shade in soil with reasonably good drainage. It is not hardy below USDA Zone 6.

Golden cypress (*Chamaecyparis pisifera* 'Filifera') is a great conifer, an evergreen shrub or small tree, six to eight feet high (but if you wait a lifetime, it often grows to a height of fifty feet). The form is a broadly conical, loose, droopy mound, like a large rag-mop, with thin, filament-like branchlets. The dwarf form, 'Filifera Nana,' is better for the small garden. They are hardy to USDA Zone 4 and were imported from Japan back in 1861.

The English hawthorn (*Crataegus laevigata*) will reach a height of twenty-five feet with a twenty-foot spread, has attractive form and foliage, white flowers in spring, followed by small red fruits, and armored with sharp thorns. Hardy to USDA Zone 5, this is a great landscape plant and if protected when young, will eventually provide its own defense.

Chinese dogwood (*Cornus kousa*) is a large shrub or a small tree with dense horizontal branching and lots of attractive leaves. Height is eventually fifteen feet with a ten-foot spread. It blooms later in the spring than the native dogwood (*C. florida*) and the pure white flowers are lovely. The species seems to be—at least so far—resistant to the dogwood anthracnose that attacks more wood-dwelling specimens. A red fruit appears in the fall. It's hardy to USDA Zone 6. While deer will look for the native dogwood, they seem to leave this species alone.

The Leland cypress (x *Cupressocyparis leylandii*) is an evergreen hybrid named for C. J. Leyland of Haggerston Hall. It's a fast-growing cultivar, eventually getting up to sixty feet, and forming an upright, graceful pyramid of soft pointed leaves, soft green when young, and a dark blue-green, and scaly when mature. This tree is exceptionally tolerant of soil, asking only for moderate drainage and not a completely dry spot. The only pest seems to be bag-worms. Deer seem to pass this one by.

Japanese flowering quince (*Chaenomeles japonica*) grows from three to four feet high with a three-foot spread. Coarsely toothed leaves grow on spreading branches and in the spring produce single, over one-inch-wide flowers of white to red to orange, followed in the fall by yellow fruits. It's a rapid grower and responds well to the pruning necessary to keep the shrub within bounds. Provide sun or partial shade in most any soil short of pure clay. This is a great plant when it comes to withstanding city conditions because the branches are very thornyk so wear gloves when pruning. Deer generally pass it by.

Sago palms (*Cycas revoluta*) are similar to palms but are a much older plant, being almost a living fossil. They are a great accent in the garden either directly planted or happily growing in containers. This is a beachside plant in Eastern North Carolina and survives USDA Zone 8 winters, where the foliage might suffer but the trunk and roots survive. In my garden it summers outdoors and spends the winter gracing the living room and is usually illuminated with Christmas tree lights for the season. That said, all parts of this tree are poisonous, the worse being the red berries, especially to dogs (cats usually know better and ignore the leaves)! And people can often have an allergic reaction if they get pricked by one of the sharp tips of the narrow leaves.

The sago palm is poisonous to most wild animals and should be carefully marked for those not in the know.

Daphne (*Daphne mezereum*) is a deciduous or semi-evergreen shrub with simple leaves but in the early spring, incredibly fragrant flowers that bloom in a spike with petal color of white to lilac to a rose-purple, appearing before the leaves and followed by a red or yellow drupe of fruit. Height is between four and five feet. This is one beautiful plant and not to be confused with the other winter daphne (*D. odora*). While glorious in the garden and not usually attractive to deer, this plant, and all parts of this plant, are poisonous. The plant or seeds can actually kill and often damage the retina of the eye.

Russian olives (*Elaeagnus angustifolia*) can be weedy and, as such, are on the danger lists of many states. That said, they are attractive small trees with small, but very fragrant, creamy-yellow flowers in spring followed by small yellow fruits with silvery scales. Their silvery-gray foliage is very attractive and Russian olives always look much older than their calendar age, thus adding stature to a garden. They are rapid growers, will do well in poor soil. Remember, you want the variety with thorns, var. *spinosa*. It's the spines that do the trick.

Enkianthus (*Enkianthus campanulatus*) is an upright, deciduous shrub which typically grows six to eight feet tall (less frequently to ten to fifteen feet). Tiny, bell-shaped, creamy-yellow to whitish-pink flowers with pink striping and edging appear in pendulous clusters (racemes) in late spring. Individual flowers resemble those of Pieris which is in the same family (heath). Elliptic, serrate, medium green to bluish green leaves (to three inches long) are crowded near the branch ends. Fall color is variable, but at its best features quality red foliage with tones of orange, yellow, and purple.

Beech trees (*Fagus grandifolia*) are big and beautiful, making splendid specimens that cast a deep shade beneath their broad, rounded crown. At maturity they can be sixty feet tall. Leaves are a bright green and turn a golden-brown in the fall. The bark is a smooth light gray. They like plenty of sun and a good soil. Often found at the margin of a woods. They are difficult to transplant so be sure to buy either a potted plant or one that has been professionally balled and burlapped. Deer usually pass this tree by, so young specimens can be easily protected with chicken wire.

Forsythia (*Forsythia* spp.) are big, beautiful, and blowsy shrubs well known for their spring display of clear yellow flowers that seem to entirely cover the plant and brighten any corner where they are planted. Forsythias are very rapid growers and can get quite over-grown if not given occasional renewal pruning, best achieved by cutting them to the ground every three or four years. They grow in an upright but spreading fountain of hollow stems; some stems get to be very long and should be nipped off, something that deer rarely do. Foliage turns reddish purple in fall. There are a number of cultivars available.

Dyer's Broom (*Genista tinctoria*) is a small shrubby plant that in my garden is about two feet high, thick with narrow pointed leaves, and in May entirely covered with yellow, pea-like flowers of such color intensity that towards twilight they almost light the border. The plants are wild in Scotland and the hills of England and sometimes along the edge of the road in the Northeast. Bright green stems are streaked with brown bark and they respond beautifully to pruning. The flowers are followed by little inch-long pea pods. When growing in fields, if cows eat the plant their milk becomes bitter to the taste. I have never observed it being eaten by deer.

At one time honey locusts (*Gleditsia triacanthos*) were grown for their wood, usually employed in making fence posts as it lasted a long time and resisted rot. Besides that quality, it's an excellent yard tree, eventually growing up to fifty feet high and having attractive feathery or pinnately compound leaves up to eighteen inches long, with each leaflet around an inch. They endure poor soil and put up with a lot of mistreatment. And they have formidable thorns that make pruning them somewhat of a misery. But a row of honey locust seedlings makes an attractive and impenetrable hedge. For the weak at heart there is a thornless variety known as *G. triacanthos inermis*. You want the old-fashioned kind with thorns.

Rose-of-Sharon (*Hibiscus syriacus*) is a shrub or a small tree, fast-growing, doing well in moist soil and standing up to hot weather. Since it is originally from China, provide full sun to partial shade in the Deep South. There will be winterkill at the northern end of the range. Blossoms resemble mallows and appear in summer. This is a shrub that is grown for the flowers so prune back in spring leaving around two to three buds on a stem. While old-fashioned plants are OK, I prefer 'Diana,' one of the newer cultivars, because unlike the species, the beautiful white flowers stay open all night and the dark-green foliage is more attractive. USDA Zone 5 is the bottom end for cold.

When I first began gardening up in Sullivan County, New York, and confronted with a continual deer problem, a number of plants escaped damage and one was a very old but vigorous: Pee-Gee hydrangea (*Hydrangea paniculata* 'Grandiflora'), with Pee-Gee simply being the initials of species and cultivar. The stems of a well-grown specimen of this shrub are strong enough to be used as walking-sticks in Japan. Eventually the shrub can become a tree up to twenty feet high. The flower clusters are often large enough to elicit surprise by garden visitors. Tolerant of soil and preferring partial shade, this plant seems to be left alone by deer.

The hollies (*Ilex* spp.) are notable plants of great beauty. Remember, there are male and female plants so you must have two sexes for fruit. A few are quite deer resistant, including my favorite, a rather rare entry known as Perny holly (*I. Pernyi*), originally from central China, a glorious plant and at home in my garden for some fifteen years. This evergreen shrub has a height up to twelve feet with a six-foot spread, and alternate light green and shiny leaves with irregular spines. Irregular here is the key; a deer cannot bite down and depend on working his or her way around regularly spaced thorns. Hardy from USDA Zone 6 through 9, providing sun or partial shade, this is one great shrub, and when it's covered with more than the average showy red fruit, spectacular is the word to use. The Native American holly (*I. opaca*) is a tree to thirty feet high with a twenty-foot spread. The leaves are garden green on top and light green beneath. The small flower is white but it's the spiny leaves and the lovely red fruit, especially when grown as a specimen plant. Deer often eat the berries, but unless truly hungry, will pass on the leaves. The inkberry (*I. glabra*) is an evergreen shrub, about nine feet tall with a seven-foot spread. The leaves are a shiny dark green, flowers are inconspicuous, and female plants produce quarter-inch black berries in the late summer. Male plants have the best winter color. Provide sun or shade, in a good garden soil. They are great background plants and excellent for naturalizing. NOTE: Even though its scientific name is *Ilex vomitoria*, the yaupon holly is a great tree to have for all wildlife, including deer, who list it as a number one browse.

Winter jasmine (*Jasminum nudiflorum*) is a Chinese native imported to the South at the beginning of the twentieth century and not as well known as it should be. It is a vining, deciduous shrub that grows three to four feet high and twice as wide. If pushed it will climb a trellis, but it prefers to cascade over a stone wall or ramble down a hillside. Usually, in the dead of winter, dozens of waxy, bright-yellow flowers open along the stems. Not technically evergreen, the arching stems stay green year-round and they grow fast so a yearling clipping by the gardener might be necessary, and not from deer. USDA Zone 7.

The junipers (*Juniperus* spp.) are evergreens from many parts of the Northern Hemisphere, including North America and China. The leaves are needle-like or scale-like and many of the species produce fragrant resins. They range in height from seventy-five feet to ground crawlers. Junipers are also favorites for bonsai. Most of the

Winter jasmine usually begins blooming in January and can continue off an on for weeks.

junipers are deer resistant, a fact easily shown by the number of cedars (*J. virginiana*) growing along roads in the eastern part of America. A favorite juniper is *J. chinensis* var. *procumbens* 'Nana,' a crawling shrub with twisted and curving branches, prickly needles and the ability to fall over walls with statuesque beauty. Sargent's juniper (*J. chinensis sargentii*) is another spreader, with a one-foot height and spreading six to eight feet. And don't overlook the shore juniper (*J. conferta*), an evergreen of up to eighteen inches in height, with a six-foot spread, tolerating low fertility and excellent on beach dunes. Creeping juniper (*Juniperus horizontalis*) is another low-growing evergreen with needle-like foliage and bearing blue berries in the fall. For years up in New York's Sullivan County, we grew pfitzer junipers (*J. chinensis* 'Pfitzeriana') along the front of the house. Named for E. H. H. Pfitzer of Germany, these shrubs grow about seven feet high with a spread of up to ten feet. The foliage is bright green and scalelike. Tolerant of soil, these plants prefer full sun and be warned, they do get very large so don't plant them in front of a foundation. They grow fairly fast and are great for carpeting a bank.

Mountain laurels (*Kalmia latifolia*) are large and robust shrubs, with bright green evergreen leaves and mounds of glorious and interesting white to deep rose-colored flowers in spring. With age, they can become gnarled and beautiful trees. This is one beautiful native shrub. Shade or sun, and does best in partial shade on well-drained, even rocky, soil. There are a number of cultivars available, usually revolving around flower size and color. Sheep or pig laurel (*K. angustifolia*) only reaches a height of three feet and often covers mountainsides from the Catskill Mountains right down the Appalachian chain. The leaves are poison and generally left alone by deer.

Japanese rose (*Kerria japonica*) represents one species of a deciduous shrub with slender stems and sparse, thin light green foliage. Flowers are yellow, bloom in early spring, and do resemble a small rose. The plants reach a six-foot height and a five-foot spread. The hollow stems are small in diameter and almost as tough as bamboo. Tolerant of soil but prefer good drainage.

A well-grown beautybush (*Kolkwitzia amabilis*) is a thing of beauty, for in early May the six-to seven-foot branches, with a spread of seven feet, are festooned with pink, tubular flowers that are pink with a yellow throat. The cultivar 'Rosea' has larger flowers. Kolkwitzias bloom in profuse clusters. The gray-green leaves turn a reddish color in the fall, they have no pest problems, and are great for a shrub border. They do not transplant well, so buy potted or professionally balled-and-burlapped plants. Because these shrubs bloom on old wood, prune after bloom, taking no more than one-third of the wood in a year. The bark on older stems exfoliates, bringing winter interest to the garden. They are hardy to USDA Zone 6.

The golden chain tree (*Laburnum anagyroides*) is a small tree with dark green leaves and in spring, pendant sprays of bright-yellow flowers, obviously members of the pea family. Native to Europe, it's widely grown in America as a specimen lawn tree, especially when in bloom. Reaching a thirty-foot height, with a fifteen-foot spread, the only requirements are sun and well-drained soil. In fact, this tree does well on rocky slopes. But the leaves and the pods that follow the flowers are highly poisonous and some care should be taken. There is a hybrid (*L.* x *Watereri*) that is shorter than the species. An added thought: This is the soft-limbed tree that is used to make a living arch in English gardens, an arch of joined trunks that then drip those pendant sprays of glorious flowers in the late spring, making the cover of every garden magazine.

We had a European larch (*Larix deciduas*) growing just above our driveway in our old Sullivan County garden, about twenty-five feet from a tall and old white pine (*Pinus strobus*), with its bottom branches making such a wide circle I always needed help to prop up those branches when cutting the lawn beneath. It sat there for twenty years and was never touched by the deer. Being a larch might have had something to do with its being spared. For as the species name indicates, this is a deciduous tree that drops its needles in the fall, after they've turned a beautiful golden tan. So about the time that deer are looking for browse, all the needles have fallen with naught left but bare branches. Various extension agents say that the European larch is occasionally badly damaged by deer but it's usually left alone. Here's a lawn tree that's worth the effort.

Himalayan honeysuckle (*Leycesteria formosa*) calls up a combination remembrance of honeysuckle, butterfly bush, and unique, almost chartreuse foliage on seven-to eight-foot tall, but strong, hollow stems that at summer's end bear pendulous blossoms that resemble the kind of earrings one of today's rock stars might wear to a turbulent music session, followed by bird-edible black berries. Provide full or partial shade. These shrubs are hardy to USDA Zone 6 (with protection) to 10.

In all my woods-wanderings in North Carolina, I've yet to see any dog hobble (*Leucothoe* spp.) that has been stripped by deer. But one species, known as the drooping leucothoe (*L. fontanesiana*),

Himalayan honeysuckle is a shrub with late-summer bloom.

is known by gardeners to be generally spared by deer. It's a graceful evergreen shrub between three and four feet high with up to a six-foot spread, the arching stems boasting alternate leathery leaves between three and five inches long, and liking, in fact demanding, part shade or shade. The plant likes a reasonable stab at drainage but otherwise will adapt to most soil conditions, but always on the acidic side. In early spring, two- to three-inch sprays of fragrant, white waxy flowers hand down and attract early-rising bees. Pruning consists of removing three-year-old canes to promote new growth from the crown. There is a beautiful cultivar known as 'Girard's Rainbow,' bearing new leaves with colors of white, pink, and copper. It's hardy from USDA Zone 6 to 9, but resents excessive heat.

Privets (*Ligustrum* spp.) are the hedge champions of all time and clippers have been trimming them in America since they were brought over from Europe (*L. vulgare*) in the 1700s and from Japan, then China, in the middle of the 1800s and even the 1900s. Unfortunately, from the point of view of native plant specialists, the privets are bad news, as their dense thickets soon crowd out indigenous species. But gardeners can use the effect to keep deer at bay. When left to grow according to their habit, privets can reach a height of twelve feet with a ten-foot spread. The lustrous dark green leaves are quite beautiful, without mentioning the clusters of small white flowers, followed by dark purple fruits. This genus does very well in many adverse conditions, including city gardens. Occasionally, they will be browsed by hungry deer but unlike many shrubs, privets respond to this pruning by growing sprouting new branches.

There are dozens of species of holly grapes (*Mahonia* spp.), but high on the gardener's list is the species from the American Northwest, specifically the Oregon grape (*M. aquifolium*). These are evergreen shrubs growing to a height of ten feet, but usually around seven. Often leggy, our mahonias are pruned with purpose once every three or four years. Alternate leaves are stiff and leathery, with spines along the margins. Bright yellow, waxy scented flowers that reveal the plant's relationship with barberries bloom in early spring. The fruits of summer are blue-black, resembling elongated grapes and favored by birds. Provide partial or full shade, in reasonably moist, well-drained acidic soil. Plants are hardy to USDA Zone 6. While deer will occasionally attack these shrubs (thus saving you the trouble), for many seasons they are left alone. American Indians used this mahonia to treat a number of diseases, and recently scientists have found that herbal extracts from mahonia can be useful to psoriasis victims.

Siberian cypress (*Microbiota decussata*) is an extremely hardy (its lowest range is USDA Zone 2) evergreen conifer that grows up to three feet high and spreads up to seventy inches, sporting good winter color, will adapt to some shade, and needs good drainage, but is quite deer resistant. Look for the newer cultivar 'Celtic Pride.'

Heavenly bamboos (*Nadina* spp.) are neither heavenly or bamboos, but earthbound members of the barberry family. Heavenly Bamboo (*Nandina domestica*) is completely unrelated to bamboo. Due to the fine lacy foliage, its common name comes from a resemblance to bamboo and the cane-like growth pattern of the stems. Nandinas are classified as evergreen, but will lose foliage if the temperature drops

Microbiota decussata is a spreading cold-climate conifer.

below 10°F. The canes will die back to the ground at -10°F, but will come back readily the next spring. During all four seasons of the year this plant provides color in the garden. In the spring, the new foliage emerges as bright bronzed red, and is soon followed by large, six-to twelve-inch panicles of creamy white flowers. As the season changes, the foliage becomes blue-green, fading to light green. Clusters of bright green berries replace the flowers. By late summer, the berries will ripen to a bright red. In the fall, the foliage color again begins to change to shades of pink and red, ending the year with bright red leaves and berries. The berries will remain until they are discovered and enjoyed by the local birds. Heavenly bamboo will slowly grow to eight feet if it is left alone. However, it can be kept at a very compact size by pruning. It is also suitable for growing indoors as a container plant. Nandina flowers attract bees while the berries attract birds. Berries are possibly toxic to cats. Shorten or remove old canes to the ground; do not shear.

Right up front, oleander (*Nerium oleander*) is a poisonous plant. All parts of the plant are harmful, including the sap. At one time this plant was featured in many mystery books, including one story about an attempted poisoning accomplished by skewering a hotdog on an olean-der stick and killing the victim who ate it. A single leaf has been known to be lethal. Even skin contact with sensitive people can cause a rash. That said, oleander is a fast-growing evergreen shrub, up to twenty feet tall and spreads about ten feet. Lance-shaped leathery leaves average about six inches long. Fragrant summertime flowers are white, pink, red, salmon-pink, or a light yellow. Shrubs should be pruned to keep a good silhouette. Oleanders have a high salt and wind tolerance so make excellent shore shrubs, plus they are drought resistant. They also do beautifully in pots. Hardy to USDA Zone 7 but must be protected or mulched in the winter. They do best in Zones 8 and 9.

The spruce (*Picea* spp.) are represented in the deer-dislike list as the Colorado blue spruce (*P. pungens*), the species name referring to piercing and sharp pointed needles. Reaching a majestic height of sev-enty to ninety feet, this spruce is a great specimen tree. Provide good soil with good drainage and full sun. There are many cultivars avail-able, including a number of dwarf conifers for the small garden. The Norway spruce (*P. abies*) can grow up to a one hundred feet tall and spread up to thirty feet. These trees transplant with ease when pro-fessional balled-and-burlapped specimens are used. There are many smaller cultivars available. According to the USDA, Norway spruce nursery stock is of low preference when white-tailed deer are involved.

There are two andromedas of note: Japanese andromeda (*Pieris japonica*) and mountain andromeda (*P. floribunda*). Japanese andromeda grows about six feet tall with a six-foot spread. The leaves are a lustrous dark green and in late winter to early spring, the flower buds that have graced the plant since fall begin to open. They bloom with waxy, white, five-inch-long pendulous clusters of great beauty. There are many cultivars. Hardy from USDA Zone 5 to 8. Mountain andromeda grows about the same in height and has the same flower-ing but it's the hardiest of the two, wintering over (with protection) to USDA Zone 5. Annual growth rate for these shrubs is less than one foot. Flowers are sometimes injured by heavy late frost. Provide a moist, acidic soil in partial shade. Lacebugs can stipple leaf surfaces with tiny wounds, making them yellow and unsightly.

Austrian pine (*Pinus nigra*) are listed by many sources as being disliked by deer. But according to USDA records about a happening in Wyoming, it seems that during a bad snowstorm, a herd of mule deer gained entrance to a conifer tree nursery where they browsed Austrian pine in preference to ponderosa pine (*Pinus ponderosa*), blue spruce (*Picea pungens*), bristle cone pine (*Pinus aristata*), and Rocky Mountain juniper (*Juniperus scopulorum*). Damage was concentrated on the lateral branch buds and needles. We had a number of Scots pine (*Pinus sylvestris*) on our old Sullivan County property and except for one year in the 1980s when ice storms ravaged the mountains, deer ignored these pines. Scots pine can reach a height of seventy feet with a thirty-foot spread. Beautiful trees, the needles are a dark green, they transplant well, and are somewhat adaptable to soil but need full sun. They are rapid growers compared to many evergreens and useful as a specimen or in masses. According to the USDA, white-tailed deer will browse Scots pine but compared to other ornamental species, this species is low on the whitetail list. Red pine (*Pinus resinosa*) grows to seventy feet, has an attractive bark, does well in colder areas (below USDA Zone 6), and makes a good specimen or accent tree. If preferred food is lacking, white-tailed deer, snowshoe hares, and cottontails will browse red pine seedlings.

Hardy orange (*Poncirus trifoliata*) is a fascinating shrub, hardy to USDA Zone 6, and ornamental all through the year. Glossy green leaves turn yellow in the fall and grow from low branching stems that are adorned with heavy thorns up to four inches long. April flowers are waxy-white, fragrant, and followed by yellow-orange fruits like small oranges. Eventual height is about fifteen feet with a twelve-foot spread. Will put up with city conditions and does well even in dry, infertile soils. When planted in a row, these shrubs make an

Young staghorn sumac in the border.

impenetrable barrier because of their vicious thorns. 'Flying Dragon' has twisted stems and sharply curved thorns.

Staghorn sumac (*Rhus typhina*) is one of my favorite shrubs or small trees for the backyard garden or even the a large spread. Highway departments hate it but horticulturalists love it (the Royal Horticultural Society gave this small tree three awards in the 1900s). This is another plant growing up in New York State that was never touched by the deer. I'm sure it would have been if hunger ruled (especially in bad years), but there were always better things to eat in my backyard. The USDA reports that white-tailed deer and moose browse the leaves and twigs while the bark and twigs are eaten by rabbits, especially in winter. But it's such a fast grower that deer never seemed to cut back any trees in the back field, and I always protect the trunks of any tree in my garden from rabbits. Alternate, feather-like compound leaves, up to two feet long, bear eleven to thirty-one leaflets and turn brilliant oranges and reds in the fall, more than enough reason for growing these beauties. The brown branches have velvety hairy resembling deer antlers. Maroon flowers are borne in upright panicles up to eight inches long. In the growing season this small tree or shrub looks completely tropical. In winter, when leaves fall, the mature fruits remain on the twigs for a great silhouette. Use this plant for holding steep slopes or mass them in places where other plants fight to survive. 'Laciniata' is a beautiful cultivar with many-cut leaves.

Corkscrew willow (*Salix matsudana* 'Tortuosa') is a cultivar introduced to American in 1923 when the Arnold Arboretum received a cutting from China. By the mid-1930s the tree entered commerce, taking the flower arrangers by the throat, as once seen in a vase, everybody wanted it. My experience with the beautiful specimen tree in Peter Gentling's Asheville garden shows the typical height to be about thirty feet. The alternate leaves are simple, lanceolate, between two and four inches long, bright green above and glaucous beneath. When young, the stems are yellow, turning olive-green, then brownish-gray with age. The contortions are always impressive. The fact that deer seem to ignore this tree is quite surprising but perhaps, again, it's not the shape but the chemical content.

Common lilacs (*Syringa vulgaris*) bloom by the cottage door, and throughout the Northeast are often found still blooming, every spring, in abandoned gardens at derelict farms. The lilac isn't even a native to North America but actually came from Turkey in the sixteenth century, but it's the state flower of New Hampshire, because it was the first state to grow them back in 1690. Everybody knows the flowers of lilacs, but to grow them to perfection, these shrubs require full sun except when grown in the Deep South. They prefer a slightly acidic soil. Most lilacs also require at least six weeks of below 40°F temperatures during the winter months. If that doesn't fit your bill, grow one of the 'Descanso' hybrids. After blooming, remove dead flowers to prevent seed formation. Every few years just remove the oldest stems, cutting back to the ground.

Leatherleaf viburnum (*Viburnum rhytidophyllum*) belongs to the honeysuckle family, grows as a shrub up to ten feet tall, and has great architectural character. Up to seven inches long, the leaves are narrowly oblong, evergreen, conspicuously wrinkled, scruffy and thick, and dark green above while paler (and slightly hairy) beneath. Showy clusters of small white flowers appear in May but you grow this shrub for the leaves and the red, then black, berries of fall (you need two plants for berries. This shrub grows fast, prefers partial shade with average soil but tolerates an alkaline soil. The cultivar 'Allegheny' has abundant flowers. Hardy to USDA Zones 6 to 8 but suffers from the heat in warmer climates.

CHAPTER TEN

Some Great Flowering Plants from a California Nursery

Years ago, when publishing was centered in Manhattan, most book editors had upstate homes or vacation retreats in upper New York State and New England so the majority of garden books had a Northeastern taint to the copy. Then to add to the mix, there were all those English garden books with all those lovely photographs of spectacular estate gardens, thus more plant suggestions appeared that just happened to be at home in much of, again, the Northeast.

Finally, the West Coast fought back and in California there appeared books, magazines, and horticultural associations devoted to all those plants—both native and exotic—that grew so well in that area of the world.

Today, thanks to improvements in shipping plant material and a wider sense of adventure found in most gardeners, we look for new and interesting material from all over the country. Now add Global Warming to the mix and today in my garden, plants winter over without added protection that would have frozen to death just a decade ago.

So a few years back I discovered a plant nursery in Richmond, California, known as Annie's Annuals & Perennials (www.anniesannuals.com); you will soon became a fan of their zippy catalog (printed or online) and the amazing choice of plants they offer for sale—not to mention, a great deal of research that went into deer-resistant plants or plants that deer actually dislike. The catalog features just a few of the two thousand uncommon varieties they grow. Fortunately for many of us in the colder parts of the country, quite a number of those plants offered are suitable for USDA Zones 5 to 8, where there are still are cold winters but gardener's hearts ache for something new for the backyard.

So here are twenty-eight plants of great beauty that are deer resistant and will survive outdoors alone and defenseless, and others

Aeonium urbicum has no common name but is an uncommon gift to a warmer garden.

that need protection and are able to sit winter out because they are grown in pots that go into protected places while those freezing winds blow. They are listed because a few are deer proof and the rest are deer resistant, and in many cases, drought resistant, too.

Again as to climate, on the web check out en.wikipedia.org/wiki/Hardiness_zone. You will find that currently "hardy to zone 10" means that the plant can withstand a minimum temperature of 30°F.

Aeonium urbicum is a species of plant in the Crassulaceae Family. It is native to the Island of Tenerife, one of the Canary Islands off the western coast of Africa and belonging to Spain. This is a most beautiful place to visit, even just for the native flora. And here is an incredible succulent that upon blooming makes one of the biggest flowering heads you will ever see. Among the tallest of *Aeoniums*, this plant can reach an un-branched four to six feet tall with a pyramidal inflorescence easily reaching three by three feet in size. The mature

Blue pimpernels add patches of great color and generally shunned by deer.

Summer forget-me-nots should be welcome in any garden.

size of the rosette head is about a foot in diameter. White or pink starry blooms appear July through August and those flowers are beloved by bees! Even when not in bloom this is a strikingly architectural specimen for a container. These plants are monocarpic and die after flowering (which takes a few years to attain) but not to worry, with all those eventual flowers you get hundreds of viable seeds and new plants. USDA Zone 9 to 10 and if you don't have the season outside, grow it in a pot. Plants easily propagate from cuttings.

Blue pimpernels (*Anagallis monellii*) bear bright gentian blue flowers, up to an inch across, with vibrant pink eyes that become a background for five bright yellow anthers. Flowers literally smother this Mediterranean annual, short-lived perennial, or dry garden perennial blooming from spring to fall. Neat and compact, this Mediterranean native grows to ten inches tall by twenty inches across,

Usually called the South African Iris, this is one of a number of fantastic plants from that area of the world.

and in warmer climates self-sows. Needs well-drained soil and is hardy in USDA Zone 9 to 11.

Call this beauty the summer forget-me-not (*Anchusa capensis* 'Blue Angel'). Mobs of intense deep, true blue "Forget Me Nots" are held in tight eight-inch clusters on this bushy, branching South African native that grows in foot-wide clusters. The flowers almost smother the foliage, creating a great mass of royal blueness for months. This plant likes a good soil and good drainage. Cut dead flowers back for a second and third round of bloom. Often grown as a self-sowing annual, it can live over and bloom in as a short-lived perennial in warmer areas. Sow seeds early indoors or sow directly outdoors when frosts are past. Like borage, every part of this plant is softly hairy, so if you have delicate skin, better wear gloves. Perhaps this is the reason that deer resent them.

Another plant with punch known as the South African iris *Aristea major* (sometimes *Aristea capitata*) produces four-foot-tall brilliant gentian blue flowers clustering on spikes rising above thin sword-like leaves. *Aristea* is a genus of evergreen rhizomatous perennials that belong to the great iris family. When in bloom, they impress with electrifying gentian blue spikes. True blue, one-inch flowers with yellow stamens form dense, crowded clusters near the top of the four-foot stalks. Plants are beautiful even when out of bloom and are highly resistant to being hot and dry, and roots are tolerant of clay but whenever possible, good drainage counts. Plants are deer resistant and disliked by snails. Cut stalks back after flowering. Hardy to USDA Zone 8b to 11.

Sometimes called rock purslane, *Calandrinia spectabilis* is a beautiful and spectacular Chilean perennial that is almost everblooming (usually from May to October) and not fussy about soil (although it approves of having decent drainage) and is close to being deer proof. This robust succulent produces a continuous supply of

Sometimes called rock purslane this is a lovely plant if offered the proper drainage.

hundreds of bright cerise, about one-and-a-half inches across shining above attractive, blue-green foliage that quickly spreads into a dense, fifteen-foot by four-foot groundcover that suppresses weeds as it grows. It's drought tolerant, too.

Velvet centaurea is a common name for *Centaurea gymnocarpa,* which has been called by Annie a "dusty miller on steroids." Striking filigreed leaves of silvery-white grow into dense mounds and from spring to mid-summer produce fluff-balls of a rosy-lavender hue. Plants are both deer resistant and very drought tolerant, plus they can grow in clay and take some shade and are best described as perennial shrubs. They are a great choice for hillsides and those neglected side yards. They are hardy to 15–20°F and meant for USDA Zone 8–10.

Honeywort, blue shrimp plant, or blue wax flower are common names for *Cerinthe major,* a herbaceous plant native to the grassy plains of countries along the edge of the Mediterranean Basin, but

Velvet centaurea works well in garden beds or in containers.

Honeywort is a plant that every gardener should grow even if it's only in a pot.

Clarkia 'Pink Ribbons' is a native of California gardens.

especially hailing from Greece and southern Italy. *Wort*, by the way, is a Middle English word for plant. Depending on your experiences with this plant it's either a hardy annual or a tender evergreen perennial, or a short-lived and half-hardy perennial, not to mention some discrete claims to it being a biennial. The clusters of interesting tubular flowers are sur-rounded by large, almost space-shaped, nodding bracts and the flowers pro-duce very sweet nectar, so in addition to being deer resistant, it's also beloved by bees. The pretty, mot-tled leaves look great when growing in pots (three gallons is suggested) and plants freely self-sow. It has average water needs, so when it's dry water reg-ularly but never overwater. You can get up to four self-sown cycles of bloom. All zones.

Commonly called *clarkia* this particular plant is *Clarkia concinna* 'Pink Ribbons' and the flowers billow over the front of a bed like a cloud of butterflies held on shiny red stems. This herbaceous clarkia is not only a California native, it's also endemic to Northern California and known to frequent the lower elevations of nearby mountains. One-and-a-quarter-inch-wide flowers look like silky pinwheels. They're a perfect choice for mixed plantings, containers, and even hanging baskets, where they'll attract all manner of butterflies and bees. These are wonderful annuals for the light shade—perfect under azaleas—and a nice change from impatiens. Plants grow about ten inches tall and twenty inches wide in average to rich soil—and no clay. They are deer resistant and drought tolerant!

Cotyledon orbiculata var. 'Flavida' can be responsible for continual oohs and aahs from garden visitors because the plants represent a great mix of horticultural interest and textural beauty: the first with eye-catching silvery-blue, chalky, finger-like leaves that form a distinctive clump of a slowly spreading groundcover that looks great all year around, and the second with the umbrella-like clusters

Everybody who visits a garden with *Cotyledon orbiculata* in bloom wants some to take home a container of their choice.

Crassula capitella 'Red Pagoda.'

The scarlet larkspur is a smashing garden perennial.

of inch and apricot bells held well above the foliage on upright foot-high stems. Plants are deer resistant and drought tolerant and outdoors hardy to the mid 20's°F. Inside they steadfastly winter over, waiting to burst forth with the following spring.

Crassula capitella 'Red Pagoda' leaps up from the ground or a container like Japanese-styled party favors. Densely stacked red-edged succulent stemlets rise up from the base to reach a height of seven inches and a breadth of eighteen. This is an easy-to-grow and fascinating small-scale groundcover, the more sun you give it, the redder it gets. In summer small white flowers followed by the top leaves drop off, which will readily root where they fall to create welcome new plantlets! Red pagoda is unexpected and unusual as an edging plant, in a container, or peeking over the edge of a hanging basket. Well-drained soil is a must.

The scarlet larkspur (*Delphinium cardinale*) is spectacular native perennial making its initial home along the California coast and the foothills from Monterey South. It blooms with showy flower clusters on three- to five-foot stems and finely dissected basal and stem leaves. The long-spurred blossoms open in clusters up to two feet in length with brilliant red sepals, while the pea-like flowers are yellow with scarlet tips. This tuberous rooted Delphinium is a boon to summer dry gardens and flowers from spring to early summer when this heat lover needs a dormant, little-to no-water period in summer to return for the next season. And it self-sows.

Drosanthemum micans is the kind of plant that can awaken the spirits after a deadly winter by offering concentrated sunshine in its masses of flowers. It's a compact perennial that can reach a height of a little over two feet and up to thirty inches across. Needle-like leaves are a rich gray-green and have been described as having a

Called the dew flower, this plant should be given great drainage and space to grow.

dewy quality, hence its common name of the dew flower. Flowers open early in the morning and close up around five, making them a clue to garden time on busy days. Provide full sun and well-drained gritty soil. Deadhead after blooming to help form new buds and cut the plants back in the fall. They are hardy to about 25°F, so in colder areas this means grow it in a pot.

One of the many kinds of hens and chickens, some common and some incredibly beautiful.

Echeveria imbricata represent one of the most stylish of the hen and chicken succulents on the market. Six inches wide and all things being equal, it can spread into a great groundcover mounting up to fourteen inches in height and about thirty inches across (in the image they are shown here with *Dyckia* 'Cherry Cola'). Summer brings arching, rosy stems and pretty little bells. Provide good drainage, a bit of annual compost, and wait for the garden crowd who will all want an offset. This plant is heat tolerant and hardy to 20°F.

Echium gentianoides 'Tajinasta' comes from the island of La Palma in the Canary Islands. The color is a true cerulean blue, its flowers held in loose pyramidal spikes blooming the first year and a wonder in the spring garden. The cup-shaped blossoms emerge from pink buds held above smooth, blue-gray, linear foliage. When well ensconced, this is an impressive plant, blooming from spring through

Echium gentianoides needs great drainage to do its best for your garden.

Just another erigeron that is beloved by bees and other great insects.

fall. A branching plant, it can reach an area of four by four feet. Cut back to thirty inches after bloom is over in the fall. Remember, this plant needs superb drainage for ultimate happiness and side dress with an inch of compost once a year. USDA Zone 9 to 10.

When *Erigeron glaucus* 'Wayne Roderick' was chosen by Dr. Gordon Frankie—bee expert of renown—because it was a super bet for attracting native bees, the nursery set to busy-bee themselves into propagating more. "After all," said Annie, "it's not just a long blooming, easy to grow, drought tolerant, super-tough perennial, and fabulous habitat plant, it also honors the legendary Californian plantsman Wayne Roderick, who passed away in 2003." This plant is just one of his innumerable contributions to botany and horticulture. Plants grow about a foot high and up to three feet wide and bear yellow-centered, lavender-blue blooms in every season but winter. Some watering in summer improves the plant's appearance. This erigeron tolerates clay, salt spray, wind, and deer. It attracts bees and butterflies! Hardy in USDA Zones 6 to 10.

Euphorbia characias 'Dwarf' is the dwarf form of the regular-sized *E. characias* but still bears the big and wondrous chartreuse flower heads that just might be to mighty for a small garden space. This cultivar grows about two-and-a-half feet high and the same in width. The flowers are just as big as the full-sized version—growing up to sixteen inches by ten inches. These plants are drought tolerant,

Euphorbia characias 'Dwarf' is one fantastic plant in the border, and if it must be netted at certain times of the year, it's worth the effort.

not fussy about soil, and added to that, both deer and gopher resistant. They will self-sow but if that extra is not needed, just cut the entire stem to the base. In hotter areas, provide some shade. And like all euphorbias, the sap of this plant can be toxic to varying degrees so protect your eyes, your skin, and never chew. USDA Zones 7 to 10.

Gaillardia x grandiflora 'Oranges & Lemons' is one beautiful blanket flower and the color is a literal splash of sunshine in the backyard. Plants bloom constantly from late spring through fall, bearing loads of three-inch golden-tipped flowers held upright above a fresh green foliar clump that grows about twelve inches across. This is a tough, reliable perennial that tolerates heat and being dry, and looks great at the front of the border or in containers. For maximum longevity, when plants show a tendency to dry out in the center,

'Oranges & Lemons' is one beautiful blanket flower and well worth the picking.

replant and remove that dead area. Butterflies and bees love blanket flowers but to ensure their continued attendance, make sure the soil supports excellent drainage. USDA Zones 5A to 10.

Graptoveria 'Crested Form' bears succulent leaves with mixed colors of amber, gold, lavender, mauve, and rose. Then add those leaves with their great sunset colors to support the intermittent crested forms and such beauty surely takes this to the top of anybody's favorite succulent list. According to Annie's encyclopedic friend David Felix, this rare stunner is a renegade form of *Graptoveria* 'Fred Ives.' The plant's habit it to create dense round mounds of tightly packed smaller leaves about a foot tall and three feet across, making it superb as an edging plant or in a container. Provide well-drained soil and once a year a bit of compost. USDA Zones 8 to 11.

The Lenten rose (*Helleborus orientalis*) is one of those plants that should be in every garden, not only for the flowers but for the great and lustrous leaves that are evergreen in our USDA Zone 7 garden. And they actually begin to bloom around the time that the Lenten season begins. But one of the most beautiful cultivars I've ever seen is 'Peppermint Ice' bearing large blossoms three inches across with double lotus-like blooms, the petals (really sepals) are edged in dark pink, then beautifully veined and spotted.

Graptoveria 'Crested Form' is marvelous in a container much less just out in the garden.

'Peppermint Ice' hellebore also makes a great cut flower (remember to slit the stems at their base).

A bonus feature is that though the blooms are pendulous (like all the hellebores), the back sides of the petals are rose and veined as well. Hellebores tolerate poor soil, clay, drought, and marauding deer. Plants are about two feet tall and two feet wide. 'Peppermint Ice' was created through meticulous hand pollination over twenty years in the making by Marietta O'Byrne of Eugene, Oregon.

Lampranthus spp. 'Pink Kaboom' has a history that goes back to a propagator at Annie's Annuals who planted a mysterious little start of this plant in their parking lot, which is described as having the worst hard-pan clay soil that can be imagined, and they never watered it. It quickly grew into a dense and rounded mound some two feet high and three feet wide with masses of succulent leaves and suddenly exploded into an astounding mass of blindingly bright perfect pink daisies. Now that it seemed to be established, they gave it some water. This survivor turned out to be a member of the

'Pink Kaboom' is an aptly named cultivar.

Woodland tidytips is the common name for this uncommonly charming bright yellow wildflower.

genus *Lampranthus*, South African plants that flower between June and August and have among its members what are called ice plants. They are pollinated by a number of insects including bees, beetles, and wasps. They are also deer resistant and drought tolerant! USDA Zone 9 and 10.

The woodland tidytips are native to the California coastline (including Contra Costa County and the Coast Mountain Ranges). These annual plants are perfectly named because the word tidy fits them like a glove. *Layia gaillardioides* is a lovely wildflower for sunny as well as partly shaded gardens. Growing about one to two feet tall, the plants are smothered with a myriad a bright yellow flowers resembling miniature blanket flowers or gaillardias. It is very popular with butterflies and native bees and reseeds nicely, too. Plants are native to the California coastline (including Contra Costa County) and the Coast Mountain Ranges. All zones.

Here is one of the many blossoms found in the passion flower family, great in gardens or in pots.

Passiflora edulis 'Frederick' is one of the exotic plants belonging to the Passion Flower Family. These plants bear flowers with a number of botanical parts that closely resemble the symbols used in the telling of The Passion of the Christ. In addition to their strange beauty, they bear lots of great-tasting fruit ready for use in salads, sherbets, or eating right out of hand. The intricate, three-and-a-half-inch-wide blossom will delight not only the gardener but also any Gulf Fritillaries in the neighborhood, with buds that open on and off from early summer to fall. Before eating the fruit you need to wait until it darkens to purple and drops from the vine. Evergreen and quick growing, 'Frederick' can easily reach a height of fifteen feet but can be kept in line by cutting back to one foot in the winter. It's is one of the hardiest of the passifloras surviving winter wet and brief frosts down to 20°F. Takes heat well, too! An annual side-dress of compost will keep it lush and happy. It is self-pollinating but doesn't self-sow.

The Cape lilac, *Plectranthus ecklonii,* is a perennial member of the mint family and a most beautiful flowering shrub from South Africa—the Cape of the common name refers to the Cape of Good Hope. The large, heart-shaped leaves are a rich green and the flowers bloom in the fall. Blossoms are exquisite on blooming spikes up to a foot long, the flowers have long and swooping blue-purple stamens and in full bloom, this shrub is truly for the books! These shrubs are easy to grow, and especially fast in that growth, so they are garden stars and great looking just as a shrub. In areas where bad frosts are due before Thanksgiving, grow this stunner in a large container and bring it into a frost-protected spot and revel in the flowers. The Cape

If there's room don't overlook the Cape lilac.

Commonly called clary sage, this is a cultivar with impressive flowering.

lilac easily reaches six feet in one growing season and should be cut back to the ground to about a foot and it will reach blooming size the next season. Provide a rich, well-drained soil, and provide at least a half-day of sun. Butterflies and humming birds adore the blossoms. USDA Zones 8 to 10.

Clary sage (*Salvia sclarea*) has a cultivar called 'Piemont' and is described by Penelope Hobhouse (of English garden fame) as being "a must for every garden." All clary sages are impressive, often reaching a height of five feet, but 'Piemont' is even more robust and beautiful. Here is a biennial, or if in a warm spot it often survives as a short-lived herbaceous perennial that is native to the northern Mediterranean and on up into North Africa and Central Asia where it has a long history as a medicinal herb and today is grown for its essential oils. The flowers appear on foot-and-a-half spikes with two-toned lavender and white flowers held in the grips of violet-purple calyces (calyces are leaf-like structures often referred to as sepals). Blooming begins in summer and continues into fall. This plant will self-sow. Because of its medicinal nature, especially when held close to the nose, these plants have a very strong, almost chemical odor, hence, I think, the unlikelihood that deer will eat much of it.

Triteleia laxa 'Queen Fabiola' enjoys the common name of Ithuriel's Spear, referring to Book IV of John Milton's *Paradise Lost*, in which the angels Ithuriel and Zephon protect the sleeping Adam and Eve from Satan. The large two-inch, beautiful, sky-facing, purple-blue trumpets are held in loose clusters above stiff leafless stems (after grassy leaves die back). The next thing to note about this perennial bulb is that it thrives in heavy clay soil, accepts either sun

Triteleia laxa 'Queen Fabiola.'

Known as fire stars in South Africa, they are amazing beauties especially because they are annual flowers.

or partial shade, blooms in the spring, is fragrant then dormant in the summer so needs no summer water, does well when planted under oaks, and is deer resistant. If you plant enough of them, they're a wonderful cut flower you certainly won't find at the florist. Native Americans would roast the corms like potatoes.

Ursinias (*Ursinia anthemoides*) are annual fire-stars from South Africa, and the cultivar 'Solar Fire' more than deserves this cultivar name. Quickly growing to fifteen by fifteen inches, the plant literally explodes into masses of two-and-a-half-inch daisy-like flowers, sporting sunny, golden-orange petals that last for months. Having a shiny maroon ring encircling the golden-yellow eye simply adds to the drama. They are both heat and drought tolerant once established and will self-sow over the seasons. In USDA Zone 10 ursinias can be planted at any time of the year because they tend to bloom shortly thereafter. They are great in containers, too.

Verbascum 'Cotswold King' have larger than average flowers and are fragrant, too.

When it comes to blooms, the *Verbascum* spp. are often a bit disappointing but the cultivar 'Cotswold King' will reward the gardener with fragrant flowers that are simple to grow and the quickest to bloom. Everybody should definitely try this extra large flowered, sweetly scented cultivar not only for the ease of growing but for the chuckles associated with the imaginary faces you can see in each flower. The floral stems reach a height of about five feet and the two-inch bright lemon yellow flowers stud the upper thirty inches of those spikes with bloom that begins in late spring. Being a biennial, the first crop needs the second spring to bloom, but once you get started the self-sowing will lead to the coming years full of these beauties. Cut back after bloom is spent, for secondary spikes in mid-summer. Provide some reasonably good soil. Flowers attract butterflies, and bees and they are, of course, snail proof and deer resistant.

Here's a mounding verbena that is drought resistant and a butterfly magnet.

In the spring, *Verbena lilacina* 'De La Mina' explodes into a super-cloud of rich lavender-blue fragrant flower clusters that in warmer climes keeps up all year long. This mounding verbena with deeply divided, medium green leaves provides months of color with its fragrant purple flowers. A drought-tolerant California native, it attracts butterflies and is perfect for planting in natural gardens and meadows. Beautiful in borders, it's evergreen and invaluable for both cottage gardens and dry gardens—or large pots. Plants make a dense mound three feet high and the same around. Butterflies and bees flock to the flowers and it's at home in a wide range of soils, from sandy to clay. This plant exists thanks to horticulturalist Carol Bornstein of the Santa Barbara Botanical Garden who discovered this selection on Cedros Island off the west coast of Baja California. USDA Zone 7 to 10.

CHAPTER ELEVEN

If You Can't Beat 'em, Join 'em

Situations exist where for one or more reasons some gardeners are slated to lose the battle for land supremacy when involved with fighting the deer. No matter what solution is tried, there are times when such solutions fail. For more about this occurrence, please see chapter 3. But assuming that you have battled and lost, kindly consider the following options. Your own yard is most likely teeming with wildlife. Over much of North America, birds, mammals, amphibians, and insects abound. To create a habitat that will not only attract and nurture the most desirable wild creatures, but also enable you to watch your own private collection of deer would most likely be a great feather in your gardening hat. And the first thing that you do is make your landscape more inviting to those that are wanted, a move that will quickly bring everything from song birds and butterflies to toads and dragonflies, from squirrels and chipmunks to creatures of the night, and then you allow the deer to join the circle of living things just outside your door.

Today most people live in and around cities and towns, but no matter where you live—in the suburbs or out in the country—each place attracts a different mix of wildlife. Manhattanites garden in the middle of a densely packed population center. But they can still watch small mammals and birds. City residents can also see a host of different insects, surprising number of animals, and many unusual plants that often grow in whatever pocket of soil their seeds may happen to find. They also are likely to observe ducks and geese flying north in the spring and south in the fall. This of course means a change in your gardening philosophies but not an end to gardening.

A wealth of wildlife thrives in the suburbs, from the deer that presently threaten your garden and prized shrubs; where birds and frogs, then butterflies, herald the arrival of spring; and where garbage cans must be tightly sealed, not for protection from wandering dogs, but to foil the efforts of raccoons, opossums, crows, and other wild marauders, including bears and even elks.

Folks who live on farms or in rural areas also run into raccoons and 'possoms and often see more deer and elk that they wish to count. Foxes—both red and gray—and coyotes are occasional visitors, and bears, moose, bobcats, and even mountain lions have been known to wander past the front door on their way to a nearby snack.

By planting certain flowering annuals, perennials, and woody plants, you can attract butterflies—almost by species—to your garden, whether you live in town or in the country. You can also choose plants that will bring a wide range of birds including hummingbirds flocking to the flowers or the hanging containers of sugar water outside your kitchen windows.

Add a protected birdbath (including a small water heater for winter visitors) and birds will choose your yard for their summer vacations. To keep them around in the winter, hang or install a bird feeder or two. Some birds like sunflower seeds, while others prefer Niger seeds or millet, but you will soon find the needed combination.

Even late at night there are visitors to the garden. For example, the pollen of lily blossoms will attract moths and a number of fascinating insects. Small bats will eat bugs on the wing, crickets sound their friendly chirps, and somewhere an owl will hoot.

One cardinal rule of nature states that everything depends on everything else. You can see this principle at work in your garden. When you begin to grow many flowering plants, all those insects arrive. Then by adding water you will attract amphibians, including frogs and toads. Even tortoises and turtles can become part of your backyards world if you garden with their needs in mind.

And that includes the deer. They rarely ravage by eating up and there are many grasses and bushes and shrubs, including roses, that will be left alone.

Finally, see chapter 8 for more on trading a grassy lawn for moss or trying container gardening.

Mapping Your Backyard

Walk out to whatever passes for your own backyard. Note things that you can change, like trees that need pruning, or lawn that is getting kind of scruffy, any natural features like boulders that cannot be removed or man-made structures dealing with electricity, water, etc. Once you are armed with that necessary information, begin the next step by drawing a map.

Mapping your yard is easy. All you need to begin your map is a sheet of plain paper and a pencil; graph paper is handy but not necessary. And remember, you need not be a great artist—just be clear and to the point.

One easy way to get a map of your property is to copy your property survey if you have one. If you don't, your municipality probably does, or you can hire a surveyor to create one.

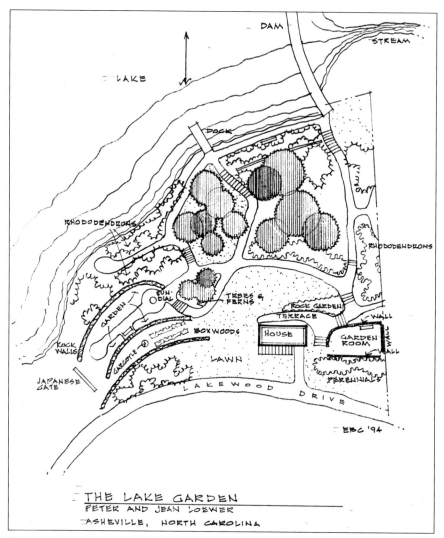

Image labels: DAM, STREAM, LAKE, DOCK, RHODODENDRONS, RHODODENDRONS, SUN DIAL, TREES & FERNS, ROCK GARDEN TERRACE, WALL, GARDEN, BOXWOODS, HOUSE, GARDEN ROOM, WALL, ROCK WALLS, PERENNIALS, LAWN, JAPANESE GATE, LAKEWOOD DRIVE, EBC '94, THE LAKE GARDEN, PETER AND JEAN LOEWER, ASHEVILLE, NORTH CAROLINA

A map of our garden on the shores of Kenilworth Lake in Asheville.
Photo courtesy of Quality Forward.

Start by measuring off your property outlines in feet, using a tape measure, and drawing the outlines on your paper. Don't forget to include some of your neighbors' property in the sketch; possibly there might be something next door that you want to conceal or an attractive feature directly adjacent that you wish to "borrow" or focus on for your property, especially if it concerns shrubs, bushes, or trees.

For example, if there is a group of trees on the property line, this might be a great opportunity to expand them. Your neighbors may even want to do the same on their property.

Add all existing buildings, driveways, adjacent streets, waterways, trees, possible windbreaks, and obstructions such as existing fences or ditches you cannot fill. Be especially aware of those that will reduce the amount of sunlight available throughout the year. Chart the direction of the prevailing winds with the help of your local weather service, and, using a compass, add the compass points for getting the correct orientation for the sun. Finally, add walkways, fences, mailboxes, and other relevant data, including slopes either up or down, areas of shade, sources of water, and even ugly views that might be hidden by your efforts.

Finally, using your digital camera (or today, your phone) take a few pictures of different areas of your yard and have enlarged prints made. Later you can try out a few garden ideas by drawing on the prints, just to give you a sense of how a particular idea might look.

You will notice that in the map of my Garden Room, the north side is now a fairly steep hill planted with a variegated bamboo that is disliked by deer, while the entire room is boxed in with stone walls and a beautiful wooden fence that measures ten feet high and fourteen feet long. This is a protected spot where I can grow all sorts of treasured plants that would be safe from all except human invaders.

Choosing a Habitat

Once you have your map and can see exactly what's on your property at a glance, it's time to start thinking about what kind of wildlife garden you want. Three of the most popular are woodland, meadow, and water gardens, then for smaller approach there are rock gardens and brush piles.

Woodland Thickets and Gardens

Woodland gardens are ideal habitats for two reasons: almost everyone has happy memories of hiking through the woods, whether with the family, at camp, or just out for a walk on a balmy Sunday afternoon, and the protection provided by a woodland garden will attract many forms of wildlife. Most of us are not lucky enough to live on large plots of land covered by stands of mature oaks and their acorns or second-growth forests, but almost all of us have a few shade trees. You can turn a few trees into small woodlands by imitating nature and under-planting with smaller understory trees, and if up against deer, you can protect new plantings with individual protections for those small trees. There are many small trees that are large enough to give protection to wildlife, even if in cages and many more that will provide flowers and fruit for them.

In addition to a number of small evergreens, there are several small maples (*Acer* spp.), birches (*Betula* spp.), service berries (*Amelanchier* spp.), dogwoods (*Cornus* spp.), redbuds (*Cercis* spp.), and a lot more.

Thickets provide cover for many birds and small mammals. You can plant them under trees or in the open. You can create thickets by planting various shrubs and bushes—and even vines—so close to each other that they become a tangled net of twigs and branches. For a quick thicket you might consider using plastic hoops (about five feet tall) and planting them with Virgina creepers (*Parthenocissus quinquefolia*), wild grapes (*Vitis* spp.), or trumpet honeysuckle (*Lonicera sempervirens*).

Meadow and Prairie Gardens

Although many gardeners think of meadow and prairie gardens as great sheets of wildflowers, the most successful such gardens mix wildflowers with grasses. Tall grasses provide great protective cover for small mammals, down to shrews and moles. When the grasses bloom and set seed, they provide food for many species of birds as well. All of the taller wildflowers are good choices, including field asters (*Aster* spp.), goldenrods (*Solidago* spp.), purple coneflowers (*Echinacea purpurea*), black-eyed Susans, or orange cone flowers (*Rudbeckia* spp.) and many, many, more. When these flowers bloom,

Rudbeckia 'Cherry Brandy' is easily grown from seed.

they attract a host of butterflies by day—and often a surprising number of moths by night.

Starting a Wildflower Garden Where the Lawn Used to Be

This is the perfect time of year to think about planning for your 2015 wildflower garden, a garden that can easily replace your lawn, thus saving on man and woman power plus bringing beauty to your neighborhood.

If your problem is not starting out from scratch but dealing with an existing field, you must spend time in preparation. You cannot (well you really can but it won't do you any good) just throw seeds into the grass and weeds, expecting them to germinate, much less survive. Those native grassroots can overpower more delicate wildflowers.

If the grasses are worth saving, but you want to add more flowers, first cut and rake the field in the fall of the year. Then you remove clumps of grass to be replaced by container wildflowers or seeds.

If your intended garden is mostly a collection of weeds, then you must plow and harrow, or at least use a professional roto-tiller. Then the earth must be raked and settled since most desirable seed will not germinate if just left on hard ground. Then the plantings must be covered by pine needles, mulched leaves, or hay to prevent their being washed or blown away by winter storms.

You might have to mow your meadow two or three times from spring to late summer during the first year in order to give the wildflowers a chance against any weedy types that show up. Once established, cutting should be either in midsummer and late fall, or just late fall alone.

Water Gardens

Water is a lure to all wildlife, but a water garden also attracts its own special inhabitants. A small pond will soon bring frogs and salamanders, which in time will lay eggs. It will also bring water beetles, water bugs, dragonfly larvae, then dragonflies, and even snails and small fish might arrive as eggs attached to the feet of various water birds. Then in high summer, the true acrobats of the air appear: the dragonflies and the damselflies—insects that not only enjoy the giver of flight but appear to enjoy the life as well.

Rock Gardens and Brush Piles

Creating a brush pile in an out-of-the-way corner of your property is an extremely quick way to attract wildlife. Instead of hauling off tree trimmings, old Christmas trees, or leaves that haven't made it to the compost heap, make loose piles of this wonderful vegetative stuff to a discrete part of your wild garden. Soon all kinds of animals will be using these piles for protection, searching for food, and perhaps even nesting in the comparative safety of their enclosures.

You may think a brush pile looks messy, and indeed, in the middle of a manicured lawn it probably would. But if you have enough space that you can put a brush pile out of sight, it can be a valuable resource. You might be able to hide a brush pile behind a garage or shed, or grow vines on chicken wire enclosures to hide the pile and make it less noticeable.

Rock piles, rock walls (even tumbling to the ground), and rock outcrops provide both homes and hunting grounds for many animals. From our favorite garden dweller the chipmunks of the North to lizards such a skinks and racerunners in the Central and Southern states, creatures delight us as they search for the insects that dash about a collection of rocks or sun themselves on a warm rock. Such gardens are also home to many harmless garden snakes, a large variety of beetles, and a host of spider species that nest in the hollows between the rocks. Chipmunks live between the rocks, too, and they love to sun themselves on top. To make a rock garden pile that appeals to this wildlife, honeycomb the pile or wall to create small cavities where creatures can hide.

Appendix 1: Wildlife and Conservation Agencies in the United States

If you have some free time at a computer—one with reasonably fast downloading—you can see for yourself just how big and full of hope this country is, even in 2015. The following websites will give you an idea of the great species distribution in the United States. And, foremost in the art work of almost every site, you will find an antlered deer.

U.S. Fish and Wildlife Service
    www.fws.gov
Alabama Fish and Game
    www.outdooralabama.com
Alaska Fish and Game
    www.adfg.alaska.gov
Arizona Game and Fish
    www.gf.state.az.us
Arkansas Game and Fish
    www.agfc.com

California Fish and Wildlife
    www.wildlife.ca.gov
Colorado Division of Wildlife
    www.wildlife.state.co.us
Connecticut Department of the Environment
    www.ct.wildlifelicense.com
Delaware Department of Natural Resources
    www.dnrec.state.de.us
Florida Game and Fresh Water Fish
    www.myfwc.com
Georgia Department of Natural Resources
    www.gadnr.org
Conservation Council of Hawaii
    www.conservehi.org
Idaho Department of Fish and Game
    www.fishandgame.idaho.gov
Illinois Department of Natural Resources
    www.dnr.illinois.gov
Indiana Department of Natural Resources
    www.in.gov/dnr
Iowa Department of Natural Resources
    www.iowadnr.gov
Kansas Department of Wildlife, Parks and Tourism
    www.kdwp.state.ks.us
Kentucky Department of Fish and Wildlife Resources
    www.kdfwr.state.ky.us
Louisiana Department of Wildlife and Fisheries
    www.wlf.louisiana.gov
Maine Department of Inland Fisheries and Wildlife
    www.maine.gov/ifw/
Maryland Department of Natural Resources
    www.dnr.state.md.us/

Massachusetts Division of Fisheries and Wildlife
   www.mass.gov/eea/agencies/dfg/dfw/
Michigan Department of Natural Resources
   www.michigan.gov/dnr
Minnesota Department of Natural Resources
   www.dnr.state.mn.us
Mississippi Wildlife, Fisheries and Parks
   www.mdwfp.com/
Missouri Department of Conservation
   www.mdc.mo.gov/
Montana Fish, Wildlife and Parks
   www.fwp.mt.gov/
Nebraska Game and Parks Commission
   www.outdoornebraska.ne.gov/
Nevada Department of Conservation and Natural Resources
   www.dcnr.nv.gov/
New Hampshire Fish and Game
   www.wildlife.state.nh.us/
New Jersey Division of Fish and Wildlife
   www.state.nj.us/dep/fgw/
New Mexico Game and Fish
   www.wildlife.state.nm.us/
New York State Department of Environmental Conservation
   www.dec.ny.gov/
North Carolina Wildlife Resources Commission
   www.ncwildlife.org/
North Dakota Game and Fish Department
   www.gf.nd.gov/
Ohio Department of Natural Resources
   www.dnr.state.oh.us/
Oklahoma Conservation Commission
   www.ok.gov/conservation/

Oregon Department of Fish and Wildlife
   www.dfw.state.or.us/
Pennsylvania Department of Conservation and Natural Resources
   www.dcnr.state.pa.us/
Rhode Island Department of Environmental Management
   www.dem.ri.gov/programs/bnatres/fishwild/
South Carolina Department of Natural Resources
   www.dnr.sc.gov/
South Dakota Department of Game, Fish and Parks
   www.gfp.sd.gov/
Tennessee Wildlife Resources Agency
   www.state.tn.us/twra/
Texas Parks and Wildlife
   www.tpwd.state.tx.us/
Utah Division of Wildlife Resources
   www.wildlife.utah.gov/
Vermont Agency of Natural Resources
   www.anr.state.vt.us/
Virginia Department of Game and Inland Fisheries
   www.dgif.virginia.gov/
Washington Department of Fish and Wildlife
   www.wdfw.wa.gov/
West Virginia Division of Natural Resources
   www.wvdnr.gov/
Wisconsin Department of Natural Resources
   www.dnr.wi.gov/
Wyoming Game and Fish Department
   www.gf.state.wy.us

Appendix 2: Deer Depredation Permits

When the first edition of the deer book was published, I found one legal reference to any state bills that dealt with the issuance of deer depredation permits to landowners who had sustained deer-related damage. It was introduced on March 16, 2001, to the Natural Resources Committee of the Iowa General Assembly, known as House File 503. Here it is below.

House File 503
Partial Bill History
Bill Introduced: H.J. 593
Complete Bill History
Bill Text
PAG LIN

1 1 Section 1. NEW SECTION. 481C.4 DEER DEPREDATION PERMITS

1 2 – FEES – RESTRICTIONS – PENALTY.

1 3 1. Notwithstanding section 481C.2, a landowner who incurs

l 4 crop or nursery damage caused by deer population may apply to

l 5 the county recorder for not more than ten deer depredation

l 6 permits for each farm unit of eighty acres where the damage

l 7 has occurred. The department shall specify, by rule, a

l 8 proportional number of permits which may be issued for farm

l 9 units based on the size of the farm unit, damage done, and

l 10 deer population. The application shall specify the crops or

l 11 nursery stock damaged, the estimated amount of damage, and the

l 12 area of the farm unit where the damage occurred. Each

l 13 application shall also be accompanied by a fee of twenty-five

l 14 dollars for each deer depredation permit requested. The

l 15 permit is valid only from September 1 through the succeeding

l 16 March 1 for taking a deer of either sex on the farm unit

l 17 specified on the application. If additional deer depredation

l 18 damage occurs after ten deer have been taken on a farm unit,

l 19 not more than ten additional depredation permits may be issued

l 20 with the approval of a representative of the department for

l 21 the same fee for each permit. A postcard shall be issued with

l 22 each depredation permit. A person taking a deer with the

l 23 depredation permit shall complete and return the postcard to

l 24 the county recorder within ten days after taking the deer. An

l 25 unused depredation permit and postcard shall be returned to

l 26 the county recorder by March 10 following the expiration of

1 27 the depredation permit.

1 28 2. A landowner who has been issued a deer depredation

1 29 permit pursuant to subsection 1 may sell or give the deer

1 30 depredation permit to hunt on the specified farm unit to any

1 31 person who is otherwise licensed, except for a deer license,

1 32 to hunt in this state. If a deer depredation permit is used

1 33 by any person other than the landowner, the name and address

1 34 of the user shall be legibly written on the permit and on the

1 35 return postcard.

2 1 3. Except during a regular shotgun season, any bow and

2 2 arrow or any legal firearm may be used to take a deer with a

2 3 deer depredation permit.

2 4 4. A person who violates this section or a rule adopted

2 5 under this section is guilty of a simple misdemeanor which is

2 6 punishable as a scheduled violation under section 805.8,

2 7 subsection 5, paragraph "e".

2 8 Sec. 2. Section 805.8, subsection 5, paragraph e, Code

2 9 2001, is amended to read as follows:

2 10 e. For violations of sections 481A.85, 481A.93, 481A.95,

2 11 481A.120, 481A.137, 481B.5, 481C.4, 482.3, 482.9, 482.15, and

2 12 483A.42, the scheduled fine is one hundred dollars.

2 13 EXPLANATION

2 14 This bill authorizes the owner of a farm unit which has

2 15 incurred crop or nursery damage caused by deer population to

2 16 apply to the county recorder for not more than 10 deer

2 17 depredation permits for each farm unit of 80 acres where the

2 18 damage has occurred. The department shall specify, by rule, a

2 19 proportional number of depredation permits which may be issued

2 20 for farm units of varying size. The application shall specify

2 21 the crops or nursery stock damaged, the estimated amount of

2 22 damage, and the area of the farm unit where the damage

2 23 occurred. Each application shall be accompanied by a fee of

2 24 $25 for each depredation permit requested. Each depredation

2 25 permit is valid only from September 1 through the succeeding

2 26 March 1 for taking a deer of either sex on the farm unit

2 27 specified on the permit. If additional damage occurs after 10

2 28 deer have been taken on a farm unit, not more than 10

2 29 additional depredation permits may be issued with the approval

2 30 of a representative of the department of natural resources for

2 31 the same fee. A postcard shall be issued with each

2 32 depredation permit which shall be completed and returned by

2 33 the hunter within 10 days after taking a deer. An unused

2 34 depredation permit and postcard shall be returned to the

2 35 county recorder by March 10.

3 1 A landowner who has been issued a deer depredation permit

3 2 may sell or give the permit to hunt on the landowner's farm

3 3 unit to any person who is otherwise licensed, except for a

3 4 deer license, to hunt in this state. If a deer depredation

3 5 permit is used by any person other than the owner of the farm

3 6 unit, the name and address of the user shall be legibly

3 7 written on the permit and on the return postcard.

3 8 Except during a regular shotgun season, any bow and arrow

3 9 or other legal firearm may be used to take deer with a deer

3 10 depredation permit.

3 11 A person violating the provisions of this section is guilty

3 12 of a simple misdemeanor, which is punishable by a scheduled

3 13 fine of $100.

3 14 LSB 3108YH 79

3 15 tj/gg/8

Fifty State Agencies Issuing Deer Depredation Permits

The fifty state agencies that consider problems associated with deer depredation permits are listed below in alphabetical order. The first entry refers to the Quality Deer Management Association (QDMA), a non-profit wildlife conservation organization dedicated to the future of white-tailed deer, including their wildlife habitat in addition to the hunting heritage of the United States. Founded in 1988, the QDMA has more than fifty-five thousand members (November, 1014) in all fifty states and several foreign countries.

Quality Deer Management Association (QDMA): http://www. qdma.com/forums/showthread.php?t=52894

Alabama: http://www.aldeer.com/forum/ubbthreads.php?
ubb=showflat&Number=65539

Alaska: http://www.adfg.alaska.gov/index.cfm?adfg=kodiakbearplan.
summary

Arizona: http://www.azgfd.gov/eservices/special_licenses/small_
game_depredation.shtml

Arkansas: http://www.agfc.com/species/Pages/SpeciesNuisanceWild-
life.aspx

California: https://www.dfg.ca.gov/wildlife/hunting/bear/depreda-
tion.html

Colorado: http://cpw.state.co.us/learn/Pages/ResearchMammalElk.aspx

Connecticut: http://www.cthuntingnshooting.com/vBforum/
showthread.php?1124-Hunting-Farmland-Deer

Delaware: http://regulations.delaware.gov/AdminCode/
title7/3000/3900%20Wildlife/3904.shtml

Florida: http://myfwc.com/license/wildlife/nuisance-wildlife/deer-dep-
redation/

Georgia: http://georgiawildlife.com/node/248

Hawaii: http://dlnr.hawaii.gov/recreation/hunting/

Idaho: http://fishandgame.idaho.gov/public/licenses/huntDepreda-
tion.pdf

Illinois: http://forums.bowsite.com/tf/regional/thread.cfm?threadid
=211599&MESSAGES=1&state=Il

Indiana: http://www.in.gov/dnr/fishwild/2718.htm

Iowa: http://www.stopthedeerdamage.com/depredation.htm

Kansas: http://kdwpt.state.ks.us/License-Permits

Kentucky: http://www.lrc.ky.gov/statutes/statute.aspx?id=2011

Louisiana: http://www.wlf.louisiana.gov/licenses/hunting-licenses

Maine: http://www.maine.gov/ifw/licenses_permits/lotteries/anydeer/

Maryland: http://www.dnr.state.md.us/wildlife/Hunt_Trap/deer/
deer_damage/ddpermit.asp

Massachusetts: http://www.mass.gov/eea/agencies/dfg/dfw/laws-
regulations/cmr/321-cmr-300-hunting.html

Michigan: http://michigansaf.org/Tours/05Deer/SurveyReport.pdf

Minnesota: http://mndeerhunters.com/en/legislation/

Mississippi: http://www.mississippioutdoorforums.com/forums/index.php?/topic/9558-depredation-permits/

Missouri: http://mdc.mo.gov/your-property/problem-plants-and-animals/nuisance-native-wildlife/deer-control

Montana: http://fwp.mt.gov/mtoutdoors/HTML/articles/2006/Depredation.htm

Ohio: http://ohiodnr.gov/

Nebraska: http://law.justia.com/codes/nebraska/2006/s37index/s3704048000.html

Nevada: http://www.ndow.org/Forms_and_Resources/Special_Permits/

New Hampshire: http://nhrsa.org/law/207-22-c-wildlife-damage-control-program-administration/

New Jersey: http://www.njfishandwildlife.com/farmer.htm

New Mexico: http://www.nmwild.org/2009/news/wildlife-depredation/

New York: http://www.dec.ny.gov/permits/28631.html

North Carolina: http://www.ncwildlife.org/Licensing/Regulations/

North Dakota: http://gf.nd.gov/wildlife/fish-wildlife/conflict/depredation-assistance

Oklahoma: http://digitalcommons.unl.edu/cgi/viewcontent.cgi?article=1448&context=gpwdcwp

Oregon: http://www.dfw.state.or.us/resources/licenses_regs/hunting_trapping.asp

Pennsylvania: http://www.portal.state.pa.us/portal/server.pt?open=514&objID=748275&mode=2

Rhode Island: http://www.dem.ri.gov/programs/bnatres/fishwild/pdf/deerdamg.pdf

South Carolina: http://www.dnr.sc.gov/hunting/depredation.html

South Dakota: http://gfp.sd.gov/hunting/depredation-hunts.aspx

Tennessee: http://www.tnwf.org/issues-impact/special-reports

Texas: https://apps.tpwd.state.tx.us/privatelands/permitDepredationHelp.seam

Utah: http://wildlife.utah.gov/hunting-in-utah/334-depredation-pool-application.html

Vermont: http://www.leg.state.vt.us/statutes/fullchapter.cfm?Title=10APPENDIX&Chapter=001

Virginia: http://www.dgif.virginia.gov/wildlife/deer/management-plan/virginia-deer-management-plan.pdf

Washington: http://wdfw.wa.gov/living/deer.html

West Virginia: http://www.wvdnr.gov/wildlife/magazine/archive/09Sum-Fall/Urban%20Deer.pdf

Wisconsin: http://docs.legis.wisconsin.gov/code/admin_code/nr/001/12.pdf

Wyoming: http://wgfd.wyo.gov/web2011/hunting-1000179.aspx

Index

305